Africa's Quest for Order

Fred G. Burke

A SPECTRUM BOOK

Prentice-Hall, Inc.
Englewood Cliffs, N. J.

Preface

This book reflects an effort to come to grips with the African Revolution. Otherwise excellent country-by-country surveys seldom provide more than a catalog of political and economic events. To understand Africa it seems imperative to identify some themes or ideas and to proceed from that point with analysis and presentation. It is much easier to be critical of an orthodox approach, however, than to establish a worthwhile substitute. One cannot escape the fact that Africa is current; that the revolution above all else involves the emergence of new states and that the significant incidents take place within and revolve about new or emergent nations. The problem then is to cover the major events that have occurred in such a way as to emphasize the recurring forces and themes which together make up the warp and woof of the African Revolution.

To do this I have employed a basic frame of reference, points of reference along the way, and finally an end or goal toward which the analysis might proceed. Some assumptions thought to be critical to what is transpiring in Africa are outlined in the first chapter about the sociopolitical process. The series of reference points include questions as to the relative significance of certain institutions and values. A number of themes and forces such as tribalism, urbanism, youth, leadership, and race also serve as references. Finally, an attempt is made to relate these themes, with the aid of the initial assumptions about the nature of the African Revolution, to what I have termed the "quest for order."

This is not an introductory book on Africa, although the Appendix provides basic information. This book assumes at least a superficial knowledge about Africa and the events which have transpired there over the past decade. Nor is it directed toward the African specialist, although we hope that he will find it interesting and worthwhile. It is, rather, written for the informed layman and student who feel the need for a thought-provoking book on Africa that will provide a more fundamental insight and comprehension than has hitherto been possible. Although our factual knowledge of Africa is considerable, our understanding of this important part of the world is not. Some will take issue with the assumptions and certainly with the conclusions, for the themes selected here are controversial—perhaps a test of their relevance. The chapter on race, for example, raises questions (but not that of biological difference, which we assume has been buried forever), which are often left unasked. As race is considered to be a major theme, possibly the most powerful of all, it receives corresponding emphasis here.

Many of the concepts and ideas advanced in the succeeding pages have been discussed, sometimes argued, on numerous occasions and in considerable detail with colleagues and graduate students in the program of East African Studies at Syracuse University's Maxwell School.

Spirited discussions with graduate students and the professor's added bonus of having access to their academic labors, is gratefully acknowledged. Three graduate assistants, one Tanganyikan and two Americans, Mr. Anthony Rweyamamu, Mr. Brack Brown, and Mrs. Susanne McCabe Zarins were particularly helpful.

Members of the Maxwell School faculty, generally, and Dean Stephen K. Bailey, in particular, provided considerable encouragement and assistance. A grant from the Maxwell School's Cross-Cultural Analysis Project made possible my most recent (1962-63) research safari to Africa.

If this volume possesses any worthwhile insights into the nature of the African Revolution they are, in the last analysis, heavily dependent upon the countless hours of assistance, information, and advice that have been given to me in Africa by friends and acquaintances too numerous to record but too important to neglect. To them I am deeply indebted.

But without the assistance of my wife who, better than anyone else, knew where and when to encourage, criticize, or cajole and who, in addition, took on the laborious tasks of typing and proofreading, this book would not have progressed beyond the professional quagmire of rough drafts, inserts, and scattered ideas.

F.G.B.

Contents

I. INTRODUCTION: THE NATURE OF THE QUEST   1

"Sociation" as an Approach to Understanding Africa, 1
Sociation and Politics, 4
Sociation and Consensus, 6

II. THE WAY OF THE QUEST   8

Cruciality of Government, 8
Liberty versus Order, 10
To Be Democratic and Modern, 11
Minorities and the New Order, 12
Violence and the Quest for Order, 14

III. TRIBES AND TRIBALISM   19

An Anatomy of Tribalism, 19
Variations in Tribal Organization, 21
Impact of European Intervention, 23
Old Forms and New Functions, 25
Some Tribal Legacies, 28
Tribalism and Nationalism, 29

IV. THE ROLE OF THE CITY   35

Look to the City, 35
The City as Generator, 37
The City as Communicator, 39
The City as Innovator, 41
The City as Integrator, 43
Types of African Cities, 44
Urbanism and Tribalism, 46
The City and the Sociation Process, 48
Some Emerging Trends, 50

V. THE EMERGENCE AND ROLE OF LEADERSHIP   52

    The Dilemma of Leadership, 53
    Sources of Leadership, 57
    The Generational Revolution, 61
    Leadership and Personality, 62
    Variations in the Emergence of Leadership, 64
    Colonial Legacy, 65
    Nationalism, Racism, and Tribalism, 67
    The Question of Responsibility, 69
    Manpower—Quantity and Quality, 70
    The Circulation of Ideology, 73
    The Africanization of Ideology, 75

VI. THE ENIGMA OF RACE   79

    Black and White, 79
    Early Contacts, 80
    Invasion and Absorption, 81
    Legacy of the Slave Trade, 82
    The Scramble, 83
    Racialism and Nationalism, 86
    The Dimensions of the Problem, 89
    The Failure of Apartheid—South Africa, 92
    The Failure of Partnership—Central Africa, 97
    The Failure of Multiracialism—Kenya, 106
    Race—A Human Enigma, 112

VII. AFRICAN UNITY AND DISUNITY   115

    Integration, 116
    Disintegration, 124
    New Nations and Old Colonizers, 129
    Pan-Africanism—Oppressed Racism or New Unity? 136
    Some Reflections, 143

VIII. AFRICA IN WORLD POLITICS   145

    Africa in the Cold War, 145
    Africa in International Organizations, 154
    The International Politics of African Development, 161
    The Never-Ending Quest, 170

APPENDIX: AFRICAN FACTS AND FIGURES   172

I
Introduction:
The Nature of the Quest

Our major concern is with that aspect of the African Revolution which can be termed "political" and "governmental." We have resisted, by and large, the temptation of modern social scientists to develop an elaborate formal methodology or approach to African government and politics, although an attempt has been made to approach the subject systematically. Nevertheless what is transpiring in Africa does have a general direction; what we seek to identify and illuminate is a "process." Our wish is to approach this process from the vantage point of its effect on people—their beliefs and behavior.

The interrelationship of the reshaping and extension of political, cultural, and social boundaries, the establishment of new nation states, and the creation of new international relations especially characterizes Africa today. The recent acceleration of this process makes Africa such an important phenomenon as to command much of our energy and anxiety. The sheer physical aspect of the situation should make us aware that when our planet's second largest land mass, long relatively dormant, begins the process of re-sorting itself into states, economies, societies, and ideologies, the remaining land masses of the planet are bound to feel the rumblings, sense the heat, and be affected by the evolving configuration of peoples, space, and ideas.

Because Africa is the last major area, and Africans are the last peoples to commence this traumatic, often violent process of disassociating and associating, the process takes place on a stage anxiously watched by all the rest of the world's states and peoples who claim an interest in the drama and its actors, and who seek to anticipate, not only the plot, but the climax as well. Furthermore, these events occur in a world in which the planet's three billion people are in constant communication with one another. What they do and say, and what each thinks of what the other does and says, is told and retold in a multitude of tongues and becomes a part of the active frame of reference of all people almost as soon as it occurs in Léopoldville, Nairobi, or Cape Town.

"SOCIATION" AS AN APPROACH TO UNDERSTANDING AFRICA

A useful theme for grasping the substance of what we call Africa and Africans is what we term "dissociation" and "association," as constituent parts of the process of sociation.[1] The essence of the so-called African Revolution—whereby old institutions are being destroyed, modified, or amalgamated, new ideas and beliefs are blended with older ones, new political entities combine and recombine and old ones disappear and reappear—is sociation.

Institutions and their organized activities are the forms that associations take. As observers of the human scene, we are concerned ultimately with changes in human behavior significant for the construction of new institutions or the alterations of old ones. A wide variety of tools and techniques for the systematic study of behavior has been developed, sharpened, and employed. As the context within which we plan to examine sociation is a particularly dynamic one, e.g., transition, change, revolution, it behooves us to settle on a definition or an approach to sociation that is itself particularly dynamic. Therefore, for our purposes, sociation is defined as a process whereby individuals shed values, beliefs, and behavior relative to membership in certain groupings; are exposed to new values and beliefs; modify their behavior and human interrelationships; and act in such a way as to form new groupings which give expression to the new or altered values, beliefs, and behavior.

Sociation is particularly related to "institution." "Institutions" as employed here refers to distinctive clusters of activity and meanings that are more or less permanent. A simple and now discarded view of the nature of the transition in Africa saw Western institutions and cultures as superimposed over indigenous forms. It is apparent to most observers today, however, that it is no longer possible, if it ever was, to export and import institutions like sacks of grain or boxes of ball bearings. In the one world in which we live, types of organized behavior and variations in the meanings that people give to what they do and say are no longer private property and cannot be isolated, nor denied entry by frontier guards or censorship.

The process of sociation in Africa is as it is, in part because the ideas, motivations, and forces that energize sociation are circulating freely in the world, not unlike the radio waves in the ether that may be captured by any receiver equipped with a proper antenna. Equally available to the African today are the ideas and words of Jefferson, Wilson, Marx, Nkrumah, Aristotle, and Toynbee. President Sékou Touré of Guinea, a Malinke tribesman educated in France, a Marxist scholar, reads Plato's *Republic* as he travels to Washington in a jet aircraft to confer with President Johnson. The forms of sociation that emerge from these alterations in behavior are not successive layers of imported veneers but resemble more nearly a chemical reaction or compound. Elements from the world's storehouse of ideas and behavior are gathered, sometimes quite

[1] The concept is not new and was developed at length by George Simmel. See *The Sociology of George Simmel*, edited and translated by Kurt H. Wolff (New York: The Free Press of Glencoe, 1950).

by accident, and then combined with existing forms that are themselves different from the way they were just a year before.

Men have always lived their lives with reference to a pattern of affiliation and belonging. Organized interaction with our kind is apparently requisite to physical and psychological security. But dissociation and/or association involves a transfer or at least a dilution of existing loyalties and beliefs. Man is naturally reluctant to part with the familiar and embrace the novel, even when it is apparent that the new associations, given a radically altered situation, are both desirable and necessary. The sociation process, then, operates through conflict and competition. Some men possess vested interest in existing patterns of membership and obligation, others in the formation of new ones. The sociation process, however, is more than the simple blending of old and new forms.

In some African areas the modern associations reflect significantly new forms of activity without seriously affecting the indigenous affiliations. Thus, for example, the Karamajong in northeastern Uganda participate in direct elections to Uganda's Legislative Council. Nevertheless the traditional social and political membership groupings of the Karamajong are little changed from those of fifty years ago. In Karamoja it might be said that a low rate of dissociation coincides with a relatively low rate of association. In other parts of Africa a high rate of association may be accompanied by a low rate of dissociation, thus often setting up a situation of conflicting obligations. There are, of course, important differences between the styles of sociation. Frequently the life of the membership units (institutions) varies independently from that of some of its members. It is conceivable, therefore, for a traditional indigenous organization, such as a clan, age-grade, or secret society to persist and continue to demand allegiance in the face of a high rate of dissociation. This we might term a low rate of organizational disillusion accompanied by a high rate of dissociation. This sociation pattern, especially if accompanied by a high rate of association, tends to build up potentially conflicting obligations wherein the individual African is required to choose between two contradictory paths of action, both of which make legitimate claims on him.

The combinations of individual rates of organizational dissolution and formation are, of course, numerous. A high rate of organizational dissolution, for example, accompanied by high dissociation and low association and a low rate of organizational formation, tends toward anomie and the absence of regulatory affiliations capable of structuring new behavior and values. A sociation style with these characteristics has typified social change for many dislocated people in the Congo in recent years.

Thus we see processes of change and consequent dislocation, conflict, and competition in the organized activity, interrelationships, and modes of thought of millions of people. We sense, however, that there is a direction to the stream of change—that the current flows, for example, from rural to urban, from parochial to cosmopolitan, from nonrational to rational, from community of kin to community of area and even to that of special segmented interest, from diffuseness to specialization, from private to public, from environmental fatalism to expectation of change, from status to class, from segment to mass, from dependence to independence, and from region to nation.

We are, of course, primarily concerned with political sociation and even more specifically have viewed this process as it gives form and substance to the nation state. The process is without beginning or end but varies tremendously in the rate with which it occurs. It serves to deprive men of their existing ties, sometimes with their consent but at other times against their wishes. From the individual's point of view the process may not always seem rational. The person's rights, obligations, and vested interests often respond to the altered status of the rapidly shifting sectors of the social and political system. Individuals find themselves moved from a relatively restricted situation to one in which almost infinite choice of behavior is possible. Individual freedom, sometimes frightening in its implications, follows from dissociation and a decline in traditional institutions. The absence of new affiliations and accompanying institutions tends toward anarchy. But even a high rate of association and a rapid formation of new institutions can produce a relative atomization of personality, for the new memberships are specialized and therefore regulate relatively less of the individual's behavior. The individual moves from a situation wherein the purposes and goals of life are determined to one in which there is freedom to choose the ends toward which he would direct his energies. Freed from the restrictions of traditional affiliation, the African can form new unions to pursue cooperatively his new values and goals or to preserve those already obtained. These may take such forms as political parties, labor unions, and fraternal societies. This thesis should not be pushed too far, for Africa is so complex that contradictory trends can also be identified. For example, some of the new associations —particularly modern religion and the political party—in some instances have absorbed the energies and values of the entire person. In fact we should have occasion to regard some of these new associations as the "new tribalism."

SOCIATION AND POLITICS

To view the phenomena of Africa today in this context, we need to employ some new ideas and symbols. For example, to say that technological change is instrumental to modernization and nation-building fails to capture the importance and affective implications of technology. Of significance is not so much the new techniques or inventions as the corresponding process wherein thousands of men redefine their affiliations and relate themselves to other men in new and powerful ways—become factory workers, union members, and professional men. Thus, forces such as urbanization and industrialization trigger sociation by which men who were formerly relatively stationary in their affiliations begin to maneuver and sort themselves into new and different groupings. People are liberated from communities that are limited by their rural tribal areas. The resultant migrations and dislocations of formerly immobile peoples act, on the one hand, to modify or destroy traditional sociations and, on the other, to initiate new ones. Although some men dissociate and associate without significantly changing their fundamental ideas and beliefs and tend to carry the values associated with their former memberships into their new affiliations, the process more often involves setting in motion new ideas, beliefs, and expectations.

An important aspect of the growth of new affiliations is a universal trend toward a mass basis of social life. Here we refer, for example, to the tendency in the new African nations to profess that governors govern in the name and with the consent of the "people." Traditional leadership was based not upon securing or manipulating mass consent, but rather on some form of inherited deference. It was not until this century that the populace in Africa really came to be invested with, or at least attributed to possess, the ingredient termed "sovereignty." This distinction is an important one, for a popular sovereignty leadership exercises authority as long as its decisions produce the values which the masses expect to receive from the exercise of authority. Ruling not by right but by the sufferance of the masses, the popular sovereignty leader must produce desired results if he is to continue to rule; he must manipulate the masses either to value what he produces or to believe that he is producing that which they value. The major difference between a democratic and a totalitarian system, then, is not so much the nature of the rule or the location of sovereignty but lies, rather, in the relative freedom that exists to compete for the support of the masses. The "political mass" in a plural society is a product of multiple segmented affiliations wherein no single unit possesses a sufficient monopoly over the individual's intrinsic values to warrant its acting completely in his name or stead.

The tendency toward mass society and mass culture does not imply, as some would maintain, a decline in the number of groups with which a person is affiliated or a drying up of the sociation process. On the contrary, an evolving type of mass society may be characterized by overlapping multiple memberships and probably coincides with a high rate of association into segmented intermediary groups. Thus significant alteration in membership configuration is required if the individual is to relate himself to the enlarged society and polity.

Sociation lies at the basis of political participation. Rarely does a person participate in the political process as an individual. He does so, instead, as a member or affiliate of a group. The Luo member of the Kenya Federation of Labor who also belongs to the Luo Union of

Mombasa and to the Kenya African National Union is viewed differently by Mr. Mboya than he is by the ward chief in his urban location. He, in turn, participates in the political process in a manner different from that of his father who has remained in Nyanza Province or that of a Kikuyu schoolteacher in Fort Hall. The nature of the sociation and the form and context of the individual's affiliation largely determine how he participates in the political process and how that participation is perceived by him and by those who seek to encourage or prohibit his participation.

SOCIATION AND CONSENSUS

In some areas consent has been withdrawn from existing organizations and from their respective leaders without a corresponding acquiescence in the exercise of authority by more modern and more inclusive organizations and leaders. This breakdown in accountability frequently results in disorder and disintegration. As important as the collective state of mind of the members of the new union, *e.g.*, the state, the labor organization, the cooperative, is the way in which the leader or would-be leader evaluates the attitude of the members, and in the way and the extent to which he feels himself required to obtain their consent.

Most traditional affiliations in Africa are peculiarly parochial and not well related to the problems inherent in modernization. They have not generally evolved as organizations capable of linking the individual to the most inclusive union of all—the nation state. When a traditional membership unit such as a large tribal kingdom has been of sufficient scope as to represent the individual capably in the new nation state, it has resisted the exercise of authority by the state and has tended, upon occasion, to compete with it for mass support. President Kwame Nkrumah of Ghana sought the disintegration of Ashanti because it posed a threat to the legitimacy of the authority he would exercise in the name of the people of Ghana. In Uganda, membership in and loyalty to the Kingdom of Buganda long frustrated the emergence of an independent and united Uganda.

Does the membership of an organization explicitly give its consent to be ruled and to obey legitimate rulers or does it signify acquiescence by simply conforming? Consent is forthcoming, or more realistically is not denied, as long as the governors wield their authority in such a way as to satisfy the values of the constituent groups, which by refusing to abide by the authoritative rules could effectively demolish the existent authority system. This is less a question of the "majority" than it is of the balance of influence between competing affiliations and the neutrality or non-involvement of others. The organizations competing for control over policy making in Africa's new states today are undergoing rapid change. Clan heads reluctantly give way to bureaucratic chiefs, and they, in turn, to local government officials who now find it necessary to share authority with regional party leaders who might themselves, in turn, be accountable to their own clan leaders. All roads are beginning to converge on the new national capitals where the national party leaders, who nowadays are more often than not also heads of state, maintain in loud and frequent voice their accountability to the "people."

The new special purpose affiliations, by their very nature, cannot represent the whole man, as did the tribe or the clan, because outside a totalitarian system it is impossible for a single organization to represent the individual in a modern, urbanizing, industrializing, large nation state. As traditional parochial segments conflict with the pre-eminence of the state, the powers of the new African nations are often used to force the dissolution of these units. Finding or substituting an intimate and all-inclusive community like the tribe or African village, which at the same time overarches the divisive multitribal, multiregional segments, persists as a major problem in much of Africa.

The mass political party is peculiarly related to the nation state and to the nation-building process. In most instances, it is this affiliation that gives birth to the new African national institutions. So powerful and pervasive is the mass party in some African countries that it has become a kind of nation-state tribe. In the new countries of Africa the lives of many men and women are almost completely bound up with the political party. It is their ideology, religion, source of income, their very home—in essence, the new tribalism. To a lesser extent, the Christian religions have supplied a similar affiliation of extraparochial dimensions, but with most of the intimacy and all-inclusiveness of the traditional parochial memberships.

A problem of increasing proportions in the newly emergent African countries is the short supply of quasi-independent pluralistic associations which might effectively protect the individual, shorn of his traditional tribal ties, from the arbitrary authority of a totalitarian state or party. The trouble with Africa, many have maintained, is the presence of too many and too small traditional cultures and societies. That in one sense, of course, this cannot be denied must not blind us to the vital role that plural political forms play in the maintenance, if not in the creation, of democratic societies and nation states. The problem of Africa is not so much an abundance of plural forms, but rather the absence of sufficient plural forms capable of constituting a modern sovereign pluralistic state and at the same time of representing the individual in such a way as to provide him with security against the state.

II
The Way of the Quest

The quest for order affects all peoples and all places as people forever maneuver and experiment to establish and to disestablish political communities, governments, allegiances, and organizations. As new values and ways of behaving and relating to the environment and to other people replace old values and behavior, men must, if they are to persist as a community, write new constitutions and laws more consistent with the new peripheries of common allegiance and common problems. Because the quest for order is a theme so central to the traumatic experience of the African Revolution, it must constitute the chief focus of this study.

CRUCIALITY OF GOVERNMENT

"Nation-building"—a concept that seems best to capture the élan of the forces at work in contemporary Africa—relies, as we shall attempt to show in the following chapters, upon a number of factors, such as nationalism, modernization, education, and leadership. In our time, however, nation-building is particularly dependent upon the presence of order. Thus the quest for order, in an important respect, is an effort to institutionalize the African Revolution; that is, to give form, meaning, and stability to national independence. Government is looked to as that institution peculiarly responsible for the provision and maintenance of order; it is the critical nation-building institution. Government in the era of nation-building in the United States, however, played a relatively minor role and was at most a partner of the private sector of the society. This, of course, was how it was supposed to have been, for it was firmly held that that government which governed best, governed least. According to this view, the function of the government was a limited and regulatory one.

The legacy of having achieved national development through a largely negative government, whose responsibility was not to initiate but to consolidate a freedom, permeates the American self-image.

We Americans have tended to perceive the new African nations in our own image; this perception significantly colors our relationship with Africa today. To be sure, some of us are prepared now to accept the necessity of primary government investment in communications and in industry. By and large, however, Americans view government principally as an instrument of individual liberty. In more recent years this negative government has been entrusted with responsibility for a wide range of social services and development but without losing sight of the basic and original purpose of the government which we were seeking. We are, of course, in the process of changing our government and system of politics as we seek to render them more appropriate to the new problems which we look to the political process to solve.

Does the African seek political forms and government for similar purposes? Are we in the West inclined to insist that the new African states settle upon a government that is more suited to the purposes of the last century in the West than to the present century in Africa? We must be aware of the fact that in Africa there is no legacy of individualism. Traditional government, where it operated distinct from other institutions, did not exist to protect the individual or to ensure his right to pursue his separate goals. In one important respect, then, the attitude of the African toward government today is quite consistent with his traditional attitude toward authority. The purpose of political authority, or government, in much of traditional Africa was to give collective voice and symbol to a people, and to discover and apply restraints on those who might deviate from rigorously circumscribed social norms.

Western influence has not seriously threatened this attitude, for the colonial interlude now drawing to a close did not so much introduce the Western concept of government as reinforce the traditional collective view of authority. The maintenance of order and the protection of property rights in the colonial period were performed, either directly or indirectly, by the colonial governor and his African and European agents. It was not until after World War II that the European colonial powers seriously began to transfer their own political institutions to Africa in recognition of the inevitability of self-government. The British Government of 1945, for example, which served as the model for the transference of self-governing political institutions to much of Africa, reflects not so much the laissez-faire England of John Stuart Mill as the successful establishment in postwar Britain of a new egalitarian welfare state. The governmental forms transferred to Africa from postwar Europe were in practice directed toward a positive role for government in the initiation and carrying out of national development.

It is understandable, therefore, that the African of today tends to expect government to provide the services he has come to deem desirable or necessary and to provide a collective symbol or voice vis-à-vis other nations and peoples. When the new government established to secure these goals appears to ride roughshod over the rights of individuals or minorities, we in the West are inclined to condemn that new government for denying the very end for which it supposedly exists. The African, on the other hand, judges his government in terms not so much of its deference to individual liberty and minority rights but its capacity to achieve the material services of modernization and to serve the nationalist or racial ego.

The early stages of political transition in Africa have been characterized by a unified determination to replace the traditional or colonial government. However, this has not often been accompanied by an agreement as to what should replace alien rule. Therefore, the real quest for order has only recently begun. The national governments of recent birth are obviously transitional. The Ghanaian Government under President Kwame Nkrumah has now had more than six years' experience. Few would question its capacity to carry out the daily functions of government. But it is equally evident that the elusive quest for order in Ghana continues; the government today is obviously quite different from that inherited from the British in 1957. The Ghanaian Government is the major instrument for the achievement of the dual national goals of modernization and international stature and eminence. However impressive its governmental superstructure, however manifest the leadership qualities of its President, the fact remains that national order and integration have not yet been achieved. Survival of the government, therefore, might depend upon the extent and the rate with which it approaches these ends, or upon its capacity to manipulate people into believing that these goals are in fact being achieved.

No African country, except the Republic of South Africa, has yet even approached the goals of modernization and nationhood, either in terms of Western standards or by whatever purposes and goals it may have postulated for itself. And we can expect more rather than less political change and instability.

The process of colonial disengagement places a heavy emphasis upon schedules, constitutions, and the other legal paraphernalia of independence and sovereignty. It may be because of our obsession with the legalities and constitutional forms of self-government that we tend often to ignore the conditions conducive to democracy. More important, possibly, than the statutory provisions for protection of individual liberty and minority rights is the amount of tolerance for conflicting opinions and of opinion permitted to flourish and to influence new governmental policy and forms.

LIBERTY VERSUS ORDER

Whatever the African's attitude toward two-party government, minority rights, individual liberty, and other elements of the Western democratic credo, he joins other men in insisting that the government he seeks be "democratic." If by democracy we mean only government based upon mass manipulation and support, then democracy has truly conquered our world. The emergence of the majoritarian principle, in one form or another, in mass-based political systems is probably inevitable. And the principle of majority rule, relying upon the righteousness of numerical supremacy, was a logical instrument of Western democracy for the African nationalists to seize upon in their struggle for national independence. Accompanying majority rule, in the Western view of democracy, is of course the value of minority rights. Despite postwar emphasis upon egalitarian social welfare government, a tendency has appeared in Africa to incorporate into the new constitutions bills of rights for the protection of minorities and individuals.

The capacity or willingness to tolerate difference, to permit disagreement, and to entertain proposals for governmental reform for altered policy and new leadership is a measure of the degree to which an existing government can either accommodate or survive the demands of an opposition. That governments voluntarily surrender ideas and power to new leaders is of course the ultimate test of a democratic system. It is difficult, indeed, to find many countries where this test is generally applied, and even more rare to find countries where it is successfully met in every instance. In the new African states the "toleration or opposition" level, short of surrendering capacity to govern, is understandably low. Furthermore, the very nature of the opposition in new nations is often such as to lead the government in power to question the opposition's legitimate intent to abide by the constitution, or its capacity to meet popular expectations were it to become the government. Thus the temptation of both the governing party and the minority opposition to act irresponsibly is enhanced.

The proliferation of bills of rights and other structural guarantees of minority and individual liberties recognize in part a tendency of both the African national leaders and the departing colonial power to abide by the rules of twentieth-century constitution-making.

The achievement of independence for the new African nations is not alone sufficient to grant the sought-after status of equality in the modern world. For in addition, the new nations must be "modern" and, more important, they must be regarded by other nations as "democratic." Although it possesses many of the attributes of greatness—size, population, and a long history of independence—Ethiopia has failed to emerge as the major leader of the new African states. In part this failure is due to the "undemocratic" and "unmodern" nature of the Ethiopian state. Because it does not have a constitutional and governmental structure resembling the modern West, its independence in African eyes is not really complete or "first class."

TO BE DEMOCRATIC AND MODERN

An interesting and significant ambivalence manifests itself in the insistence, on the one hand, that the new governments or states be regarded as democratic, and on the other hand, that an independent personality be demonstrated by downgrading Western culture and institutions. Thus democracy in Africa, it is maintained, is not only not derived from the West, but is in many respects superior to Western forms. This leads to the curious, and at times frustrating, situation wherein Africa's new leaders label as "democratic" institutions and behavior that contradict the meaning of the term as it is understood in the West and then justify this on the basis that it is an expression of "African" democracy. Possibly the most frequently heard explanation of why African political practices can deviate sharply from those of the West and still be regarded as democratic relates to the peculiar nature of Africa's struggle for independence and development. For example, as long as the activities of government are directed against the remnants of colonialism or toward modernization, they are obviously in the interest of all the citizens, and consensus can be taken for granted. Therefore a multiple-party system, a free press, and other institutions capable of giving expression to diverse points of view and to the policy of an opposition are not really requisite to democracy.

Like water seeking its own level the governments of Africa are still in the process of establishing more permanent forms. Therefore, viewed from the point of view of the political scientist, one should not technically speak of modern African governments as political institutions. The new states inherited a ready-made order of frontiers, governmental forms, and operating patterns. These, however, are not the end of the process but the very beginning. We can expect the African to experiment and to vary the inherited order as he seeks to establish a system consistent with his perception of public problems and values. Therefore, we should regard practices inconsistent with the model governments bequeathed by the colonial powers not as deviations but rather as the establishment of precedents in the current quest for order. In the future sufficient precedent will have been established to firmly institutionalize African government and politics. Whether these institutions will be democratic in the Western sense it is too early to determine. Thus, the quest continues compelling the African to establish his personal equality and dignity through the instrument of his new state and to reject outside institutions while seeking a government that sufficiently resembles Western forms to warrant its being regarded as "democratic" and "modern." The problem then remains one of finding a government which is both "African" and which measures up to the standards of the modern world that Africa would join but not emulate.

MINORITIES AND THE NEW ORDER

European colonial powers prefer not to disengage completely from their former dependencies. They attempt to perpetuate their institutions and to protect their commercial interests and investments as long as possible. Thus, some constitutional provisions in new African countries reflect a deliberate effort on the part of the decolonizing power to protect those individuals, minorities, and investments most clearly associated with its own values and interests.

We must also remember that near barbaric treatment of minorities and individuals accompanied the past war. World opinion expressed, for example, in the Covenant of Human Rights compels the new African states, if they are to win the respect and status they desire in the world community, to proclaim the rights of minorities and individuals. Furthermore, the willingness and inclination to recognize and at least pay lip service to these individual liberties also reflect, in part, the nature of the social revolution throughout Africa where the individual, as opposed to the clan or tribe, is becoming more and more important. On the other hand, an examination of the new constitutions and governmental structures reveals also the inclusion of provision for minority rights for traditional regions or groups. Not only is such recognition often required if unified support for the new multitribal state is to be forthcoming, but it also reduces the likelihood of a postindependence growth of divisive element. The conflict between individual and minority rights and the authority of the sovereign state to guard itself against subversion is as old as popular government. The ambivalence of this contradiction is strikingly revealed in the Nigerian Constitution. Articles XXII-XXIV of the new constitution specify in admirable detail the prohibitions of governmental action and outline the twentieth-century freedoms familiar in similar documents in constitutional democracies throughout the world. These rights and safeguards are followed, however, by a clause stating that "nothing in this section shall invalidate any law that is reasonably justifiable in a democratic society—in the interest of defense, public safety, public order, public morality, or public health. . . ." [1]

The important question, of course, is not the legal and constitutional safeguards, or even the observance or violation of these safeguards, but rather the extent to which they are incorporated into the social fabric and fundamental belief structure. In one respect, African diversity and extreme social fragmentation, which has long hindered development and political integration, gives effect to the principles of toleration, difference, and opposition. For the new states, without exception, consist of unions of different and often conflicting cultures. Association of many small-scale societies into a single nation state has tended to necessitate governmental forms which recognize the existence of the traditional constituencies and which thereby guarantee them a right to continued existence and to some home rule privileges and rights.

In the last analysis, however, the requirements of modernization, nationhood, and international dignity demand that the government, if it deems it necessary, be prepared to sacrifice the individual, the ethnic or racial minority, and even the traditional constituent unit. Deliberate planned modernization may be inconsistent either with highly decen-

[1] The Constitution of Nigeria, Article XXIII, paragraph 4.

tralized government or with the presence of an opposition which may, or may not, be loyal. Because his mentors hold these libertarian values in high regard, because the African leader himself has been exposed to this philosophy, and because sophisticated and respectable behavior in the world community requires that lip service at least be paid to the libertarian ethos, the leaders of the new African countries generally seek to protect or establish a posture of protecting minority rights and of countenancing a political opposition. However, when the chips are down and a choice must be made by the government in power between survival and a toleration of minorities, the latter, most often, are expendable.

VIOLENCE AND THE QUEST FOR ORDER

As man is never without some form of order and constantly in search of new forms, it follows that the search implies a dissatisfaction with the existing system on the part of some and a desire to replace that system with something different. All government, however, serves to protect or promote the values of one or more groups or elements in the society to the relative disadvantage of others. Therefore any existing government serves vested interests and will naturally abhor any change which might lead to its demise. Thus the quest for order not infrequently is accompanied by conflict between those who seek to establish new forms and those whose interests are served by the existing system. During periods of rapid political transition violence lurks close to the surface.

Conflict and violence have accompanied the quest for order in Africa no less than elsewhere in the world, but unlike North and South America, Southeast Asia, and Oceania, there has been comparatively little revolutionary violence directed against the European colonial powers in Africa.[2] In part this can be attributed to the absence in traditional Africa of large-scale organizational skills capable of effectively opposing European intervention and colonization. Even though these skills now exist, violence has been the exception rather than the rule. The reason for this is that the African's will and capacity to achieve independence have coincided with a willingness on the part of Britain and France to disengage—in part of course, in recognition of the existence of this new capacity. Thus, conflict has centered not around the question for self-government but around the issue of when and for whom.

The Portuguese, on the other hand, have refused to accept the necessity of disengagement, and in Angola the African has had recourse to violence in order to establish his right to seek his own government, while in South Africa violence is forever latent and, when it seems to give promise of success, tends to become manifest.

It would be inaccurate to leave the impression that the African Revolu-

---

[2] For a different point of view see Jack Woddis, *Africa the Lion Awakes* (London: Lawrence and Wishart, 1961).

tion has been particularly bloodless, for it has not. Violent conflict in postwar Africa has generally taken one or a combination of four forms.
1. *Traditional Tribal Feuds and Warfare.* This form of armed conflict, characterizing much of Africa before the advent of European penetration and hegemony, is restricted today to those few areas that have been little affected by the West. Thus, the Karamajong in Uganda's remote northeast, upon occasion, continue to wage war upon the Turkana. Although this form of traditional violence is nearly extinct, there is some evidence that the dislocation accompanying independence might serve to revive intertribal warfare. For instance, independence in the former Belgian Trust Territory of Ruanda has led to a revival of the conflict between the Watutsi and the Bahatu. Uganda's independence brought into the open the smoldering conflict between the Batoro, Bamba, and Bakanjo. Before the final demise of traditional tribal warfare in Africa, a brief revival of this primitive form of conflict is likely to occur.
2. *Riots and Revolts Against Constituted Authority.* This form of short-lived but often bloody violence characterized conflict in many colonial areas in the period immediately following World War II. In 1944, for example, rioting in Uganda was directed against the Buganda Government faction which was ostensibly supporting British rule. This type of conflict is a protest not necessarily so much against the colonial power as against the authority of indigenous chiefs and other rulers. Thus, riots against constituted authority sometimes reflect elements of civil strife as well. The 1949 riots in Buganda, Uganda, were as much a protest against the chiefs and influential African elite as against the British. The Bukedi riots in the same country in 1960 were clearly directed against local chiefs and not against the central government. Riots of this nature are often sparked by economic distress brought about by a fall in commodity prices, a change in labor conditions, or by the assessment of increased taxes.

In 1961, election rioting in Zanzibar led to the death of more than seventy persons and caused serious injury to three hundred. The situation warranted the bringing of troops to Zanzibar from Kenya and Uganda to restore order. This conflict revolved around the struggle for power between the dominant Arab minority and the more numerous Afro-Shirazis. As this situation and as numerous riots in the Republic of South Africa illustrate, race, too, serves as the basis of violence against constituted authority. The riots in Nyasaland in 1959 were more directly a protest of the Africans against alien authority and arose in opposition to Nyasaland's forced inclusion in the Central African Foundation.
3. *Civil War.* Although Africa has been spared the long and tragic civil wars that have plagued other continents, it has not escaped entirely. The short but violent mutiny of southern troops in the Republic of the Sudan in 1955 which pitted Arab north against African south certainly

had the earmarks of a civil war. In Liberia, the constant tension which erupts into violence at election time between the coastal descendants of the original American Negro settlers and the indigenous up-country Africans can also be included within this category, as might the conflict which terrorized the newly independent Cameroon Republic in 1960.

4. *Wars of Independence.* Although this type of violence has been the exception in Africa, for reasons that we have already noted, the revolt of the Angolan people against Portuguese rule should certainly be classified as a war of independence. The uprising against French rule in Madagascar (Malagasy) in 1947 was also obviously a war for independence, even though an unsuccessful one.

Thus the violence accompanying the quest for order in Africa has tended to pit African against African. To simply say, as some critics of African independence are inclined to do, that internecine warfare is the natural state of African society, is to ignore the fact that civil strife in Africa on a large and deadly scale is by and large a product or legacy of colonial rule, and, some would add, of neo-colonialism as well. Belgian hegemony in the Congo effectively dislocated tribal groups, urbanized a large population, and rendered hundreds of thousands of Africans dependent upon complex economic and political organizations which they were never instructed in operating before independence was thrust upon them. The civil war in the Congo, even if U.N. troops and Katanga mercenaries had not been present, can hardly be regarded as simply a revived form of traditional intertribal warfare.

Violence as an element in the pursuit of independence has undergone significant changes since World War II. On the one hand, the increased fire power and effectiveness of modern weapons render it somewhat easier for an existing government (colonial or African) to resist efforts to overthrow it. On the other hand, the major colonial powers are now relatively weaker and less able to mount and sustain major defensive wars than they were before World War II. More important, of course, is the new balance of international power. Neither the USSR nor the United States is a colonial power and both have a long tradition of opposing colonialism.

A factor not often observed is the impact of World War II on the attitudes of Africans toward Europeans and toward being ruled by European powers. Thousands of Africans served in the military forces of Great Britain and Free France during World War II. The veterans returning to the villages and farms were wise in the ways of the outside world and less mystified and intimidated by colonial rule than they had been before they left. They had learned, and subsequently told others, of the defeats that the Europeans had suffered at the hands of the colored peoples of Japan. They knew—some of them from the original source— of the defeat of France and Belgium and the isolation of Great Britain.

At the same time, they themselves had learned to shoot guns and engage in organized strife. To this we must, of course, add the impact upon the African intelligentsia of the numerous wartime proclamations, such as the Four Freedoms and the promise of Indian and Philippine independence. In short, the postwar world witnessed both an absolute and a relative decline in the capacity of the European powers to employ violence in order to retain their holdings. This decline was accompanied by an enhanced awareness and increased capacity on the part of the African to employ violence, expel the colonial regime, and establish governments of his own choosing in Africa.

The prospect of slaughter in this age of technological warfare is distasteful to Frenchmen and Englishmen whose memories of sacrifice and bloodshed are still vivid. Only the Portuguese Government, relatively free of the dictates of public opinion and not restrained by recollections of war, has chosen violently to defend the status quo. Yet it is evident, even to many Portuguese leaders, that a reactionary government is today unable to sustain its moral and political position in the face of the ever-rising material and human costs of violence. Portugal must be prepared to face the increasing antagonism and hostility of a world which, although divided on many important issues, is of a single mind in viewing colonialism as an anachronism in our time.

Furthermore, American and Soviet successes abroad have made it amply clear that it is no longer necessary to control the government of a territory in order to influence its policy and people. Also, isolated instances of violence such as the Mau Mau incident in Kenya severely damaged the integrity of the colonial power and thus acted to prejudice adversely its future relationships with Africa. The British painfully discovered in Kenya that violence is costly, raises the price of administration astronomically, and tends to divert personnel from the task of development and preparation for independence to nonproductive security measures. Large numbers of Africans hitherto apathetic or even sympathetic to colonial rule are swept by violence into the trauma and emotion of conflict and hatred. The ensuing dislocation seriously affects the European's capacity to govern, for colonial administration has always relied upon the consent of a passive Africa rather than upon force. An environment of violence and warfare activates and mobilizes far larger sectors of the population in opposition to the regime than the colonial administration can effectively cope with.

The real task of the major colonial powers since World War II has been to delay independence as long as possible in order to build those institutions that might both ensure a capacity for self-government along the lines of the metropolitan power and secure the rights of the metropolitan country's minorities and investments in Africa. To delay too long would be to risk the danger of violence and to forever preclude any influence in the new country or any rights for the European minorities resident there. To grant independence too quickly would be to risk chaos and disintegration. The game of successful disengagement is a complex one, and the relative absence of violence between the colonial powers and the Africans is a credit to the skill with which both have played the game.

III
Tribes and Tribalism

It is likely that the tribe, which still serves as an organized means of regulating interrelationship of countless thousands of men, was once the dominant form of human association over much of the inhabited earth. Today, something romantically or derisively termed "tribalism" is with few exceptions directed toward Africa or Africans. Anthropologists are not agreed upon the precise meaning of the term "tribe," but it is usually used to refer to a certain type of human group and organization. Tribalism, however, is an emotive symbol used by African nationalists and Western journalists to refer to those elements of the social and political system which would seem to frustrate "modernization," or it is applied to almost any form of behavior on the part of Africans which cannot be explained or understood within the framework of the observer's own culture.

Mau Mau, ritual murder, traditional dress, physical mutilation, naked torsos, unity, and disunity have all been regarded at one time or another as aspects of tribalism. Thus, like democracy, which to many people means anything that is not communism or totalitarianism, tribalism often is but a residual category collectively explaining the inexplicable.

AN ANATOMY OF TRIBALISM

We cannot begin to understand what is meant by "tribalism" without first examining tribal forms of political and local organization. Most scholars agree that "tribe" refers to a cluster or group of people sharing a common language, culture, and territory. To qualify as a tribe, other anthropologists would require the group to possess an ideological unity or a shared dogma as to tribal origins as well. Important for our purposes is the fact that one of the critical aspects of tribe is a considerable solidarity or "we" feeling, wherein the collectivity or group tends to be more important than any single individual. In contrast, in Western civilization, the social and political systems place a high premium upon the individual. If the individual in Western society is in possession of his normal faculties and is of legal age, we assume that he possesses a wide range of personal choice for which he is then held responsible. The liberation of the individual from the protective, although confining, bonds of the tribe and other kinship groupings is a fairly recent historical phenomenon and in many areas of the world is still under way.

Tribal life was, and in some areas of the world still is, the major form of corporate and communal existence, involving as it often does the sharing of a common religion and a belief in a common origin.[1] It is difficult for us, immersed as we are in our own culture, to conceive of an intense human unity based not upon contiguity but more upon dogma and ideology; the tribe is much more than an association of individuals empirically linked together by a common interest. Ideally, for the individual, there is no life or reason to exist outside the tribe and its constituent units.

Modernization in Africa, among other things, has penetrated deep into the substance and ideology of tribal organization and solidarity. The social revolution currently underway throughout Africa is much more complicated and involved than the observers and writers who speak glibly of "detribalization" would have us believe. We shall attempt to show that tribalism, or the value and behavior patterns that can be attributed to tribal organization and life, is not so much disappearing or reappearing as it is changing in form and substance. Some observers, including a number of Westernized Africans, feel that the tribe is inconsistent with modernization and its persistence is a constant stigma and symbol of a primitive past. On the other hand, certain romanticists and a few colonial administrators (who themselves may be seeking to escape from the present) are enamored of the noble savage, tend to deify tribal institutions, and look with pain upon alterations in the social and political system that evolves in response to new conditions.

There are three broad principles or ways in which men tend to associate together, which in turn require political regulation: kinship, residential locality, and special interest association. Grouped together in one or a combination of these three ways, men tend to form associations which have a life existence separate from and greater than any one or a combination of their constituent members. The predominant form of corporate group in Africa is the kinship or descent group termed "clan" or "lineage" by anthropologists. The three basic aspects of kinship which serve as the basis of the traditional political systems are descent, filiation, and marriage. In most societies descent, and thus the authority and obligation inherent in the society, is unilineal; that is, it is reckoned on one side of the family only. The lineage members trace their descent to a known ancestor, whereas a clan is a unilineal descent

---

[1] The extent to which the tribe, especially as a political unit, is based upon kinship, is contested by various scholars. Schapera, *Government and Politics in Tribal Society* (1956), p. 29, argues that there are a number of tribes which do not share this real or fictional kinship. He would suggest that to Maines' two principles of political association—kinship and local contiguity—we add a third, namely, personal attachment to a common leader.

group whose members claim common descent from a single ancestor but cannot trace all the steps between the living members and the ancestor founder. Generally a lineage consists of from two to seven generations, whereas a clan may be composed of ten or more generations. "In many African societies, individual discipline and by extension community order is the responsibility of the leaders of the descent groups, who are often also the political leaders." [2]

As the kinds of situations or collective problems for which men design forms of political organization change, the nature of the organization, if the system is to persist, must also change. Tribal organization, with its emphasis upon kinship, age, dogma, the natural environment, and a subsistence economy, in its traditional form no longer provides an adequate, organized manner of coping with many of the social problems arising out of the radical and rapid alterations in the world in which the Africans now find themselves living. Problems of sanitation, erosion, and markets now exist side by side with the traditional concerns of inheritance, bride price, and kinship regulation. On the other hand we must not forget that there exists a considerable number of traditional social conditions for which the elements of traditional tribal forms continue to be appropriate. Therefore, it is not surprising that the political systems of much of Africa are composed of elements of both modern bureaucratic government and of traditional institutions.

Any form of human organization that involves a differential distribution of authority acts relatively to deprive some and reward others; it is in the nature of those who profit from an existent pattern of power distribution to be found in the vanguard of its defense. Not a small part of the conflict and dislocation accompanying rapid transition in Africa can be attributed to this struggle between the holders of traditional authority and the younger men who seek to replace them as leaders. Often the conflict manifests itself in a struggle for power and influence between the chiefs and the younger, frequently better educated and more radical, political party leaders. Few Ghanaian villages in the Ashanti region, for example, were spared the intrigues of the struggle for power between the traditional chiefs and the local representatives of Nkrumah's Convention People's Party.

VARIATIONS IN TRIBAL ORGANIZATION

Tribal organization in Africa varies so radically from one place to another, both in scope and form, that we are reluctant even to venture any generalizations. The anthropologists' indecision as to the precise meaning of the term "tribe" is certainly understandable in view of this extraordinary variety. Some tribes are very small and their members number only in the hundreds. Others are very large and may incorporate more

[2] Simon and Phoebe Ottenberg, *Cultures and Societies of Africa* (New York: Random House, Inc., 1960), p. 32. Copyright © 1960 by Random House, Inc.

than six million people as do the Ibo of Nigeria. The Yoruba in the
same country are nearly as numerous, with five million members. East
Africa, too, has its large tribes, including the Baganda in Uganda and
the Kikuyu in Kenya. Some of these larger tribes, such as the Baganda and
Zulu, possess a long illustrious history and a national or, should we say,
tribal consciousness of collective identity and patriotism.

Studies of African political systems have not been numerous and
nearly all available works are relatively recent. One of the first, and
certainly one of the most influential, was Rattray's work on the Ashanti
(in present-day Ghana) in 1929. Herskovits, too, was an early contributor,
having examined the governing system of Dahomey in 1938. Also to be
included among these early pioneering studies is Nadel's study of the
Nupe of Nigeria and Evans-Pritchard's works on the Nuer of the Sudan.[3]

With some notable exceptions, the larger tribes generally possessed
more highly developed political systems wherein a paramount chief or
divine-right king ruled the tribal nation through the agency of a
hierarchy of lesser chiefs and special-purpose authorities. Early British
explorers and missionaries discovered the existence of sophisticated
tribal nations of this description both in the Lake Victoria region of East
Africa and in the northern regions of Nigeria. In fact, British influence
and control throughout much of tropical Africa was extended by granting recognition to these tribal nations and by the convenient incorpora-
tion of their governmental system into the over-all pattern of colonial
rule. This expedient, whereby traditional governmental forms were continued but made subordinate to the administering foreign power, is
termed "indirect rule" and has received considerable attention as a
political invention.[4]

These former tribal nations, possessed of a unique culture, a long
history, and a dynasty of rulers which they often traced back to the days
of King Alfred or Louis XIV, have naturally resisted the efforts of their
European mentors to treat them as administrative provinces or districts
in a larger, more inclusive African nation state or colony. The price of
modernization and nationalism for the traditional leaders of the large
tribal nations such as the Kabaka of Buganda and the Asante of Ashanti,
has come very high indeed.

The term "tribe" is also affixed to grouping of people who, although
speaking a similar language and sharing a common culture, do not
possess large-scale or specialized political systems and who, before the
arrival of the Europeans, were only dimly conscious of their exclusiveness. Although small-scale organization is generally characteristic of the

---

[3] Melville Herskovits, *Dahomey* (New York: J. J. Augustin, Inc., 1938). S. F. Nadel, *The
Nuba* (Oxford: Oxford University Press, 1947). E. E. Evans-Pritchard, *The Nuer*
(Oxford: The Clarendon Press, 1940).
[4] In reality, indirect rule is as old as the "conquest" theory of the state and is less
a political invention than an administrative expedient.

smaller tribes there are significant exceptions. The Iteso in Uganda, the Dinka and the Nuer of the Sudan, although quite large for tribes, were diffusely organized and lacked large-scale centralized political institutions. Not all of these small-scale political systems are organized solely or even primarily on the basis of kinship. In some diffuse traditional societies the personal or familial relationship of the member of the community to the chief constituted the authority system, whereas among some of the Nilo-Hamitic tribes of East Africa the age-grade unit took precedence over kinship as the primary basis of political authority.[5] It is commonly believed that tribe or clan organization based upon kinship dominated African social and political life, but even among the less highly developed African tribes kinship was not always the primary element in the political system.

Of course it really is not possible to separate the political from other aspects of social organization in these small diffuse uncentralized tribes. In reality all social institutions exercised considerable influence and were an integral part of the political system. The numerous small-scale socio-political systems that characterized these diffuse tribal societies were nearly autonomous and periods of cooperation were followed by feud and conflict.[6] Complete anarchy, however, was avoided by the tendency of these many small segments to overlap one another. This overlapping of kinship, residence, and age-grade provided the basis for a rudimentary larger-scale organization that was often capable of mediating between conflicting smaller segments.

IMPACT OF EUROPEAN INTERVENTION

When these diffusely organized areas fell under colonial rule, often through the connivance and assistance of the military forces of their better organized and more powerful neighbors, the European power was faced with the problem of administering an area which, in Western terms, did not appear to possess a government and which seemingly existed in a state of confusion and anarchy. Needless to say, the natives of these diffusely organized tribes were as unaware of this confusion as they were of the fact that they did not possess a governing system. This seeming disorganization and disintegration frustrated and challenged the ability of the colonial powers to administer these areas indirectly through the agency of a native chief or king as they had so successfully done in the larger-scale societies. Therefore they were often faced with the necessity of ruling these diffuse cultures, subcultures, independent

[5] Age-grade or age-set refers generally to an organizational structure common in Africa whereby the population is divided into segments of approximately the same age. Thus persons of the same age-set go through life together, moving from less to more mature positions of responsibility at regular intervals.

[6] Possibly the most thorough analysis of the small-scale African political organizations is presented in the work by John Middleton and David Tait, ed., *Tribes Without Rulers* (London: Routledge & Kegan Paul, Ltd., 1958).

lineages, and families directly as occupied territory. But more often the colonial power superimposed the political system of a neighboring larger-scale and more specialized tribal kingdom over these "tribes without rulers." It is somewhat ironic that in the process of administering these areas and defining their respective boundaries, the British in East Africa, for example, gradually created a consciousness of tribal identity and exclusiveness that did not traditionally exist. In part, this was achieved by designating the area inhabited by this complex of peoples as an administrative district or local government. This new tribal nationalism has posed a handicap to later unification into modern nation states.

Tribal organization, in both the small- and large-scale socio-political systems, is undergoing radical change as it is called upon to cope with new problems and conditions. We would not disagree that tribal forms of sociation are becoming relatively less important throughout most of tropical Africa as the nation state with its attendant political party and local government sociations become increasingly important. More important than the demise of "tribe" is its modification and its assumption of new roles. For example, in many areas in Africa the clan, or another segmentary unit, serves unofficially (and was sometimes unbeknown to the European colonial official) as the lowest tier of administration. In this capacity it directly links the official administration to the individual or kin group.

It is difficult to understand the way in which the complexities of modern bureaucratic government are interpreted and translated by a village chief or elder. He serves as a sort of broker of modernity for the great mass of the people who retain their traditional beliefs and practices. Relevant to this internal role is the peculiar manner of settlement of much of Africa. With some exceptions the African village, of which so much is written and so little known, is not a concentrated cluster of houses geometrically located along a path or road. The romanticist often conceives of the African village as a cross between a Grandma Moses Christmas card scene of the New England village and a hectic beehive or ant hill. Although there were, and still are in West Africa, a few traditional cities of considerable size and complexity, of which we have something to say elsewhere in this study, Africa has been and still is characterized by a settlement pattern to which the term "village" has been applied.[7] Although these villages tend to be separated from other villages by natural barriers or by relatively unsettled spaces, the residents of a given village are not usually concentrated cheek to jowl but are more apt to be scattered in what at first glance may seem to be isolated family homesteads. Yet this seemingly haphazard form of residence does not seem isolated or haphazard to the African.

It is usually the village chief who must translate outside governmental

[7] See Chapter IV.

policy or bureaucratic regulations (planting and harvesting rules, tax collections, sanitation and health rules) into meaningful commands which will be obeyed and which will effectively alter human behavior in the desired direction. If this is not accomplished, policy is meaningless and consists of no more than plans. So important are these unofficial segmentary leaders that in some parts of Africa the village chief uses some of his own income to pay a small salary to his unofficial assistants.

OLD FORMS AND NEW FUNCTIONS

It is at this parochial and local level that we can best perceive the changes taking place in political legitimacy. At the local level the African, on occasion, will find his loyalty split between obligations owed to his traditional segmentary leaders, who are generally of a kinship variety, and the obligations he owes to local government officials and representatives, or to local representatives of the central government. If this is not sufficient to generate anxiety, we need only add the new obligations connected with a political party, cooperative, and church membership. In those areas where chieftainship is not a part of the traditional political system but has been imposed upon the people or has been adopted for the purposes of administrative convenience, the elected local representative on the local government council is sometimes regarded more as a traditional leader than is the official civil-service chief.

The significance of this coexistence at the local level of modified traditional and modern bureaucratic forms is that even though they may conflict they effectively combine to provide community order and to serve as the matrix within which social and political transition takes place. At this important level one form of political authority seems to blend with another until the end product resembles neither. The segmentary leaders (clan leaders, elders, age-grade heads) have been deprived of most of their traditional authority by the modern bureaucratic government. These traditional leaders are no longer permitted to force their former subjects to behave in certain traditional ways. Of course this is not to say that these individuals are powerless, since they continue in many cases to be the recipients of the legitimate consent of the great mass of the peasant population. But to a significant degree, even though they still possess legitimate authority in the eyes of their subjects, they no longer possess the coercive force to back up that authority. On the other hand the official bureaucratic chief or other government functionaries sent down from a higher level to the village do possess both the capacity and the authoritative power to coerce. They do not elicit a sufficiently high degree of local consensus to obtain a desirable level of conformity to the alien and bureaucratic rules. Thus, each of the two systems needs the support of the other and a natural alliance is often formed between the official bureaucracy and the traditional kinship segments at this parochial, but vital, level of society and politics.

After World War II the colonial powers, and in particular Great Britain and France, came to realize that the days of external colonial rule were not unlimited and that their future relationship with their dependencies would rely, in large part, on the progress they were able to make in preparing these territories for self-government before independence was gained. That much of the preparation would have to take place at the local level was evident. One of the most significant policy changes was a shift from indirect rule to the development of local governments generally patterned on the system existing in the European metropole. The advent of democratic local government, particularly in those African territories having experienced British rule, has resulted in the establishment of thousands of local councils. In some British territories there existed as many as six tiers of representative councils. In parts of Uganda, for example, there are village, parish, subcounty, county, and district councils at the local government level plus the legislative council in the capital city. As these councils, patterned as they are on the British model, have tended to be large—with a membership in some instances exceeding fifty—it is not unusual for the village kinship segments to evolve unofficially as constituencies. Therefore in some localities it is possible to find lineage or clan leaders serving simultaneously as village and county councillors. This blending of new and old at the local level has helped to instruct the African villager in the ways of representative government and thereby has eased some of the problems of political transition. But it has also served to perpetuate parochial loyalties and his substituted a modern arena for the continuation of traditional parochial conflicts.

Although direct election has been introduced in much of Africa for the national legislatures, the principle of indirect election is still widely used at the local and provincial level. Therefore many local and regional councils are composed of representatives who were elected by and from the membership of lower councils. When we add to this the fact that the constituent areas of many of the lower councils often coincide with traditional parochial constituencies (tribe, clan, secret society, lineage, age-set), it is possible to see how the blending of territorial representation with kinship and other traditional segmentary associations characterizes not only village level organization but is an element at all levels of political organizations. This intimate interrelationship of traditional and modern political ideologies and systems illustrates how tribalism, rather than disappearing or reappearing, is in fact continually being molded and blended with imported ideas of territoriality and bureaucracy into a uniquely African governmental-political system.

Some tribal institutions such as witchcraft, on occasion, are employed and modified to cope with problems and interpersonal conflicts that are not soluble by the modern councils, courts, or chiefs. In this way traditional institutions perform a vital function, for they provide a means of mediating potentially disruptive conflict for which no other method exists. The amazing capacity of traditional tribal institutions to meet these new requirements should certainly testify to the necessity of viewing African social and political institutions as dynamic and not static. Only the romanticist now believes that African institutions have remained static for centuries and now suddenly are subjected to radical change in response to outside cultural influence. We must constantly bear in mind that these African institutions have always been in a state of flux and that the significance of the present is the increased rate and the direction of change.

The rules, ordinances, and laws passed by the modern councils and administered by the large-scale bureaucracy sometimes require the support of the remnants of tribal institutions. For example, in Uganda, district councils (prior to independence), on the urging of the British Administrators and a few educated councillors, passed ordinances limiting the wealth that could be exchanged as dowry or bride price. The exchange of money, cattle, or other valuables at the conclusion of the wedding contract has long been a vital element in many local African economies. Rules regulating the amount that can be legally paid could conceivably disrupt the local economy and social structure. Sometimes the African feels it necessary to call upon a traditional institution to render a new bureaucratic rule or ordinance operable. The manner in which witchcraft, for example, as a traditional aspect of tribalism interacts with the modern rule making authority of the new local governments is illustrated in the following case.

In an administrative district in Uganda, which coincides almost exactly with the domicile of a single tribe, the district council, upon the initiative of British Administrators, passed an ordinance limiting bride price to fifteen cows. As any male is aware, however, some women are worth more cows than others, and as most economists realize, there exists a relationship between supply and demand from which neither women nor cows are exempt. As might be expected some women did in fact, if not in law, bring more cows than the limit specified by the district council ordinance. Among most African tribes it is required that the father of the bride return the bride price to the father of the groom if, for certain justified reasons, the bride leaves the home of her husband or dies. When this type of situation actually occurred the question arose as to whether or not the father of the bride should return all of the cows that he had received or only those which the ordinance specified he was legally entitled to receive. Obviously there was no modern legal way in which the father of the groom was able to enforce the return of the part of the bride price which he was not legally entitled to receive. Faced with this situation the groom's father solicited the services of a witch doctor, paying him to lay a spell on the family of the father of the bride to force the return of the cows which had been paid in excess of the legal limit.

We have observed a number of cases of this type; in every instance witchcraft worked effectively to provide the coercive power behind a modern legislative ordinance, whose enforcement, without witchcraft, would have been most unlikely.

We have also seen cases where witchcraft was used to enforce the payment of gambling debts and to ensure the fulfillment of contractual arrangements completed outside the modern legal system. There exist innumerable transitory situations involving a variety of tribal institutions which call forth the cooperative interaction of modified tribal practices with modified modern bureaucratic governmental structures. It should be evident at this point that tribalism is neither disappearing nor being revived but is reacting to the demands placed upon it as it has through the centuries.

SOME TRIBAL LEGACIES

More often than not the tribal groupings led a migratory life. Africa of the seventeenth and eighteenth centuries was a land in motion wherein transient segmentary groups were thrusting their numbers into the domain of other tribal areas. These in turn moved into territories occupied by still other tribes thus causing considerable culture contact, conflict, and interpenetration of peoples. This long history of tribal movement to and fro in search of water, food, and adventure has left some important legacies which, if not always apparent, often lie latent beneath the surface. Many of Africa's tribes and segments do not reside in neatly concise areas but are spread, like the roots of a tree, deep into the territory occupied primarily by other tribal groups. The occupation of the continent by the European powers put an abrupt end to traditional forms of tribal conflict, migration, and convergence, thereby cutting off, on occasion, the advance sections of migratory tribal groups. This has often acted to isolate them from the parent group and to expose them to traditional tribal enemies. This condition, plus the convenient policy of attempting, wherever possible, to draw political administrative boundaries to coincide with tribal groups, has acted in many areas to perpetuate tribal differences and to preclude traditional means of solving these vexing differences. Thus the new tribalism, often a by-product of administrative convenience, tends to accentuate the fracture of the developing nation states into feuding groups and sections. The international boundaries, originally drawn to separate European spheres of interest, now often separate people of the same tribe who seek, now that the European is gone, to restore their lost unity. Viewed in this manner it is just as evident that tribalism can be a unifying as well as a divisive force insofar as it attempts to break down artificial international boundaries. But while it seeks to ignore national boundaries it also often opposes national unity in order to maintain and enhance tribal unity. An understanding of these contradictory but often simultaneous forces and their interrelationships is required if we are to grasp the complex nature of the political evolution underway in Africa today.

Possibly the most powerful factor that has worked to weaken parochial tribal ties and to substitute for them a sense of national unity and purpose, is, ironically, the presence of alien European domination which with independence will disappear. The presence of alien colonial rule provides one of the few factors that all tribes and tribal leaders can agree to oppose.

TRIBALISM AND NATIONALISM

That tribalism persists and frequently is more intense after independence and the withdrawal of colonial rule is becoming increasingly apparent as more and more African nations win the right of national self-determination. This relationship has been perceptively described by Elspeth Huxley. "Colonialism was the glue that stuck these human units [tribes] together into a shape recognizable in an atlas. . . . Now the glue is dissolving and many of these units are falling apart." [8]

Possibly the most striking, and at the same time the most tragic, illustration of the persistence of tribal solidarity and its tendency to become manifest once the "glue" of colonialism dissolves can be seen in the Congo. It was as late as 1959 that the world received its first indication that Belgium's rule over its huge multitribal African territory might soon come to an end. A man little known to the outside world at that time, but a household name among the Abako tribe of the lower Congo, was already setting the stage for events to come. Mr. Kasavubu, who in 1959 was the president of ABAKO—a predominately tribal political association—was then demanding autonomy for a lower Congo state, which he predicted would recapture the grandeur and glory of the sixteenth century tribal empire of Don Affonoso, King of the Congo. So powerful was this ancient tribally based empire that it had maintained ambassadors in Europe. This movement threatened the future political unity of the Congo as did tribal separatism in Katanga, but it also served as a unifying factor, for President Kasavubu sought to incorporate into this new tribal nation Bakongo tribesmen whom the European imperialists and geographers inadvertently had located in Portuguese Angola and in the former French Congo.

Kalonji, the leader of the Baluba tribe, also had dreams of re-establishing a large tribal state in the Kasai region. He proposed to include in his new tribal nation those portions of Portuguese Angola where many of his tribesmen, isolated from the main group, had long resided. The Baluba, a warrior people resident in Kasai, have long contested and fought the Lulua. This conflict reached such an intensity that in February of 1960 a formal peace convention was signed in Brussels between

[8] Elspeth Huxley, "Africa's First Loyalty," *The New York Times Magazine* (September 18, 1960), p. 14.

Belgium and representatives of the Lulua and Baluba tribes whereby the Baluba, living on Lulua tribal land, were required to return to their ancestral homes in southeastern Kasai Province. Tribal jockeying for position and influence, just prior to independence, was little noticed at that time despite the fact that more than 100,000 Baluba were uprooted from their homes and resettled at a great distance. But the most dire implications of tribalism in the Congo awaited independence.

Independence Day celebrations for the Congo were accompanied by rioting and renewal of tribal warfare. And before the Independence Day celebrations were over Bayaka warriors from the upper Congo were looting stores owned by the Bakongo, and in Luluabourg, the capital of Kasai Province, fighting between the Lulua and the Baluba broke out again; the glue was already becoming unstuck!

Africa's nationalist leaders—that is, those individuals who have been able to rise above tribal obligations and elicit the support of more than a single tribe—have tended to come from the small, relatively insignificant tribes. Patrice Lumumba, for example, the only political leader in the Congo who had a truly national following, came from one of the smallest tribes in the Congo, the Valetla. Like the members of many other small tribes in West Africa, the Valetla are commercially minded and more inclined to leave their tribal lands to engage in trading and merchandising ventures that take them the length and breadth of the country.

Although the environment, imperial history, and factors leading up to the situation may vary, the renewal of tribal conflict in other parts of Africa bears a striking resemblance to that in the Congo. For example, in November of 1959 in Ruanda-Urundi—the Belgian administered trust territory in East Central Africa—fighting broke out between the Batutsi ruling minority, which sought to retain a feudal system in that heavily populated area and the Bahutu, the majority agricultural people over whom the Batutsi have ruled for centuries. The Mwami—paramount chief of Urundi and of course a Batutsi—resisted efforts to confine his role to that of a figurehead in a constitutional monarchy. The more numerous Bahutu of lower status, led by a few educated members of the tribe, were determined to seek majority rule or at least equal status with the aristocratic Batutsi before self-government was granted and the dominant position of the Batutsi received constitutional as well as traditional legitimacy. The status difference between the Batutsi and Bahutu is so great that when Kigeri Mwami of Rwanda was in New York to testify before a General Assembly Trusteeship Committee meeting, he refused to take his place alongside the low status Bahutu petitioners who were also in attendance. In November 1959 the tall, regal Batutsi warriors, composing only one-fifth of the population, were all but swamped by the more numerous, embittered Bahutu. It is estimated that more than 500 tribesmen lost their lives in the fighting, while entire villages went up in flames as the tribal war spread rapidly throughout the country. Many Batutsi refugees escaped across the border into Uganda. In all, more than 150,000 tribesmen fled their tribal homes during the fighting, and a refugee problem of major proportion resulted.[9]

Tanganyika, for example, has resettled approximately 15,000 Rwanda refugees in its West Lake Region, while Uganda plans to make permanent provision for as many as 35,000.[10]

As a consequence of this conflict the Mwami was deposed and Rwanda was proclaimed a republic. It has been suggested that Belgium deliberately supported the Bahutu and that there was collusion between the Bahutu and the Belgians to destroy the supremacy of the Batutsi.

In 1962 the General Assembly of the United Nations appointed a special commission to investigate the differences between the tribal factions in Burundi as well as in Rwanda. It was hoped that a union of these two small, although heavily populated, states could be achieved. However, both President Kayibanda of Rwanda and Mr. Muhirwa, the Prime Minister of Burundi, informed the United Nations Commission that they were unable to agree on the proposals for the unification of their two countries. Reluctantly the United Nations Commission reported its findings to the General Assembly, which subsequently confirmed July 1, 1962, as Independence Day for both Burundi and Rwanda.

An independent republican government for Rwanda has not brought an end to tribal strife. The thousands of Batutsi refugees in western Uganda still regard the deposed and exiled Mwami (king) as their rightful ruler. Border forays are frequent and the situation is sufficiently tense to lead the Uganda Government in August 1962 to prohibit the deposed Mwami from holding political meetings in Uganda.

The situation in Burundi is only slightly less plagued by tribal differences and intrigue. The Belgians, in 1961, formed a coalition government dominated by the Bahutu. The issue in Burundi, moreover, is further complicated by a traditional division between two ruling Batutsi families.

Elections in August 1961 brought the Party of Unity and National Progress to power and secured the Prime Ministery for Prince Louis Rwagasori, replacing the coalition led by Jean-Baptiste Ntidendereza, son of Chief Baranyanka, the head of the rival Tutsi family. A month after his party won office and he became Prime Minister, Prince Rwagasori was murdered. At the subsequent trial held under Belgian administration one man, a Greek national, was found guilty of firing the fatal shot, was sentenced to death, and was executed on June 30, 1962, the day before Burundi's independence. On July 2, twenty-four hours after independence, the Burundi Legislative Assembly voted to reopen

[9] *London Times* (Nov. 13, 1959), p. 12.
[10] *Tanganyika Standard* (Dec. 25, 1962).

the case with the result that the opposition party leaders implicated in the earlier case were to be retired. At a subsequent trial, Jean-Baptiste Ntidendereza, former Minister of the Interior and leader of the opposition Christian Democratic Party, and four accomplices were sentenced to death. An appeal in January 1963 supported by Amnesty, the international organization for political and religious freedom, was abruptly ended by the Prime Minister. Despite international criticism the executions were carried out in January 1963.

Although conflict between tribes within a newly independent nation is most common, independence may also spark an effort to bring outlying tribesmen, ruled by another power, into the new state. Thus, although national homogeneity lessens the likelihood of internal strife within Somalia, the presence of Somali people across the frontier in Ethiopia and Kenya has led to the possibility of external violence and war. The Somali claim that the Ogaden region of Ethiopia is not only inhabited by Somali-speaking people but that it legally and rightfully belongs to Somalia. Self-determination for Somalia brought independence to only two of the five Somali-speaking territories of East Africa (formerly Italian and British Somaliland). Match boxes on sale in Mogadishu, capital of former Italian Somaliland, the largest of the Somali-speaking territories, portray a Somalia flag flying not only over the now unified and independent former British and Italian colonies, but over the Somali-speaking regions of Kenya, French Djibouti, and the Ogaden Region of Ethiopia as well.

The seeds of irredentism sown by imperialist competition in the last century do not augur well for the stability of contemporary Africa. Inter-tribal competition, conflict, and tribal irredentism did not vanish with independence but are now vented in political party struggles, international disputes, United Nations debates, and in religious controversy.[11]

The seeming ease with which African tribal groups have been able to transform themselves into political parties has come as a surprise to many observers. For example in the Congo the Baluba tribe became the BALUBAKAT Party and its tribal opposition, the CONAKAT Party. Independence and the withdrawal of the colonial power, in some regions, has permitted a resumption of the struggle against neighboring tribes which, it is hoped, will lead to the righting of long-standing real or fancied wrongs preserved in song and epic poem. To the more tribally oriented African, nationalism has tended to imply the withdrawal of external authority, not only that of the European district officer but of the African chief and other indigenous officialdom as well. Independence does not so much mean freedom of religion, speech, or press as it does the promise of less restraint and a better living standard. If nationalism fails to meet these often inflated expectations it may be rejected in favor of a revival of traditional forms of tribalism.

[11] Irrendentism as effected by tribalism is more fully covered in Chapter VII.

Even among the educated Africans, who generally deplore tribalism, there exists a recognition of its pervasive force and of the necessity, at least in part, to conform to its obligations. Educated Kikuyu girls who have not undergone the tribal circumcision rites, for example, are often shunned as mates by even the educated males.[12] Would-be political leaders educated in the West have found it necessary, upon their return, to submit to various initiation rites which they objectively perceive as barbaric, but which they realize are required if they are to be eligible for positions of leadership.

The extraordinary capacity of latent tribalism to spring to the fore as an element in national political evolution is vividly demonstrated by recent events in Kenya. Few would have predicted before 1960 that Kenyan independence would be delayed by party factionalism based upon intertribal conflict. Unlike Uganda, and to a lesser extent Tanganyika, Kenya's tribal structure was characterized by small-scale diffusely organized societies. Neither of the two large tribes—the Kikuyu in central Kenya and the Luo in the north—possessed a tradition of centralization and historical exclusiveness comparable to that of the Baganda and Banyoro of Uganda or the Wachagga of Tanganyika. Until 1960 when it became apparent that Kenya would become independent as an African dominated state, the racial issue was paramount and tribal conflict was latent. In March of 1960 Kenya-wide parties were once again permitted; the rapid domination of KANU, the first party to be established, by Kikuyu and Luo leaders, triggered the formation of KADU, composed of a coalition of the territory's smaller tribes. To defend its many constituent tribes and its probable minority position KADU espoused MAJIMBO—a form of regional federation calculated to protect the smaller tribes from Kikuyu and Luo domination. Despite opposition from KANU, which favors a strong unitary state, MAJIMBO was accepted as the basis of the new constitution at the Lancaster House Conference of February 1962.[13] The semifederal constitution for Kenya requires a two-house legislature and the delineation of six constituent federated regions. During the fall of 1962 a special Regional Boundaries Commission gathered evidence and heard tribal testimony in its task of reconciling the now manifest tribal enmities with the delineation of the constituent regions. The ensuing debate, fired by the interests of the two major parties and by the activities of politicians with personal interests at stake, has combined to bring to Kenya a higher degree of tribal consciousness and intertribal hostility than ever existed in the past.

Predictably the report of the Kenya Regional Boundaries Commission left many tribal groups dissatisfied. Threats to "sharpen spears" and

[12] Elspeth Huxley, "Drums of Change Beat for African Tribes," *The New York Times Magazine* (Nov. 29, 1959), p. 27.
[13] Report of the Kenya Constitutional Conference 1962 (Command 1700).

"resist to the last drop of tribal blood" to prohibit the formation of regions as specified in the report, brought Kenya to the verge of large-scale violence. Tribal histories, ancient migrations, and nearly forgotten wars and alliances have been revived and presented as counterclaims and evidence of right of occupancy.

No modern association has been spared the bitterness and confusion of this newly released and strengthened tribalism. The Kenya Federation of Labour, the Kenya Students Association, the Kenya Farmers Association, and countless others are divided and plagued by tribal suspicion, fear, and factionalism.

The tribal alliances which form the two major parties have themselves become victims of tribal strife. The large and, in an electoral sense, potentially decisive Kamba tribe late in 1962 broke off from KANU and under the leadership of Paul Ngei established the African People's Party. The Luo, the second largest tribe in Kenya, threatened to split away from KANU and form their own party (Luo United Movement). The Kikuyu, plagued by a richness of political talent and skills and by their association with the activities of the Land Freedom Army, managed to win the fear and suspicion of nearly all Kenya tribes. In Kenya's far Northern Frontier Region, Somali tribesmen, supported by the Somalia Government, are threatening civil war unless they are permitted to secede from Kenya and join with their brethren in a greater Somalia. Nationalism, tribalism, and interstate relations are inextricably interwoven. In Chapter VII the preponderence of intertribal strife as a factor in Africa's interstate relations is discussed in detail. The critical role of tribalism in the politics of nationalism in Kenya is illustrative, and comparable other examples are numerous.

Tribalism as a form of social and political organization—as a way of providing the integrative forces which are required to maintain aspects of traditional society—will probably be retained, at least as long as the kinds of problems for which it provides solutions continue to exist or are not adequately provided for by other and more modern affiliations. In not a few instances the tribe and its constituent units provide a form of security for the members of the numerous and differing African societies which the modern political structures of the nation state and its subdivisions are not yet able to supply. Nor does tribalism simply linger on within the more remote rural regions of Africa, for as we shall see it possesses a vitality and has been able to alter its forms and purposes sufficiently to play an important role in the new African cities as well.

IV
The Role of the City

LOOK TO THE CITY

Nearly everywhere in Africa today, young men and women are pulling up stakes—leaving behind the lands of their kin as they head for the bright lights of Nairobi, Léopoldville, or Dakar. So important is the urban migration under way in Africa that it would not be an exaggeration to conclude that without the city there would be no "Uhuru!" no "Free-dum!"—for truly it is the city in modern Africa, as it was in Attica and in medieval Europe, that "makes men free."

Both the problem and the promise of the African Revolution are sharply posed in the life and complexities of its mushrooming cities. Tribalism, for example, is not unique to the rural traditional countryside but today is an urban phenomenon as well. And many of the forces working to alter and reconstitute tribalism can best be seen within the context and the culture of the city.

The city in Africa today, as it was on other continents in other eras, is a Pandora's box spilling out riches and poverty, freedom and violence, and beauty as well as ugliness. The young men who founded and who now staff the African nationalist movements and parties are not to be found in the huts and gardens of the peasant village. Even though the city as a place to live, as a culture, or as a way of life is an alien form of sociation to Africans, it is the home of the political ideas and tools that are being forged and wielded to transform an entire continent.

The view that the city is sinful, dangerous, and an unnatural habitat for men is a thread which runs deep within America's national character and is reflected in our politics, literature, and art. This subconscious national characteristic may explain our tendency to view urbanization in Africa as a corruption of tribal society, but it contributes little to our understanding of one of the most powerful migrations under way in the world today.

Long before the advent of Western influence and hegemony, the people of Africa were on the move. Although the direction and composition of the current urban migration differs from the traditional movements and countermovements of whole populations, it would be misleading to think of urbanization as something inherently un-African or uniquely Western. Every man's life span is broken into memorable, often ritually symbolized events. The significance of a person's movement from one domicile to another is not the simple fact of relocation, per se, but the human experience and emotion that accompany the severance of old and the establishment of new ties, loyalties, and relationships—in short, new associations. Social change, including urbanization, is not something which has a beginning and an end but is rather a process which occurs at a given place or era at varying speeds. The rate of social change appears to be intimately related to the process of accommodation to change, with rapid alterations in human behavior and values tending to be found in conjunction with personal insecurity, conflict, hardship, and violence.

The rate of urbanization measures fairly precisely the speed with which Africa is being transformed. Twenty years ago the adult male urban population of the then Belgian Congo, for example, was less than 10 per cent; today more than a third of the adult males in the Congo live in its major cities. The simple view held by many persons that all Africans live in tribal villages and that the major urban centers are inhabited solely by Asians and Europeans is inaccurate and dangerously misleading. Few people are aware, for example, that about a third of a million Africans live in the urban compounds of the Republic of South Africa's Rand mining area alone.[1] The African populations of Ibadan and Addis Ababa are approaching one-half million each, while more than two hundred thousand Africans live in such cities as Dakar, Léopoldville, Salisbury, Lagos, Khartoum, and Tananarive. There are today more than one hundred cities in Africa with a population in excess of ten thousand.

Of course it would be equally misleading to picture Africa as a land of city dwellers, for in reality it is the least urbanized continent of all and less than 10 per cent of its population is estimated to be living in cities of five thousand or more. But more important than the number of city dwellers is the rate of urban increase. It is worth recalling that except for the ancient trading cities along the trans-Sahara routes, such as Timbuktu and Kano, and a few Arab-Portuguese port settlements along the East African coast, there was hardly an urban settlement throughout all of Africa at the time of the arrival of the Europeans.

Thus the African city, with very few exceptions, is a modern response to the forces of change—forces that had their origin primarily outside of Africa. At the same time, the city serves to focus and ameliorate these alien forces and to attract from the hinterland the hundreds of thousands of Africans who come to the city and are affected by the force of innovation and who in turn scatter the seeds of this change throughout the continent.

The thrust toward national unity in the West was often achieved at the expense of the semiautonomous cities and more than a few of these ancient medieval towns remained, for long periods, autonomous islands in a sea of new kingdoms. In Africa the process is reversed, for the thrust

[1] Lord Hailey, *An African Survey Revised* (Oxford; Oxford University Press, 1957), p. 566.

toward national unity has its origins in the cities and tends to lose momentum in the rural areas, as the distance from the national capital or other sizeable cities increases.

THE CITY AS GENERATOR

The capital city's near monopoly of nationalist activity and attitudes conflicts with the orthodox view of the nation state as a land mass delineated by sharply drawn boundaries. The educated habits of our formative years often make it difficult to perceive of nation states in other than a geographical sense. Thus the Republic of the Sudan conjures up a large, more or less triangular, arid country south of Egypt. Say the name of a nation state and chances are the image evoked is a geographical one of political boundaries and dominant physical features. But if we direct our attention toward the process of nation-building or toward the fabrication of political and related institutions, the new nations assume a different form. The Sudan is no longer a large pink land mass but rather the city of Khartoum with tentacles of influence and power radiating outward, the longest tentacles reaching to lesser centers of political authority such as Juba in the south and Dongola to the north. These lesser power centers, in turn, radiate even lesser lines of authority and influence outward from their respective centers.

In most of Africa this process of extending the lines of authority and influence from a single center to subcenters is currently under way. The process resembles the construction of an extensive hydroelectric grid. Although the enormous tracts or areas lying between the tentacles or lines of authority fall within the legal sovereign territory of the new African states, the thousands of people inhabiting these areas are only dimly aware of their legal nationality and think and act more as Masai or Karamajong than as Kenyans or Ugandans. Nation-building involves the extension of the political grid to bring within the system effectively those areas which are now a part of the nation in name only.

When firmly established, a political grid becomes relatively inflexible and, once a certain point is reached, it becomes increasingly difficult to extend the lines of power further because of the likelihood that they will collide with those of another system. In the new states of Africa, however, the political power grids are in their formative stages and there is still considerable room for the extension of the grid outward from the national capital. As the numerous proposals for union testify, the final over-all configuration of the many evolving power grids is yet to be determined. National frontiers, or what might be termed the hypothetical boundary lines of power, drawn by Europeans at the turn of the century to arbitrarily demarcate imperialistic spheres of influence, are not insurmountable barriers to the extension of the political power grid. There has never been a Maginot line on the Niger-Upper Volta border! In fact, even the cartographer has not been able to determine exactly the location of this and other African frontiers. Nor has the African nationalist come to think in terms of motherland or fatherland. In the minds of Africa's new leaders independence is not necessarily circumscribed by existent territorial boundaries. It is more than likely that we can look forward to the extension and linkage of power grids in a manner and with an ease that the history and culture of the other continents had made all but impossible. Nor must the systems to be linked necessarily require that the states adjoin one another. Modern communications technology, plus the sharing of a common British or French language and administrative system by a number of African countries, even though they may be separated by wide distances, makes it possible to link power grids of new states in the absence of a common frontier. The proclaimed union of Ghana, Guinea, and Mali suggests that variations in colonial origin will not necessarily preclude eventual linkage of this sort.

It is to the booming, dynamic capital cities that we must return, however, to comprehend the manner in which this power is generated and then fed into the power grid. For it is the capital cities that house the political power plants—government bureaucracies, representative institutions, political parties, and other related sociations. Here decisions are made that switch power and influence to the urban substations in the up-country hinterlands. At these up-country points local administration, branch political parties, schools, and local governments transform the centralized power into new patterns of human behavior, values, memberships, meanings, and loyalties. The intensity of influence tends, like voltage in an electrical distribution system, to decrease as distance from the generator or transformer increases. Political power, unlike the electric power plant, must contend with social forces as well as with physical distance; Africa is not a power vacuum waiting inertly to be filled by the expanding grid of national power. The persistence in many African countries of powerful, traditional centers of tribal authority, such as Kumasi in Ghana, conflict with and resist the extension of political influence from the capital city or from its provincial "transformers."

Competition between rival urban power centers, an obstacle to the extension of national power and influence not unknown in the West, also acts simultaneously to channel and to limit the extension of political authority from the African capital city outward. Some of the new African states, or soon-to-be independent states, possess a single identifiable center of political authority, whereas others are characterized by more than one sizeable urban center. No one would deny, for example, that Nairobi is the "powerhouse" of Kenya and that the major power transmission lines tend to flow out from Nairobi. There are, of course, other cities of significance in Kenya, namely Mombasa on the Indian Ocean and Nakuru in the White Highlands, but the orientation of these cities is primarily toward Nairobi. The type of power grid that evolves in a country dominated by its capital city is quite different from that in the Congo, for example, where political power is generated and transmitted not only in Léopoldville, but in Stanleyville and Elizabethville as well. These large booming cities of the Congo are not only major transformer stations designed to boost and extend the political power in their own right. The influence of these cities, as recent events have so vividly shown, may conflict with, and in some instances even neutralize, that of the national capital.

Dar es Salaam, the capital of Tanganyika, shares its urban status and influence with Mwanza, a Lake Victoria port, about 800 miles to the northwest; with Tanga, the sisal shipping seaport to the north; and with the rail and road transport centers of Tabora and Moshi. Competition between these power centers is inevitable, and it is already evident that the immediate postindependence political opposition to the new government was based among labor union leaders in Tanga and Tabora.

Some of these up-country cities were initially founded as administrative subcenters for large, tribally homogeneous provinces or districts. In situations of this sort, independence tends to activate the latent tribally oriented power centers in opposition to that of the national capital. A power grid of this nature with competing centers of influence in Ibadan in the west, Kano in the north, and Enugu in the east dictated the adoption of a federal form of government for an independent Nigeria. Although a federal system can explicitly allocate power among the regional capitals so that no one center can dominate the others, it cannot, as events in Nigeria have revealed, preclude a struggle for power. Ibadan, the capital of the Western Region and spiritual center of the six million strong Yoruba tribe, in 1962 was the center of a plot to overthrow the central government.

The peculiar pattern of potentially conflicting centers of influence and political power that characterize the new states may also evolve in response to aspects of the modernization process. In Tanganyika, for example, the labor movement has its center in the transport and rail city of Tabora and in the sisal port of Tanga, while TANU, the dominant political party, operates out of Dar es Salaam.

THE CITY AS COMMUNICATOR

In Africa today, planes fly regularly between the major cities; roads, some better than others, now link the capital cities with outlying provincial towns and headquarters. Often the roads are paralleled by phone and telegraph lines and in more and more parts of Africa by high-tension electric power lines as well. Thus the African political power grid, which we have described, has its physical counterpart. In the new state characterized by a single major capital city all roads, phone lines, and other forms of communication lead to and radiate from the capital city.

The new values and practices transforming the life of millions of Africans, and the meaning that life has for them, penetrate the fabric of

African society from the outside world through the medium of the major cities. But more important, these new behaviors and beliefs are given their peculiarly African content and meaning within the city.

Communication technology is playing an even larger role in the transmission of the symbols and values of nationhood to the parochially oriented hinterlands. Radio and more recently television programming and transmission, emanating primarily from the capital city, is a powerful conveyor of national ideologies. In a mass-based political system, wherein only consent of the people justifies the exercise of authority, leaders and would-be leaders compete for popular support. In many new African states, radio transmission is regarded as a critical factor in winning and retaining the support of the politically conscious public. Control over radio programming and transmission is thus germane to the political process; competition for access to this vital instrument is an integral part of African politics. Although the number of radio receivers in Africa by Western standards is small, the relative effectiveness of those that do exist is considerable.[2]

National boundaries, frontier posts, and custom agents may effectively limit the exchange of peoples and materials, but radio transmission is oblivious to national frontiers. For example, Tanganyikans living in the Moshi and Arusha area of their country are able to receive Nairobi, Kenya, television broadcasts. The full implications of situations of this sort must await Kenyan independence and the evolution of the East African Federation discussions currently under way. Tanganyika itself has already demonstrated in its radio broadcasts, beamed at The Rhodesias, the political significance of transnational electronic capacity.

Not only do African leaders compete for the ear and support of the African masses, but voices from outside Africa also seek to influence Africa's awakening millions. Thus, every week Red China beams more than one hundred hours of radio time into tropical Africa in six languages; Soviet transmitters located in the Caucasus and elsewhere burden the air approximately fifty-five hours a week urging a Communist brand of modernization and sociation upon nearly every African country. So powerful is the modern technological capacity to project the voice of authority, or would-be authority and influence, that the new African governments understandably seek to monopolize radio transmission and programming, while revolutionaries pursue, as one of their first goals, the capture of this powerful urban-centered instrument. The influence of radio, dependent as it is not only upon its reception, but its comprehension as well, is limited by the absence of a lingua franca in most African countries. Transmission time is therefore often divided among the major language-tribal groups and over-all effectiveness is considerably reduced.

[2] There are about 142 radio stations and 3 million radio receivers in Africa south of the Sudan, reaching about 10 per cent of the population.

Competition for vernacular transmission time is an important issue of contention in a number of African countries; although the propaganda and ideas that are transmitted seek to promote a sense of national unity, multiple vernacular transmission often acts to perpetuate tribal differences and parochialism. Thus while radio, programmed by nationalists and transmitted outward from the national capital, attempts to extend the lines of national political influence and power, a built-in resistor of language and culture partially blocks its effectiveness by perpetuating linguistic and cultural differences.

THE CITY AS INNOVATOR

New ideas and ways and manners of behaving are carried by men whose livelihood requires them to move back and forth from the urban areas to the smaller towns and cities. These are the marginal men, "the culture brokers"—the cab, bus, and lorry drivers, preachers, extramural teachers, government agents, veterinary and agricultural representatives, salesmen, professional political party and other sociation leaders—all of whom carry the word from the city center to the outlying towns, which in turn distribute and interpret the message to an even larger audience. In Tanganyika, for example, each town and village has its TANU headquarters which in turn services the surrounding region.

It is not only because both technological and human means for distributing the new ideas and behavior patterns originate in the city that urban areas serve as centers of this process. More important factors are the heterogeneity of its population, its relative freedom from the confines of tradition, and its receptivity to external influences. The independence movements and political parties of Africa have their origins in the beer halls and slums of the major cities. Even Mau Mau, which many have regarded as largely traditional, did not spring from the rural soil of Kiambu or Fort Hall, but was born instead in the suburban slums of Nairobi. Nor need the city necessarily be located within the revolutionary country. The headquarters of Frelino, the Mozambique Liberation Movement, is in Dar es Salaam, while Angolan Liberation Organizations are based in Léopoldville and Conakry.

Any alteration in the facilities providing for an increase in the movement of people to and from the city and hinterland extends a knowledge of the city's values and mores. Ten years ago in Nairobi, the majority of Africans wore no shoes; outside Nairobi only chiefs or other important persons wore shoes. Today it is rare to see an African in Nairobi in bare feet (except in the bars and hotels which cater to American tourists, where high-salaried African waiters patter about in bare feet). The wearing of shoes, minor as it may seem, spreads along the communication-political power grid to other towns and cities and from each into the most immediate hinterland. It is in this fashion that one can also observe the extension of cash cropping, political party membership, nationalist agitation, the construction of schools, and other sociations oriented more toward national than parochial values.

Urban sociation, unlike membership in traditional clan or tribal segments, demands that the city dweller be able to speak and understand a common language. This need of a common tongue has rendered imperative the learning of French or English. In some parts of Africa, however, a single African vernacular such as Swahili in East Africa rivals English or French as the predominant multitribal language. Nevertheless, it is unusual for a single language and accompanying social system to extend over a large population or an extensive area. More often, language and cultural groups are small, parochial, and relatively isolated by the rigors of the physical environment or by the relatively low level of communications between isolated rural societies. When a tribesman from a remote rural area migrates to the city, one of the first things he must do is to achieve a facility in the city's lingua franca. Failure to do so renders him ineligible for any except the most menial jobs, and precludes participation in those circles for which he decided to give up the security of rural life and to take his chances in the city. He is caught up in a new and powerful world wherein novel and exciting ideas and ways of doing or not doing things travel at the speed of sound. The congestion of the city also facilitates communications. For example, Tom Mboya could hardly have addressed forty thousand Africans at a political rally on a single night anywhere else in Kenya but in Nairobi. Even radio, which is regarded as a major link with the rural areas, conquering as it does both problems of space and density, is a much more effective instrument of communications in the city than in the countryside. More people take advantage of a single radio receiver in the city, and the broadcaster can count upon a mass audience all able to understand the language in which he is speaking. A large vernacular campaign poster in a rural area will communicate with relatively few people. A similar poster placed on a bus loading center in Lagos, written in English announcing a political rally, will be seen within an hour by thousands of people whose experience in an urban milieu inclines them to act accordingly.

Most African economies are dependent upon a single or a combination of crops or metals, the production and development of which was initially financed and administered from the capital city by non-Africans. Thus the capital or dominant regional city tends to possess a monopoly over the financial and monetary system. The few banks that do exist in the smaller cities and towns are invariably branches of those located in the capital city. Furthermore, the city is generally the site of the head offices of the cooperatives, labor unions, transport companies, development corporations, import-export firms, commodity marketing boards, and the like. Economic decision-making power is centralized in the capital city along with political power, and the combination and interaction of the two is a major source of over-all urban power. In short, it is the city that is connected to the outside markets, serves as the hub of the internal power distribution grid, is the major source or clearing house of capital and finance, and most important, is the dwelling place of those Africans who are rapidly embracing new work ways, language skills, and values.

The city cannot be viewed alone; it requires a rural hinterland wherein it can extend its lines of influence and power, for this is the very basis of its existence. The interrelationship of city and countryside is a subject which has received considerable scholarly attention. The dependency of the city upon an adequate food supply, for example, is a maxim of urban development. In Africa this has meant the development of surplus cash food crops and a transportation network to bring the foodstuffs to the city. Surplus income in the hands of the food growers provides a market for urban services and industry and, more important, in the developmental stage, a ready source of taxation. Taxation in turn enables an extension of governmental services and influence even farther into the hinterland, extending in the process the national power grid.

THE CITY AS INTEGRATOR

The ties between the new urban cities and rural countryside in Africa are unusually close. A knowledge of this intimate association is necessary to an understanding of political evolution. Often what appear as purely rural uprisings or agrarian social movements will be seen, if examined closely, to have originated in the city. The Kenya Government in the 1950's sought to enforce land consolidation in Nyanza despite a lack of consensus among the rural Nyanza people. Opposition to this policy in the rural areas was widespread but feebly organized. The thousands of Luo tribesmen living in Nairobi and Mombasa were in direct communication through their para-tribal associations and effectively defeated the Kenya Government's early program for land consolidation.

Possibly, of even more significance in the dissemination of new ways is the location in the capital cities of the new universities and colleges. Educational centers in the West took root, in many instances, long before the nation state and its single capital city rose as the center of national life. In Africa, however, the capital cities are the obvious centers of higher education, and most African universities are located there.

Government in the new African states is assigned primary, and in some countries almost sole, responsibility for economic and social development. The new African countries are, above all, social welfare states, some such as Guinea being self-proclaimed socialist republics. Whatever the degree of government involvement in the economy, it is evident that everywhere in Africa there exists an intimate relationship between political authority and national development. The new universities, unlike those of the West and more like those of the Communist world, are charged with the responsibility of preparing persons to serve the state. Threatened as they often are by an opposition that seeks to convince the masses that it can meet their expectations better, the new regimes are inclined to regard the universities as a part of government and to insist that the ideas and methods taught be such as to perpetuate and not threaten the power position of the existent elite.

So far we have tried to sketch briefly an over-all view of the role and significance of the growing urban centers to the sociation process generally, and, more specifically, to the building of new national institutions. To complete the picture it is necessary to enter the heart of the metropolis and focus on the men and women who are swelling Africa's urban centers. Then we must examine how they affect the city and how it in turn affects them.

TYPES OF AFRICAN CITIES

The impact of the city upon Africans, or Africans upon the city, varies profoundly from one country to another and depends upon a complex welter of factors. An important element everywhere, however, is the economic and administrative composition of the city. A port city like Lagos in Nigeria differs greatly from an administrative inland capital such as Bamako in Mali. The traditional culture of the area in question is also an important factor. Ibadan, for example, has always been a predominantly African city, inhabited, by and large, by people who were born there and whose fathers before them earned their livelihood in the city. The young up-country Yoruba tribesman venturing to make his fortune in Ibadan will be confronted with fewer obstacles than will a Ndebele who seeks his fortune in European dominated Salisbury. The racial composition of the city is also an important factor about which we shall have more to say later. An aspect of race to be noted here is ethnic homogeneity. A city in a province or region dominated by a single tribe does not always readily absorb migrants from other tribes and areas. The language barrier slows integration; in many instances the traditional relationships of the tribe or origin of the migrants to the dominant ethnic group of the urban region have been hostile.

The range and frequency of migration to and from the city are relevant here. Some cities such as Addis Ababa and Kano, although experiencing rapid growth, have always housed a core of permanent African residents. Other cities, primarily those dominated by European and Asian commercial, industrial, or extractive industries, are populated by Africans who are more inclined to view urban residence as a temporary expedient and who look forward eventually to returning to their rural tribal homes.

In the newly dependent African states the city is no longer regarded primarily as a dwelling place for Europeans and Asians and secondarily as a place in which the African works. In Accra, Lagos, Khartoum, Dakar, and Conakry, one no longer finds departments or bureaus of "African" administration, "African" housing, or "African" welfare. These have been replaced by departments of public housing, local administration, and public welfare. The dominant Europeans in the Federation of Rhodesia and Nyasaland, the Republic of South Africa, and Kenya toward Africans living in and associating with the city historically viewed the African's presence as necessary but unfortunate and to be held to the absolute minimum. This view is rapidly changing—but not everywhere in the same direction. In the Republic of South Africa, the government is seeking to expel Africans from the major cities whereas in Mombasa, Nairobi, and Lusaka, African urban housing is being built and efforts made to encourage the Africans to settle permanently, albeit in what remain in effect segregated quarters.

The greater part of the residents of the new cities still do not regard the city as their permanent home, and it would be difficult indeed to find many persons—black, white, or brown—who anticipate dying in the city. One of the most striking things about the new African cities, even when we take into account their relative youth, is the notably few places and institutions of burial.

It is not only the African who has one foot back in the land of origin, for the Indian in the East, the Lebanese in West Africa, the Frenchman, Englishman, Portuguese—these men of varying hue, wealth, and occupations—tend, more or less, to retain strong ties with a distant land which in one language or another is called "home."

In much of Africa, and particularly in those cities located in non-independent countries still dominated by Europeans, there exists a peculiar relationship between the urban dwelling African and the rapidly growing urban institutions. Many of the new associations, such as labor unions, political parties, clubs, welfare societies, are perceived by the migrant African as urban amenities to be "used," rather than as membership associations in which to participate or to belong. The new urbanities flow in, through, and often out from them, and in a fundamental sense, have not considerably altered their traditional rural values and beliefs. Viewed in this fashion, some urban institutions in the new African cities are not an integral element of the culture of the urban resident but are more like a convenient Salvation Army canteen or YMCA. Upon arrival the urban migrant tends to gravitate toward his respective tribal, ethnic, or racial quarter, in a manner reminiscent of Polish, Italian, and Irish immigration into New York, Boston, and Philadelphia about a century ago.

Even though famine upon occasion stalks the countryside, urban life is viewed by many Africans as being more precarious and insecure. The fickle nature of a wage economy, the fear that goes with living among stranger-enemies, the absence of elderly wisdom and authority—all these things tend to promote insecurity and anxiety. This insecurity and the intense communal nature of traditional society and obligations in most cities, tend to reinforce communications and a sense of solidarity with one's land and people of origin. In short, urban residence significantly affects traditional tribal ties and associations but not always in the expected direction and not always with the same intensity or consequences.

URBANISM AND TRIBALISM

Rarely is urbanization in Africa discussed without reference to something termed "detribalization." In Chapter III we suggested that the values and behavior implied by "tribe," "tribalism," and "detribalization" are most complex and varied. For example, it is too often assumed that the tribesman, when he comes to the city, discards completely his tribal cloak and then suffers for a time a state of cultural undress while he painfully puts on a new suit of urban stripe. If there were not considerable truth to this assumption, it would not be so pervasive a part of the literature of Africa and African urbanization.

Nevertheless, the process of dissociation that accompanies urbanization in some localities is extremely rapid and violent, whereas in other cities the new urbanites, although now affiliated with many new urban groupings, do not necessarily dissociate from their traditional memberships. The various combinations of the process of dissociation and association depend not only upon the nature of the urban environment but also on the peculiar nature of the tribal culture that the urban-bound African carries into the city with him. For example, some traditional tribal ties are not intimate or intense and therefore may not conflict with the sociational demands of life in the city. In some tribes, for example, the initiation rites of the young men lie at the very heart of the tribal sociopolitical system; in others the initiation ceremonies are less demanding and may be overlooked with relative ease. Initiation rites involving circumcision among the Kikuyu youth in Kenya are an integral aspect of the tribal social system. So important is this rite today, even among the highly educated, that Kikuyu students in New York have been known to gather, with the assistance of modern surgeons, to perform the Kikuyu initiation ceremonies. Tribal customs that act to isolate tribe from tribe or which conflict with the values and altered behavior patterns called forth by city life are a serious hindrance to nation-building in much of Africa. Nation-building in Kenya, for example, eventually will require the breakdown of these aspects of tribal separatism that deny nationalism and preclude the evolution of an over-riding national culture.

It is to the city that one looks for the first signs of this cosmopolitan solidarity. And surely there are many indications of the growth of extra-tribal values and institutions which one might with some validity describe as Kenya nationalism.

Nevertheless, the perpetuation of certain customs and rituals by many tribal groups renders national integration extremely difficult. Differences in the requirements of eligibility for marriage and in the sexual customs of the Luo and the Kikuyu, the two largest and most influential tribes in Kenya, are such that even in the relatively cosmopolitan cities inter-marriage between the two is not common. So long as eligibility to wed involves circumcision and the two tribes' customs on this score differ radically, one cannot expect rapid national integration.

Certainly there is much evidence that new trans-tribal associations of an occupational, locational, recreational, and political nature are grad-ually gaining the segmented allegiance of the urban African. Nevertheless, there continues to exist, in most cities, a sociational structure based upon tribal and other traditional origins. These para-traditional groups, remodeled and reorganized to cope with an alien urban environment, require the exercise of new skills and leadership talents if they are to compete successfully with other urban tribal groups for jobs, markets, and political influence. So well organized and powerful are some of these migrant para-tribal groups that they have on occasion come to dominate the lives of the older permanent urban residents in a manner reminiscent of Irish influence and power in some northeastern American cities. Nor is their influence limited solely to the city, for often the emergence of these para-tribal organizations in the cities is paralleled by a decline in the influence and authority of the rural-based, more traditional, socio-political system. Thus it is not unusual for a para-urban tribal group, whose organization and leadership differs radically from the parent organization, to dominate large portions of the life of the city and also to exercise considerable influence in the area of tribal origin.

For reasons that are peculiar to their respective cultures, or in response to the administrative practices and customs of the colonial power, some African tribal groups, resident in the cities, have established a near monopoly over specific occupations and trades. This new parochialism does little to further ethnic and tribal integration in the process of nation-building. In the towns and cities of Ghana, for example, the Jema tribesmen have a firm grip on the marketing of firewood; throughout Nigeria the Ibo tend to have a near monopoly in urban commercial enterprise; the Kamba of Kenya are that nation's recognized woodcarvers, and the Kikuyu its clerks. In Uganda the Bahima of Ankole are cattle herders; nearly all nursemaids and servants are Batoro; the Baganda are the nation's bureaucrats.

In an effort to present an objective and balanced assessment of the impact and processes of urbanization, we must not ignore some of the more obvious implications of dissociation or those aspects of dissociation termed "detribalization." Crime rates in most African cities are high; delinquency and prostitution are commonplace; violence and drunken-ness are ever present. A breakdown of tribal mores—the absence of tradi-tional tribal authority, myths, elders, sanctions, and intimate face-to-face relationships in the exploding urban areas and slum suburbs—is common throughout Africa today. Family solidarity and family norms tend to disintegrate in the face of a wage economy, a monetary income, and commensurate purchasing power going to the individual, irrespective of age, rather than to the family head. Although most Africans send some money back to the village, the subsidization of those left behind is apt to build a dependency of the traditional elders on the absentee youth and thereby further distort the traditional distribution of authority and obligation.

THE CITY AND THE SOCIATION PROCESS

Urban employment, work hours, recreation, marketing—all these involve new forms of interpersonal relationships which, given sufficient intensity or frequency, become structured in terms of an association. Urban life for the African has invariably required participation in new associations related to his new job, to his leisure time, and to the city or its neighborhood as a political and social entity. All organized human associations that specify how, when, and how and when not the member is to act, also specify the forms of coercion that will be employed to encourage conformity and to punish deviation. Forms of coercion, to be effective, deprive a person of something he values highly. Thus the urbanized African loses a day's pay or may be discharged for failing to work the specified regular hours. Failure to abide by the universal rules laid down by the urban government or by the location chief, as the case may be, results in a fine or imprisonment. If the African only had to accommodate himself to new forms of interrelational behavior and sanctions, the problems of adjustment would still be acute; traditional ties, however, also make demands upon him, and a failure to conform to the requirements of traditional tribal groups can also result in severe coercion, which conceivably can deprive the African of equally important values. The generally accepted norms of the urban milieu prohibit theft, even from strangers or from men of another tribe. Traditional obligations to support or to otherwise assist relatives and members of one's age-grade or tribe may take precedence over the more recently acquired obligations of urban life. Normlessness, insecurity, and crime, so characteristic of most new African cities, result not so much from an absence of behavior-regulating norms, but as a consequence of seeking to cope with the anxiety born of that conflict. One alternative is to withdraw from the obligations of both systems and thereby become truly normless, while another is to create new behavior patterns and norms.

Although it is extremely rare for a tribe to be completely unrelated to a corresponding territory, it nevertheless is not so much restricted to territory as are Western requirements of citizenship. The Luo tribesman, for example, who migrates to Nairobi to seek his fortune is certainly aware of the fact that he has left his tribal land, but the simple fact of moving into Nairobi does not, in his estimation, make him a Nairobian, or for that matter, any less a Luo. He retains his tribal citizenship, and as a matter of fact he probably joins his fellow Luo in Nairobi in an expatriate tribal association. In one sense the African carries his corporate responsibilities and loyalities with him wherever he goes. There would seem to be an interesting similarity between this concept of extra-territorial obligation and citizenship and that of the corporate white-collar migrant American who today carries his obligations and corporation loyalties with him as he moves from branch office city to branch office city.

These neo-tribal affiliations serve to introduce the immigrant into the urban culture, shielding him as much as possible from the culture shock of what is loosely termed "detribalization." The urban tribal organizations assist the newly arrived African to find housing, food, and employment. These expatriate tribal organizations undergo an interesting change and are quite different in their urban composition and function from the parent groups in the tribal location. By and large, it is the young, and primarily the young males, who leave the tribal land to journey to the city, plantation, or mine. The role of the elders, so basic to traditional tribal organization, is replaced in the city by a leadership reflecting more the composition and values of the new environment. Education, urban experience, and cosmopolitanism replace age and a knowledge of tribal law and custom as the criteria of leadership. So important and representative have some of these neo-tribal groups become that in some cities they are even given formal and legal recognition by the urban government and granted the status of advisory councils.

In the process of organizing to cope with what are predominantly urban and modern problems, the urban tribal associations in part have come to resemble fraternal and guild organizations. Mr. K. A. Busia, the eminent West African social scientist, has carefully documented a tendency toward increased urban specialization on the part of tribally organized sociations. He found that some urban, although predominantly tribal, organizations in Ghana were involved in schemes of unemployment compensation, health insurance, financial assistance, scholarship programs, and the like.[3] In East Africa as well, it has been found that these urban-tribal groups sometimes serve as lending agencies, assist their members to establish commercial enterprises, serve as charitable agencies, sometimes provide burial services, and have even been known to act as insurance trusts. Affiliation with these tribal segments of the urban culture may of course lessen civic and national ties and solidarity. Insofar as each urban-tribal group maintains order among its own members, it contributes significantly to over-all municipal order, if not to meaningful urban and national integration.

Thus urban tribal organizations, in one respect, have slowed down the

---

[3] K. A. Busia, "Social Survey of Sekondi-Takoradi," *Social Implications of Industrialization and Urbanization in Africa South of the Sahara*, UNESCO International African Institute (1956).

assimilation of urban migrants into a national culture as did the ethnic associations in the major cities of the United States during the early 1900's. However, it is debatable that the adaptability of these traditional tribal associations to an urban milieu is responsible for the relatively orderly transition that characterizes urbanization in Africa.

The role of the urban para-tribal groupings, like the ethnic clubs of urban America, will probably linger on for many years but will gradually decline in significance as they are replaced by functional trans-ethnic organizations. There is already considerable indication that urban para-tribal organizations are replacing traditional sociations. Less than five years ago there were in Nairobi, Kenya, more than five hundred tribal or other traditional "locational" sociations based upon area of origin, kinship, or age-grade unit. A recent study in that city found it difficult to locate as many as twenty organizations of this type.

As communications between the urban center and hinterland improve, as more and more persons flow through the city and back to the rural areas, the urban migrant will be less likely to enter the city completely ignorant of its culture. To this extent he will be less dependent than earlier migrants upon those urban-tribal affiliations. The image frequently drawn of the African ruralite coming to the city in bark cloth and bare feet—a bewildered country bumpkin—is not now consistent, if it ever was, with reality. Today even before the migrant leaves his village, the chances are he has already established ties with close friends and relatives who preceded him to the city. Vivid, although possibly often exaggerated, descriptions of life in the big city are a part of the dialogue these days in most of rural Africa. It is this knowledge of the city, although vicarious, that in fact often inspires the ruralite to leave home and to seek his fortune in the town.

Another stereotype of the urbanization process is the ruralite moving from an area of purity, plenty, and security into the filth and insecurity of the city. Recent studies have made it clear that the urban African possesses greater security, with respect at least to food and shelter, than do his tribal brothers. The urbanite standard of living is so much higher that the city dweller is looked to for assistance by his less fortunate family back in the area of tribal origin.

SOME EMERGING TRENDS

The importance of this reciprocal relationship between country and city is not well understood. The evolution of viable nations in Africa will depend, in part, upon the presence and role of a few politically and economically stable but creative cities. These in turn will depend upon the presence of many competing countervailing organizations—or stated otherwise, upon a highly developed urban pluralism. Many African cities today lack a variety of overlapping memberships, affiliations, and loyalties. A major finding of the Sofers in their study of Jinja in Uganda was the notable absence of participation and the paucity of voluntary associations.[4]

Only in a few cities in West Africa is it possible to discover a viable growing middle class. In most cities the huge African populations, as in the Middle East, resemble more and more an unintegrated proletarian mass. The African urban dweller of moderate means is often besieged by requests for assistance from his relatives and fellow tribesmen who have stayed behind. The discrepancy between standards of living in the urban and rural areas added to the continued viability of traditional obligations has skimmed off much of that surplus wealth and initiative that might have lent itself to the evolution of a sizeable middle class.

The growth of social class, in response to the relative variation and pluralism of urban life, is regarded by some as the factor that eventually will weaken and destroy urban neo-tribal ties. There is considerable evidence that variations in income, politics, taste, and education are in fact having this effect. But the obligations of traditional culture, the monopoly in some cities of all but the most menial positions by non-Africans, residential restrictions, and a growing sense of racial solidarity act to slow the trend toward a class as opposed to a tribal and, more recently, a mass culture. Economic competition in Africa has not led to an identity of interests between Asian and African merchants but has promoted instead the formation of separate organizations pursuing similar purposes for each racial group.

[4] C. and R. Sofer, *Jinja Transformed—A Social Survey of a Multiracial Township*, East African Studies, No. 4, p. 112. East African Institute of Social Research, Kampala, Uganda (1954).

V
The Emergence and Role
of Leadership

Traditionally, African society was ruled by the eldest generation, whose role was not to legislate new rules and laws but rather, in close communion with the deceased, to execute and stand guard over universal and timeless norms. As knowledge and power over the mystic forces that affected life and death, sickness and health, and war and peace tended to lie in the domain of the ancestors, it is not surprising that the elders—those members of society closest to the ancestors—often exercised predominant influence. But revolutions, dynamic leadership, the engineering of rapid social and political change—these phenomena have always required the strength and audacity of young hands and young minds. The African Revolution is not an exception. Possibly the most striking aspect of the current African scene is the generational revolution that is both caused by and is causing the political and social upheaval. It is not only the authority and influence of the colonial powers that have been successfully challenged. Possibly even more important is the decline of the traditional elders and the rise of the young intellectuals. The Mau Mau terrorists directed their vengeance not so much against the British as against the older leaders exercising authority and influence as agents of the colonial power. A major contention of the young revolutionaries nearly everywhere in Africa is that the Europeans have perpetuated white minority rule by supporting conservative chiefs.

African nationalism has passed through a number of chronological stages. The early days of nationalist agitation and modernization also had their young intellectual leaders. Some leaders of the period before World War II continue to exercise considerable influence, particularly in West Africa, where both colonialism and nationalist agitation came at a much earlier date than in East and Central Africa. In this category of African elder statesmen belong such eminent persons as M. Houphouet-Boigny, the President of the Ivory Coast, long a member of the French Chamber of Deputies and formerly Minister in the French Government, and Kwame Nkrumah, President of Ghana. In those coastal areas of Ghana, Sierra Leone, and Liberia that have experienced a prolonged contact with Europe, a Westernized native elite has existed for a number of generations. Along the coast of what is now Ghana, for example, there still live a number of wealthy, Western oriented families from which sprang many of Ghana's early leaders (although not Nkrumah, as these aristocrats are quick to note). Dr. J. B. Danquah, the patriarch of Ghanaian nationalism, belongs in this category, as does Nnamdi Azikiwe, the vivacious leader of the National Council of Nigeria and the Cameroons (NCNC). At fifty-seven, Azikiwe has retired (at least temporarily) from active politics and now looks down upon the political scene from the lofty position of Governor-General. Nor can we omit Jomo Kenyatta, now seventy-two and still one of the most powerful political figures in all East Africa. It is worth noting that the influence of these grand old men of African politics is today everywhere challenged by the enthusiastic appeal of younger and more forcible leaders. Houphouet-Boigny, who once stood head and shoulders above all French West African leaders, must now share the mantle of power and influence with such young men as Sékou Touré, President of Guinea. Kwame Nkrumah of Ghana, at fifty-five, is old for an African politician, but certainly much younger than Joseph Danquah (sixty-eight), leader of the United Party, whom he has completely eclipsed, just as Kaunda in Northern Rhodesia has eclipsed Nkumbula and Nasser Neguib.[1]

THE DILEMMA OF LEADERSHIP

Leadership, as it relates to culture, society, environment, and to the peculiar nature of the "sociation" process under way in a given country, is a complex subject. Who should lead? On what basis should authority be granted and wielded? How and why should men consent to being ruled? This is the stuff of which both practical politics and political philosophy are made.

The leadership patterns in a given country affect the attitudes and capacities of a people to alter their social and political institutions. The shattering of old affiliations and the formation of new ones alters the patterns of human behavior as well as the explanations and reasons that men give for the ways in which they do behave. Not only is leadership a prime mover in initiating change, but new behavioral patterns and ideologies in turn influence the type of leadership that evolves.

As Africa today is in the throes of relinquishing its traditional ideologies and myths as to ruler and ruled, it becomes a fertile ground for the cultivation of new ideologies and myths. Western and Communist spokesmen and their respective disciples (the new missionaries) toil feverishly to lead the African nations toward political and economic salvation according to one dogma or another.

[1] Two new works on African leaders, which provide information on their origins and character, were published recently: Rolf Italiaander, *New Leaders of Africa* (Englewood Cliffs, N.J.: Prentice-Hall, Inc., 1961). Translated from the German by James McGovern. Copyright © 1961 by Prentice-Hall, Inc.; and Thomas Patrick Meladay, *Profiles of African Leaders* (New York: The Macmillan Company, 1961).

The interesting thing about these twentieth-century ideologies as they compete for influence in transitional Africa is that, unlike the indigenous or traditional varieties, they demand a high degree of mass participation and consensus in the political process. In the relatively highly developed and large tribal kingdom-states, before the arrival of the English, authority was wielded by divine right king-chiefs and flowed down the hierarchy through lesser chiefs responsible to the king-chief. Often a clan or other kinship system paralleled or interlaced the authority hierarchy and thus elders and clan leaders tended also to be involved in politics and government. The number of persons that ruled was small, whereas the number of persons that obeyed was large. As the king-chief or elder ruled by a divine or mystical right, the explicit consent of the subjects was not required. Authority was exercised in the name of the higher chief or the ancestral gods by an aristocracy or autocracy. The rule of the Omukama (king) of Bunyoro, in Uganda, was traditionally regarded as being divinely inspired. The extraordinary influence wielded by the present Omukama, despite his relegation to the position of a titular head of government, indicates the tenacity of traditional forms and beliefs. In sharp contrast, both Western democracy and Marxism, although differing in the way in which they seek and obtain consent, proclaim that they rule in the name of the people. The masses of Africa—if we may so term them for this purpose—are having popular sovereignty of a sort thrust upon them without having sought or fought for it. And many Africans are surprised, confused, and possibly somewhat flattered to learn that their support is necessary and that the purpose of the ruler is to serve them—that is, the people—"muntu."

Today, except for pockets of extensive traditionalism like Ethiopia, Portuguese Africa, and the Republic of South Africa, leaders exercise authority to some degree with the sufferance and consent of the people. These new leaders rule not so much out of a right, supported by a myth of divinity, royalty, or age, but exercise their authority and are secure in the seats of power only so long as they manage to meet the socio-economic expectations of the people—or manipulate the people to believe that they are in fact meeting those expectations. This is so in part because the ideals of modernization and development are replacing traditional values. The goal of political transition—of new governmental institutions—of "uhuru" is the acquisition of personal dignity and equality to be acquired through the agency of modernity as attested by its most demonstrative symbols—a high level of material consumption, highly developed education and technology, and international recognition and status. If to this we add the modern necessity that the ruler obtain the support of the ruled, that is if he is to retain his position, it is possible to understand how and why political leaders and would-be leaders compete with one another for mass support by promising more and better "modernity" and "dignity."

The pinnacle of leadership in a mass-based political system, particularly where the masses are politically unsophisticated and unpredictable, is a risky and insecure position indeed. Nevertheless, competition for positions of leadership is intense. Political office in a mass-based political system has long been recognized as an escalator for those who would be mobile in their ascent. In the budding African nations the rewards of political office in contrast to life without them are so desirable as to be worthy of constant struggle and sacrifice. Competition for power in the new African states is frequently unrestrained and the would-be leaders, in their efforts to topple an existent elite, are not beyond making wild exaggerations and promises that would bring a blush to the countenance of even the most hardened American politician. If these maneuvers secure the positions of authority, then the problem of delivering the goods upon which leadership depends becomes even more difficult. As leaders of men have always sought scapegoats to explain their failure to meet expectations, the tendency to continue to flail the colonial horse or to turn frustration against a minority ethnic or racial group or against the remnants of colonialism in other regions of Africa is at times irresistible.

To protect itself from being outbid in promises of the good life, an existent elite must often change the rules of the democratic game to eliminate or neutralize its opposition. The instruments of state power are sometimes employed to curtail the activity of the opposition by removing its leaders from the scene. More important possibly is recourse to traditional ideologies and myths to legitimize and further sanctify the rule of the existent elite.

In Ghana, we have witnessed in recent years a steady whittling away of the effective right of the opposition legally to become the government, or for that matter the right to exist legally as an opposition. In 1958 the CPP (Convention People's Party), dominating Parliament under the strong leadership of President Nkrumah, tightened the laws to increase to fifteen years the permissible sentence for sedition, the definition of which was then broadened to include "inciting hatred or contempt of the government" or "permitting feelings of ill will or hostility between classes." The Preventive Detention Act passed in the fall of 1958 allows the Ghana Government to detain for what amounts to an indefinite period of time without trial those persons charged with acting in a manner prejudicial to the security of the state. In 1962 the Foreign Minister and the Minister of Information were imprisoned under this act. The Industrialization Act, making it all but impossible for union members to strike, has effectively neutralized organized labor as a source of political competition. In 1959, twenty-one members of the opposition United Party in Ghana were jailed in the aftermath of disturbance attending a special election to fill the seat of K. G. Busia, the self-exiled eminent anthropologist and opposition party leader.

In many respects Ghana's ruling party and its elite pose the classic example of the newly emergent African state. They face the triple dilemma of meeting the expectations built up during the independence struggle, of welding together diverse, historically conflicting cultures and people in the absence of the integrating force of a colonial administration, and of maintaining the power to rule in the face of growing opposition.

Since its independence in March of 1957, Ghana attempted to cope with these problems while playing a leading role in the liberation movements of neighboring African territories. To contain and repress a regionally based opposition (the United Party), which challenged the ruling CPP's record of meeting inflated expectations, Nkrumah and the CPP employed the coercive resources of the state. But whereas behavior can be coerced, the human will is difficult to control. Each act of repression tended to be followed by an incident of rebellion, which in turn called forth further repression. Successive acts of repression tend progressively to destroy existing legitimate channels of opposition, requiring the leaders of the opposition to rely upon illegitimate, violent means.

A proclaimed army plot against the Prime Minister and government in 1958 provided a pretext for the deportation of Muslim political leaders, a prohibition of political parties based on religion and tribalism, and, more important, led to the dissolution of the regional assemblies—the constitutional repositories of tribal opposition. The inherited parliamentary system proved incapable of providing the instruments necessary to integrate a multitribal state, or to guarantee to the existing elite perpetual office. The plebiscite of 1960 and the subsequent adoption in July 1960 of a republican constitution with Kwame Nkrumah as the first president was designed to meet this problem. Nonetheless, opposition persisted. Armed with its new executive powers, Nkrumah's government in October 1961 arrested Joe Appiah, son-in-law of the late Sir Stafford Cripps, one time confidant of Nkrumah and later leader of the opposition United Party. Appiah was jailed under the Preventive Detention Act along with fifty other "subversive" members of the opposition, including J. B. Danquah. Instead of improving, however, matters became worse. Driven even more deeply underground, the opposition had increasing recourse to violent means and 1962 became for Ghana the year of the bomb. In August of that year President Nkrumah narrowly escaped assassination as a series of bomb explosions in Northern Ghana killed 15 and injured 250 bystanders. Two more ministers were detained while K. A. Gbedemah, former Minister of Finance, fled to the United Kingdom. Explosions in the capital city of Accra occurred with such frequency in 1962 that a state of emergency was declared. August bombings brought September repressions, and in an attempt to circumscribe further an opposition no longer visible or overt the Foreign Minister, Mr. Adjeu, and the Minister of Information, Mr. Adamafio, were arrested and detained. The CPP-controlled Parliament approved the adoption of a single-party system, thereby proscribing all other political parties. The assembly also adopted a motion that Dr. Nkrumah remain president for life. The Preventive Detention Act was amended to provide that prisoners were not necessarily to be freed after five years detention. In December 1962, a hand grenade hurled in the Accra sports stadium, moments after President Nkrumah had left, killed 4 and injured 85 persons. Ghana's neighbors, particularly Togoland—a haven for those fortunate enough to escape arrest and detention—were accused of complicity in the repeated bomb attempts on the President's life. On December 29, Ghana warned Togo of the "dangerous international consequences" which could result from the Togolese Government's provision of "shelter and encouragement" to those conspiring against Ghana.[3] Three weeks later President Olympio of Togoland was assassinated and what had begun as a tribal issue had become an international incident.

Another way in which an existent ruling elite seeks to perpetuate its leadership is to add to its mass support elements of legitimacy associated with traditional authority. Thus Kwame Nkrumah fosters and promotes an image of himself as a semidivine leader possessed of supernatural powers. His countenance adorns the nation's stamps and coins; captured in marble, it looks down upon the crowd in Accra; and strategically imprinted on ladies' attire it adds color and a moving symbol of his eminence in the market places throughout Ghana. The flavor of this emotional appeal is suggested by a stanza of a poem singing the praises of Nkrumah, published in the *Accra Evening News*.

> O revered, beloved son of Africa;
> O great redeemer of Africa,
> Thy wisdom has wrought things many and wonderful,
> Thou seemest a Savior come from God.[4]

SOURCES OF LEADERSHIP

The length to which an elite is prepared to go to perpetuate itself depends in part upon the nature of the leadership, which in turn is in part a product of the "sources" from which it springs. Changes in the society affecting the sources of leadership often preview significant changes in the key institutions within a country or region. For example, if we sought to predict where one would find future or potential leaders of the United States, we might well study such institutions as political parties, labor unions, corporations, universities, and the military. Indeed, C. Wright Mills' *The Power Elite* employs this approach to analyze the power structure of the United States.[5] One of the major characteristics

[3] *Tanganyika Standard* (Jan. 11, 1963).
[4] Italiaander, *New Leaders of Africa*, p. 238.
[5] C. Wright Mills, *The Power Elite* (Oxford: Oxford University Press, 1956).

of the modernization process in Africa is the demise and transformation of old institutions and sociations and the evolution of new forms. Therefore, before attempting to speculate intelligently about who Africa's future leaders will be, we must first know something about the process of institutional change. Obviously the greater part of the crop of new national leaders will not come from the ranks of traditional tribal institutions. In the Middle East and in Southeast Asia, for reasons peculiar to the nation-building process there, national leadership increasingly emerges from the higher ranks of the military. To date, this pattern is less apparent in Africa, in part because military institutions have not loomed so large and have not been granted the status and prestige characteristic of the Middle East, although there is some evidence that a pattern of military recruitment may evolve in Africa as well. An example of the emergence of national leadership from the ranks of the military in Africa can be seen in the Sudan. There, in November 1958, General Ibrahim Abboud and the army toppled the democratic regime of Abdullah Khalil and substituted a military dictatorship. General Abboud, as President, continues to ignore the demands of opposition leaders for the restoration of civilian rule. The government, the general says, "has to further the aims of consolidating national unity and ensuring a highly respected place for Sudan in the international community." [6] On July 11, 1961, General Abboud's government accused fifteen former important officials and political leaders, including two former Prime Ministers (Abdullah Khalil and Ismail el Azhari), of "dark conspiracies—fabricating lies, distorting facts," that were sufficient to lead to their arrest and imprisonment.[7]

It is somewhat ironic that in Egypt and the Sudan, as in Pakistan, Turkey, and Korea, corrupt or inefficient "democratic" regimes have been toppled by "puritanical" military leaders, most of whom received their military training in the democratic West.[8]

Strong party government in new nations has been characterized by a concentration of political power at the national capital and by a decline in regional and tribal autonomy. It is more than accidental that the military autocracies in Sudan, Turkey, Egypt, and Pakistan have all adopted a policy of decentralization of administration to regions, provinces, and local governments.

An emergent political leader is likely to come from that segment of society that is relatively predisposed toward "change." Here too the emphasis is upon youth and education; the role of young university stu-

---

[6] *The New York Times* (Dec. 11, 1960), p. 9.
[7] *The New York Times* (July 12, 1961), p. 12.
[8] It is worth noting that whereas the political-nationalist leaders emerged from the urban centers in the new countries the higher military posts tend to be filled by young men from the rural countryside.

dents and university groups is prominent throughout the postwar pattern of revolution and violent change. Governments have been toppled and threatened by popular student-led movements in a score of countries since World War II. And in the United States it is the Negro youth who have forced the pace and stolen a march on the older NAACP leaders. Youth movements in Africa have played and continue to play a major role in the process of nation-building. Youth movements and trade unions are two major forms of sociation that cut across territorial, national, and tribal boundaries and thereby exert a powerful force in the direction of unity, federation, and Pan-Africanism. Before the breakup of the French Community states in West Africa which followed upon De Gaulle's referendum of 1958, the entire region was dominated politically by a single party, the Rassemblement Démocratique Africain (RDA); a single major labor organization, the Union Generale de Travailleurs de L'Afrique Noire (UGTAN); and a single youth federation, the Conseil de la Jeunesse d'Afrique (CJA). Overlapping leadership and an emphasis upon youth characterized these organizations. Sékou Touré, President of Guinea, in 1958 was at the same time President of the Confédération Nationale des Travailleurs de Guinée (CNTG) and of the Guinea branch of the RDA. The youth organizations may not initially have been formed for political action, but once an organization of angry young men exists, use of its organizational skills for political purposes is irresistible. The Ashanti Youth Association, for example, was involved in a wide variety of activities and affairs in Ghana. Nearly all youth associations oppose traditional leadership institutions. In Ashanti it was the Ashanti Youth Association that led the way in opposing the traditional authority of the Ashanti chiefs. In Tanganyika the TANU Youth League was in the forefront of the struggle against the traditional chiefs.

Frequently youth associations revolve around an educational institution. These may be purely student associations or they may take the form of alumni groups, such as the Association des Anciens Elèves des Pères de Scheut in the Congo, which in 1953 elected as its vice-president a young man named Patrice Lumumba. The short-lived ten years' career of Patrice Lumumba illustrates well the emergence and significance of leadership. In 1951, he joined an Evolué club in Oriental Province (Association des Evolués de Stanleyville). In the same year he was elected secretary-general of the Association of Postal Workers of Oriental Province—a new association reflecting the rapidly changing occupational pattern of the Congo. In 1953 a student alumni group elected him vice-president (Association des Anciens Elèves des Pères de Scheut). In 1955 he was made chairman of a trans-tribal association termed the Association du Personnel Indigène de la Colonie, in effect the African civil servant association of Stanleyville. A year later he took the initiative and formed the Amicale Liberale de Stanleyville. Soon after, this slight, relentless, moustached young man moved to the capital city of Léopold-ville, where he hoped to give free reign to his genius for organization and national expression. There he quickly formed the MNC (Movement Nationale Congolais). In 1958, his political activities and the Stanleyville riots landed him in jail where he acquired his P.G. (Prison Graduate) degree, another attribute of revolutionary leadership. In 1958, Patrice Lumumba was elected president of an urban para-tribal association (Association des Batetilas de Léopoldville), a cluster of small but related tribes. In the same year he founded a study "circle," an association combining youth, urban residents, and school graduates (Centre d'Étude et des Récherches Sociales). All of this culminated in Patrice Lumumba's becoming the first Prime Minister of an independent Congo and ultimately led to his assassination on February 10, 1961.

Lumumba is often depicted as the only truly national Congolese leader, one who was able to rise above tribal parochialism and politics. Although his party, the MNC, claimed adherents over most of the large and complex territory termed the Congo and was opposed by powerful tribal-party associations such as Kasavubu's ABAKO, Lumumba also relied upon tribal organizations and solidarity for support. In a manner calculated to appeal to the most perceptive New York politician, he carefully balanced his ticket to include candidates from those tribal groups whose support he sought and selected the leaders of his party branches with the same purpose in mind. Links with purely tribal communities inclined to support Lumumba for traditional reasons were also forged. In common with the mass party leaders in Ghana, Mali, and Guinea, he relied primarily upon women and youth organizations and modern groups, such as teachers, unions, and civil servants. The major youth group in the Congo—Alliance de la Jeunesse Congolaise—was firmly in Lumumba's camp and was an important element in his initial national appeal.

It would be misleading, however, to maintain that these youth movements, which have proven so crucial to African nation-building, are completely oblivious to traditional tribal ties or loyalties. Even in the cities and universities, chapters of youth groups can be found organized primarily on the basis of tribal origin. Although these associations may claim that their goal is the preservation of traditional culture, they also tend to be instrumental in the reformation of aspects of that culture which conflict with the new nationalism. For example, LaGoumbe, a youth association composed primarily of members of a northern Muslim tribe but located in the port city of Abidjan (Ivory Coast), has been instrumental in effecting the emancipation of women "back home"; has acted as a mutual aid society to raise dowries; and has sponsored its own recreation and music.[9]

[9] Thomas Hodgkin, *Nationalism in Colonial Africa* (London: Frederick Muller Ltd., 1956), p. 89.

THE GENERATIONAL REVOLUTION

To concentrate upon the emergence of youth in positions of influence without noting the effect of this upheaval upon the traditional wielders of authority is to neglect what is possibly the most important scene in the drama. Old men everywhere have habitually shaken their heads, mumbled curses, and sadly remarked that when they were boys things were different. Rarely has an elder generation of predominant influence and power undergone such a rapid reversal of role and influence as the traditional rulers of many African societies. There are exceptions, however, and the amazing thing about leadership in some of the large-scale traditional-tribal political system is not its backwardness nor its immutability but rather its remarkable capacity to accommodate itself to rapidly changing environment.[10]

Frederick Mutesa II, the Kabaka of Buganda, is a Cambridge man, dresses impeccably, speaks correct English, and can tell droll tales of how his grandfather fed Christians to the royal crocodiles. Nevertheless, he regards seriously his role as head of the forty-eight Buganda clans and of the tribal kingdom of Buganda. The Kabaka, his ministers, and council (*Lukiko*) like to see their tribal kingdom as an independent state that agreed to British protection in 1900. Not only did the Kabaka's government pose a roadblock to the unity of Uganda, but it continues tenaciously to resist the replacement of its traditional aristocracy by a mass-based democracy. There are in Buganda a number of bright young men who have sought in vain to reform the Buganda Government, both from within and from without, some of whom are today a bit sadder and wiser.

With the exception of the relatively large, powerful, and amazingly viable traditional states like Buganda and Ethiopia, which, as we have noted, have been able to absorb into their governing systems most of the young, educated would-be reformers, traditional forms of social and political leadership are rapidly giving way to the new nationalism. Today throughout much of Africa the voices of the nationalist political party leader and not that of the chief is more often heard and respected in the hundreds of district and regional councils. At the parochial level the local schoolteacher or cooperative society chairman competes with the tribal elder for influence and prestige. The secondary schoolboy, home on a holiday, is inclined to ridicule the simple gospel of the old uneducated mission-trained preacher. The ruralite who has completed eight years of primary school regards himself, and is regarded by others, as being quite superior to his cousins who do not possess the Standard Eight Certificate. More important, he often feels superior to the village elders

---

[10] For a detailed and excellent account of the way in which traditional systems accommodate themselves to transition, see David Apter's recent study of the Baganda, *The Political Kingdom in Uganda* (Princeton, N.J.: Princeton University Press, 1961).

who have not been to school. For it is to him, and not to the village chief or clan leader, that the widow brings the complex and mysterious government compensation forms, the letter from a son at the University of Chicago, or the newspaper clipping sent by a daughter from Nairobi. The elders, however, are not always hostile to the new values. One cannot help but be touched by the belief of many older people that education is simply something which one absorbs through exposure. We recall the attendance, night after night, of a very old man at an adult education extramural course in northeastern Uganda. This elderly gentleman could not understand or speak English but firmly believed that if he attended the sessions regularly he would somehow be touched by the magic of education. For the power and wealth of the European settler and departing colonial ruler is attributed almost mystically by many Africans to their possession of this magic "education." The importance of education can hardly be exaggerated or grasped by those from a culture where it is taken for granted. To the African youth education means power. It means the difference between ruling and being ruled; between hunger and plenty; between psychic superiority and embarrassing inferiority; between racial inequality and racial equality; between parochialism and cosmopolitanism; and between boredom and adventure.

It is these young men, possessed of a minimum of education but able to read, write, and speak the European tongue, who can be found laboriously typing or penning a letter for the illiterate village chief to a higher headquarters; arrogantly wielding a rubber stamp authorizing an illiterate peasant to sell his cotton; patiently and often inaccurately interpreting the vernacular into French or English for a visiting bureaucrat (black as well as white); spending his salary of fifteen dollars or so a month on a bicycle or transistor radio, the symbols of status or dignity.

It is relatively easy to identify, interview, and study those men whose names appear daily in the local papers and nowadays in *The New York Times* and *London Times* as well. But the crucial level of influence and leadership—that stratum upon which future order and national integration will ultimately depend—is difficult to comprehend and know. Here we are referring to primary schoolteachers; assistant agricultural, veterinary, cooperative, or community development officers; court clerks; railroad bookkeepers; regional and local party leaders. It is these middle and lower level nontraditional roles that are critical to the nation-building process and about which we know so little.

LEADERSHIP AND PERSONALITY

In the absence of a sophisticated electorate, but with the requirements of obtaining mass support, leadership in Africa is more a dynamic of personality, vitality, and ambition than it is an agency for the expression of an underlying and motivating ideology. Only if we are aware of the personal as opposed to the ideological nature of political leadership in

Africa can we understand the extraordinary gyrations of African party leaders as they form and break alliances overnight and take what appear to be contradictory ideological stands from one day to the next.

Given this personal or charismatic milieu within which political leadership operates, it is possible for an extraordinarily ambitious leader to shape the political destiny of a territory and a people almost single-handedly. On February 12, 1961, the people of the Southern Cameroons (British), supervised by a United Nations plebiscite team, voted to decide whether they would federate with Nigeria to the west or with the Republic of the Cameroons to the east. Observers predicted a close vote which might have gone either way. The people of the Northern Cameroons in the November 1959 plebiscite had already voted against joining with Nigeria, preferring continued status as a trust territory. In February 1961, it was assumed that the Northern Cameroons would vote to federate with the Cameroon Republic (former French mandate); when the ballots were all counted, under the watchful eyes of the United Nations Commission for Supervision of the Plebiscite, it was discovered that by a close vote the Northern Cameroons had elected to join with Nigeria.[11] Even more surprising was the overwhelming victory of the pro-Cameroon and anti-Nigeria party in the Southern Cameroon plebiscite. There is little doubt that this extraordinary two-to-one decision for union with the Cameroon Republic (only seven of the twenty-six plebiscite districts voted a majority in favor of union with Nigeria) is largely attributable to the organizational skill and vigor of John Foncha, then Prime Minister of the semiautonomous Southern Cameroons and leader and founder of the Kamerun National Democratic Party. Admittedly he was able to draw upon the distrust of the Southern Cameroon people for the Ibo across the Nigerian frontier, but had Foncha lent his skill and personal following to the cause of union with Nigeria, it is likely that the people of the Southern Cameroon would today fly the Nigerian flag.

The greater the incidence of traditional conflict, the more likely it is that personality on the one hand and tribal solidarity on the other, in contrast to party ideology, will set the objectives of political action. Leadership skills in societies rent by tribal, religious, or other segmented factions are often dissipated and therefore not available for the crucial process of nation-building. One of the most persistent characteristics of the African Revolution has been this waste and spoilage of scarce leadership skills. In the Republic of South Africa, South-West Africa, Portuguese Africa, and to a lesser extent in the Rhodesias and Nyasaland, the evolution of political leaders capable of national administration and guidance has been deliberately retarded by the European minority. Leadership talents are sometimes deliberately diverted into less threatening activities, such as church, club, tribe, and crime. These transitional

---

[11] The Republic of the Cameroons has protested the election, claiming interference by Nigeria.

sociations do provide channels—sometimes the only ones available—for the development of modern leadership talents and potential in those territories where the dominant white elite holds a monopoly of governmental leadership positions. In countries not beset by minority racial domination, leadership talents are sometimes consumed in the pluralistic struggle of tribe against tribe, Catholic against Protestant, African against Indian, or region against region. Those new or modified institutions which provide valuable experience for the evolving leaders and which meet the requirements of responsible large-scale organizations often provide the source of future nationalist leadership. In short, some institutions provide greater access to political influence than do others. A surprising number of Africa's young men of power have emerged from labor unions —Tom Mboya, R. M. Kawawa, Sékou Touré, and J. K. Tettegah. From journalism have come Kwame Nkrumah, Nnamdi Azikiwe, and Ignacio Muzazi; from the cooperative movement, P. Bomani and A. Z. N. Swai.

Although not primarily directed toward the acquisition of political power, these associations present a base from which would-be political leaders can operate and thereby gain access to the political realm. Possibly more important is the manner in which these supposedly nonpolitical membership units provide a base from which the nationalist leaders can operate sub rosa. When political parties or other nationalist types of organizations are finally permitted in the emerging nations and the movement for national self-determination is regarded as legitimate, these transitional associations are ready and able to provide the great bulk of the new nationalist leadership. The cooperative societies in Tanganyika, for example, served as covert bases of TANU organization and activity.

VARIATIONS IN THE EMERGENCE OF LEADERSHIP

How did Africa's new men of influence capture power? Why was it Sékou Touré and not someone else who gained control of the UGTAN? Is it possible to identify leadership attributes or situations which have tended to further the careers of some and frustrate those of others?

By manipulating an existent traditional elite, it is sometimes possible for a would-be leader to maneuver himself into position to assume the mantle of authority as it slips from the hands of the previous elite. In Katanga, Moise Tshombe was able to place himself in the strategic position of natural heir to Belgian authority. Other leaders have emerged on the crest of a crisis situation largely because of their ability to manipulate that crisis to their own advantage. Holden Roberto, a leader of the African rebels in Portuguese Angola, illustrates well the way in which a crisis situation can cast up a nationalist leader. Colonel Mobutu of the Congo and General Abboud of the Sudan have shown how control over the coercive organs of society (military, police, economy) pave the way to personal power. Of course, no single set of circumstances, personal attributes, or skills explains how, why, and who becomes a leader. Obviously individual merit, efficiency and brilliance, as demonstrated by Dr. Mondlane, the leader of the Mozambique National Liberation Front, are sometimes major factors. It is more likely that the interrelationship of these attributes and conditions most precisely explains the emergence of political leadership. But here we must insert a word of caution. The acquisition by a would-be leader of predominant influence in a single institution does not necessarily ensure ready access to the positions of political power in new states. The Asian commercial elite in Uganda, Kenya, and Tanganyika, because it is a racial minority in a new nation wherein power is determined by the weight of numbers, is precluded from turning its economically elite status into corresponding political status.

Furthermore there is evidence that some of Africa's best potential leaders are inclined not to enter the political wars or to accept positions of political leadership because of the insecurity and even personal danger inherent in the politics of emergent nations. Some secondary schoolteachers, university professors, as well as a sizeable number of young men serving in district and provincial administrations, have demonstrated an aversion to partisan politics. As the standard of living increases, there does seem to be a tendency for potential leaders to forego political office and to seek a career in the relatively more secure organizations of the military, bureaucracy, and professions.

COLONIAL LEGACY

Schools are unevenly distributed over the African continent and even within the individual territories are usually concentrated in the urban centers or in regions of minority racial domination. For example, less than 1 per cent of the population of Ethiopia attends school, whereas the proportion in Ghana is greater than 13 per cent (the comparable figure for the United States is about 20 per cent and for Brazil about 1 per cent). As recently as 1958, there were less than 450 government primary schools in Ethiopia—a country of about 20 million—and fewer than 1,000 young Ethiopians were studying to become teachers in teacher training establishments.[12] In independent Liberia, which has had the benefit of long and close association with the United States, only about 4 per cent of the population is in school, in contrast to Uganda, which has about twice as many children per thousand population in the classroom.

Exploration patterns are also significant. For example, during the mid-nineteenth century, it looked for a time as if the interior of East Africa would be opened up by penetration along the Nile to Lake Victoria. But the Madi Rebellion in the Sudan closed off the Nile route to British expansion into what is now Uganda, Kenya, and Western

[12] George H. T. Kimble, *Tropical Africa*, Vol. 2. Anchor Books, Garden City, 1960, p. 129.

Tanganyika. The unpredictable mood and ferocity of the Masai warriors were equally effective in blocking the passage of the competing Roman Catholic White Fathers and Protestant Christian Missionary Society missionaries from approaching Lake Victoria on a direct line from the East African coast. These facts plus the momentary military pre-eminence in the Lake Victoria region of the Kingdom of Buganda in the late nineteenth century served to focus in that kingdom initial British interest and organization as well as missionary influence and education. As a consequence the Baganda experienced as much as twenty to thirty years more exposure to concentrated missionary education and British influence than the peoples in the distant territories to the north—some of whom were not "pacified" until nearly 1920. Buganda became the transport, educational, administrative, and economic hub of all of Uganda, and the Baganda (people of Buganda) are considerably wealthier, better educated, and more sophisticated than the people of the other constituent tribes and regions of Uganda. Makerere College, until very recently the only institution of university standing in East Africa, is located in Kampala, the capital of Buganda and principal city of Uganda. As one would expect, the number of Baganda youth attending Makerere since its founding is disproportionate to its population. A major obstacle to independence for Uganda was the disproportionate wealth and influence of the Baganda. Their traditional leaders, many of them Makerere graduates, look upon the other districts and tribes with some disdain as backward and inferior, while the tribes and regions to the north and east both emulate and fear Buganda. In short, the nation-building process in Uganda—in East Africa for that matter—cannot be fully understood without reference to the levels of education and opportunity that have fallen to some groups and not to others. In Kenya the Kikuyu tribe, again for reasons of fortunate location and a sympathetic traditional culture, became the favorite, and through the years it has been the Kenya Kikuyu students that have rivaled and at times surpassed the numerical pre-eminence of the Baganda at Makerere. Mau Mau and the long period of "emergency"—aspects of which still linger on in Kenya—certainly slowed the phenomenal rise of the Kikuyu tribe to dominance and provided an opportunity for the outlying and equally numerous Luo to begin to catch up. But with few, although certainly notable, exceptions, the Kikuyu today tend to monopolize leadership roles in Kenya, as do the Baganda in Uganda.

A comparable situation can be found in nearly every emergent African state or dependent territory. The relatively inaccessible northern regions of many of the new countries in West Africa—Ghana, Nigeria, the Ivory Coast, and the Cameroons—have experienced a similar developmental history. Many of the coastal peoples were characterized by small-scale social and political organizations relatively vulnerable to European influence and penetration. The northern tier territories in many West

African countries on the other hand, are primarily Muslim and are characterized by semifeudal, large-scale socio-political systems. They did not embrace alien educational and political memberships as rapidly as their neighbors to the south, who subsequently came to dominate the political life of the new countries. Suspicion and sometimes overt hostility between the coastal people and the more traditional and conservative people in the northern reaches of these West African countries is a constant threat to stability and national integration.

NATIONALISM, RACISM, AND TRIBALISM

Modernizing institutions have been highly concentrated and have given some peoples an extraordinary advantage over their countrymen. This has contributed to the problem of nation-building by emphasizing both regional and tribal differences and traditional animosities. Young men who leave the distant, backward, hinterland tribes to study or to make their fortune in the universities and cities are separated from their own people by great distances—cultural as well as geographical. In most areas extraordinary progress is being made to improve communications between the parochial illiterate masses and the new urban elite. The capacity of more and more people to read about and to relate events from the outside world increases as education becomes more widespread. Equally important are the tremendous strides being made in some countries to facilitate the physical conveyance of words, ideas, goods, and people through the extension of radio transmission, the building of roads, airlines, and increased printing and distribution of newspapers. If we were forced to identify a single key to African development and nation-building we might do worse than to settle on the interrelationship of communication and education as the singly most important cluster of factors.

The young educated Africans have heard of Little Rock, although perhaps not of Chicago or San Francisco. They have traveled to the European-dominated cities and been exposed to racial discrimination. They have read and brooded over the American Declaration of Independence which declares all men to be created equal and over the Christian dogma that all are brothers in Christ. The fierce, obsessive drive which arouses these young African intellectuals to ride roughshod over the niceties of democratic ethics in pursuit of the holy grail of national independence cannot be separated from the question of racial identity and exclusion. Racism is a powerful strain running clearly throughout African nationalism. The opening declaration of the Afro-Asian Conference at Bandung is a forceful reminder:

> Let it be said that it is actually the unanimous desire of the countries and the awakened people in Asia and Africa to fight racial discrimination. . . . We are all interested in racial equality. I believe that to be the touchstone

for those who are here assembled and the people they represent. There has not been, nor is there now, any Western colonial regime, although they differ in their systems and methods, that has not inflicted on a larger or lesser scale, on the populations they dominate, the doctrine of their racial inferiority.

Presidents and premiers of independent states meet on equal footing whatever the color of their respective populations, and each state, whatever its size or level of development, speaks with an equal voice in the General Assembly of the United Nations. The crusade to achieve racial equality and dignity on the coat-tails of national sovereignty gives to African nationalism its extraordinary drive and its unique character. And this in turn is one major reason why education is so highly regarded. It is the magic which has maintained European domination and African subjugation. Education gives knowledge of the verbal skills of the dominant whites and an insight into their mores. Education, in short, is a training in the acquisition and use of the tools of power. In the territories where education has not provided access to positions of political influence and equal status, the educated African reacts with an almost pathological bitterness and tends to belittle those things associated with European statutes. He often responds by seeking to "return" to traditional values, to the use of force if necessary, to attain those things due him as an equal human being and citizen of an independent nation.

To make a unified nation from a welter of races, ethnic groupings, and tribes requires a trans-racial, trans-tribal leadership. The claim of African nationalists in Kenya, the Sudan, and northern Uganda that the policy of the European powers and settlers has deliberately fostered tribal conflict to preclude a united attack upon alien domination is widely believed. Although tribal and other parochialisms dissipate leadership and frustrate nation-building, the presence of a sizeable non-African elite also provides a rallying point about which unity can be achieved. Thus, although the Europeans in Kenya, to consolidate their own position, may have divided in order to conquer, their very presence and influence was a force which the Kikuyu, Luo, Wakamba, and even the Masai could agree to oppose. But racialism like tribalism can become a dangerous crutch sustaining an otherwise irresponsible African leadership. For a would-be African leader can seek mass support by appealing to tribal instead of trans-tribal support, and the same aspiring office-holder can also attempt to outbid his more responsible opponents in the area of race. Thus some Kenya candidates for the Legislative Council in 1961 reputedly sought votes on the basis of promising their would-be constituents the neighboring European's farm, car, and cattle. The story of the African who politely comes to call in order to look over his future land and possessions may be preposterous, but it is a serious reminder of the potential implications of mass-based politics in an area characterized by an unsophisticated electorate and an irresponsible would-be elite.

In a democracy, politics have always been a good way to get ahead. The influence in American politics of the Irish at first, then the Italians, the Polish, and more recently the Negroes is but the American version of the universal phenomenon. This in part explains the extraordinary interest in political life taken by vast numbers of Africans since as a group they have long been denied the social and economic kingdom and now believe with Dr. Nkrumah that if given the political kingdom, all others will follow.

THE QUESTION OF RESPONSIBILITY

The manner in which traditional leaders in much of Africa are held accountable, and to whom they owe responsibility, is not defined with exact precision. Whether or not the transitional or modern leader is accountable to the traditional culture often depends on whether it will benefit his career. The range of alternatives and decisions open to new leaders is not limited either by the formal requirements of their office or by custom or popular consensus. Aspiring political leaders, unlike their traditional predecessors, must secure the active support of the masses and are inclined to make use of ethnic and racial associations in their quest for positions of leadership. Even when he holds a Ph.D. from an American or British university, an aspiring African political leader often pays homage to traditional elders, worships at a pagan shrine, and wears the traditional dress of the leader class in his attempt to lay claim to both traditional and modern legitimacy. In this way, much of the lure of traditional culture is reinterpreted and becomes symbolic of the new legitimacy, in the process sanctifying the rule of the modern leaders. This interlocking or traditional and modern justifications for leadership roles is a complex subject but one that must be understood if we are to be able to project the future patterns of leadership. But even while the new leaders pay lip service to the traditional values in their pursuit of political power, the gap between the educated class and the masses continues to grow. If it is a function of leadership to bridge this gap, the fact that the gap is still unspanned must be viewed with alarm. Increasingly, the masses will come to resent this situation.

Highly educated African families almost invariably live in the urban university centers. They have little in common with the illiterate bush people and are inclined to seek out other educated young couples. This makes for class conflict and for an African version of the age-old urban-rural conflict. One can detect a growing fear on the part of the countryman toward the city dweller. Sometimes this fear can be seen in the relationship between the traditional elders and the young intellectuals. The older Africans, and particularly those traditional leaders who live in the hinterland, are afraid of the radical ideas of the educated young people, who, they feel, will destroy the sanctity of the traditional system and in the process bring chaos upon the heads of their people. The Baganda riots of 1945 and 1949 were set off by a combination of the illiterate rural clans and the growing urban proletariat in opposition to the wealthy, educated, and less traditional elite.

It is fascinating to watch the rapidity with which new urban-centered associations, like labor unions and political parties, break down the traditional status distinctions between superior and subordinate tribes, clans, classes, sexes, and age-groupings, and at the same time give rise to Western socio-economic classes, mass-based organizations, and political elites. As these new associations level the distinctions of traditional society, they sow the seeds of future status differences and potential group conflict.

The ruling elite in the new African countries is under constant pressure from its supporters, competing elites, and foreign governments and publics to "produce" or "achieve," to meet varying and often conflicting expectations. This pressure tends to make the new leaders hypersensitive to criticism, which in turn encourages them to abandon democratic procedures in order to meet or stifle conflicting demands and expectations.

MANPOWER—QUANTITY AND QUALITY

The continued emphasis—the near obsession—with education, even in those countries that have gained their independence, reflects an interesting but subtle aspect of the nature of sovereignty in the new African nations. Kwame Nkrumah, Sékou Touré, and other African leaders have said time and time again that they will be neither independent nor free until they are no longer dependent upon their former rulers, who often continue to occupy as many positions and offices as they did before, although now theoretically under African authority. To the average African peasant in Northern Nigeria, Katanga, Tchad, or Niger, the distinction between a dependent colonial and an independent free man is not always very clear. If "uhuru" (freedom) is the most powerful slogan in dependent Africa today, then "Africanization" is its counterpart in the newly independent countries and in those scheduled to receive their independence in the near future. It is important to draw attention to the mood underlying the insistence that young men and women be educated immediately to replace those non-Africans, who of necessity hold positions of authority and influence even in the newly independent countries. Of the more than 200 members of the senior staff of the Northern Region of Nigeria, two-thirds are expatriate Britishers. Uganda, which achieved independence in 1962, only recently appointed its first African District Commissioner. Of the more than 1,600 servants in the administrative and professional classes of the Kenya Civil Service, only 42 at the end of 1960 were Africans.[13] Unfortunately, Tanganyika illustrates this problem well. In May 1960, a United Nations report stated that the major problems facing Tanganyika were: (1) establishing of a competent corps of officials and sufficient numbers to provide for growing needs, (2) financial

[13] Author's survey of public service training in Kenya (August, 1961).

and technical assistance, and (3) expansion of education and essential services. As recently as 1958 most observers of the African scene would have agreed that this large multitribal United Nations Trust Territory would be the last area in East Africa to achieve independence. The reasons for this view were many. Most compelling was the fact that Tanganyika was the poorest territory in East Africa. Although tremendous progress has been made, the fact still remains that economically and administratively Tanganyika is still the poorest, least developed, and most backward territory in East Africa.

Tanganyika's steady but rapid march toward independence is regarded as a model of political transition—a showcase of the successful transfer of authority from a European power to a native people. General elections were held for the first time in 1958, and it was not until 1959 that ministerial government was introduced. The following year elections were held which returned a majority of African members to a national legislature. No serious efforts were made to prepare Africans to replace Britishers as district officers before 1957. At the end of 1958 there were only four African district officers. There are about four thousand senior and middle grade posts in Tanganyika, less than 1 per cent (380 as of July 1960) were filled by Africans. Six years ago only five Americans in Tanganyika held positions at this level.[14] Unfortunately, the problem is not primarily one of facilities for training Tanganyikans to assume these important civil service positions. There simply are too few candidates possessed of the educational requirements either to fill the positions or to qualify for specialist training. In 1962, only 106 students in all of Tanganyika received higher school certificates.

Although this problem exists at every level and function of government, the most immediate and serious situation, if this distinction can be made, is at the level of provincial and district administration. A capacity for modernization with political stability in an emergent but backward country, larger than Texas and New England combined, is acutely dependent upon capable administration at the provincial and district level. As of 1959, only one of Tanganyika's fifty-eight districts was administered by an African District Commissioner. In 1961, there were about five. By independence day British District Commissioners were replaced by Africans, and responsibility for over-all district and provincial administration was in the hands of the relevant African ministries in Dar es Salaam. A year later only three European District Commissioners remained.

In 1962 the administration of the country was drastically reorganized. Career provincial commissioners were replaced by politically appointed regional commissioners, some of whom are at the same time members of

[14] The rapidity with which an African Government can Africanize is demonstrated however by the fact that by January 1963 the percentage of Africans in these posts had increased to nearly 40 per cent of the total.

Parliament and of the national TANU executive. These new commissioners—all Africans—are ex-officio Secretaries of TANU within their respective regions. The politicizing of the administration was subsequently extended to the district (area) level with the political appointment of TANU leaders as area commissioners. And the proclamation of a single-party state in 1963 further extended the process of integrating party and administration.

To many Africans in responsible governmental positions, the future is viewed as a race between education and national disaster. If these young leaders are to retain positions of power, they must provide the services that a world-wide competitive communications system has led the masses to believe is their due. To do this they must find the men to staff the positions required to administer a complex, twentieth-century social welfare state. Yet, to satisfy the psychic need for racial equality they must often staff these positions with Africans not yet sufficiently trained and experienced to assume responsibility. To do this with even minimum efficiency they must somehow, almost overnight, turn hundreds of thousands of uneducated young men and women into dedicated, technically competent, and efficient civil servants. It is therefore understandable that men like Julius Nyerere, Sékou Touré, and Hastings Banda look to the outside world for assistance in meeting these immediate and critical needs.

Nearly five thousand African students attended American universities and colleges during the academic year 1962-63.[15] This was a 25 per cent increase over the number studying in the United States in 1960-61 and a 69 per cent increase over the previous year. The pilgrimage of African students to the portals of Western universities was dramatized in 1959 by the Kenya Airlift, which brought to the United States nearly three hundred East African students whose transportation was financed by a $100,000 grant from the Joseph P. Kennedy Jr., Foundation.

The Ford Foundation and other bodies have done much in recent years to raise the standard of education in Africa and to increase teaching personnel and facilities. In a reverse airlift in 1961 and again in 1962, three hundred carefully selected and trained young Americans were flown to East Africa to spend two years teaching in Tanganyika, Uganda, and Kenya. In Nyasaland, Somalia, Ethiopia, Liberia, Tanganyika, Sierra Leone, Senegal, Ivory Coast, Ghana, and Nigeria, the Peace Corps teachers are making an extraordinary contribution. The United Nations (UNESCO) too is aware of the critical race between education and social and political chaos. At a UNESCO-sponsored conference on African education held at Addis Ababa in May 1961, African countries submitted an inventory of their teaching and physical plant needs. Other countries are also providing assistance. More and more African students are attend-

---

[15] This number includes students from the United Arab Republic and from the Republic of South Africa.

ing West German universities. Israel recently opened a school to teach Africans the techniques of democratic planning and economic development. In spite of these developments the major base for overseas higher education for most young Africans continues to be the metropolitan countries of Great Britain and France. The necessity for young Africans to obtain the tools and techniques with which to transform a continent rapidly is leading them not only to Columbia, Cambridge, and the Sorbonne, but to Prague, Moscow, and Peiping as well. In 1960 nearly three hundred African students—more than there were holders of American government fellowships—attended the Institute for Economic Studies at Prague. Nearly six hundred African students attended the 1957 Youth Festival in Moscow. At the Cairo Afro-Asian Peoples' Solidarity Conference, the leading Russian delegate told the participants, "We are ready to help you as brother helps brother." Russia's expanded interest in Africa is reflected in Soviet scholarship on the subject of Africa. An Institute of African Studies was established in the Soviet Union in 1960 under the directorship of Professor Potemkin, the Soviet's leading African expert. Moscow's Friendship University already has enrolled hundreds of African students, and African students are to be found in other Russian universities as well. A growing number of African-Muslim scholars are studying in the University at Tashkent, the capital of the Muslim Soviet state of Uzbek.

THE CIRCULATION OF IDEOLOGY

African students in the United States carry back to their developing country a knowledge of American engineering skills or principles of constitutionalism and federalism. They take with them too the saga of Little Rock, a recollection of restaurants that would not serve them and landladies who suddenly had no rooms, and a memory of Negro slums and degradation. Nor are only modern techniques imparted in the educational process. Education opens the door to the entire storehouse of human ideas, ideologies, and doctrines. The young African who ponders long about Socrates' drinking of the hemlock or about John Locke and the rights of the revolution, or who studies the American Declaration of Independence (noting that it not only proclaims the right to abolish and to institute new governments, but that it also declares that all men are created equal) will find motive and meaning to give force to social and political change. We must be careful not to liken the young intellectual African nationalist to Thomas Jefferson or James Madison. Our planet seems to spin much faster now than it did in the eighteenth century. There is little time nowadays for relaxed comtemplation of the wisdom and relevance of the words of Harrington, Locke, and Rousseau to nation-building. Carefully written letters, tracts, and essays which later generations cherish as native philosophy are the product of more leisurely revolution and transition than is currently under way in Africa. The African national leader dictates his speeches to a shorthand stenographer as he prepares to meet the Soviet or American ambassador. The world has undergone a communications transformation; the words of Jefferson, Marx, Roosevelt, Lenin, Rousseau, and De Gaulle are pouring in upon Africa from hundreds of radio transmitters. Tons of printed words arrive daily in Mombasa, Léopoldville, and Dakar. A group of interested Americans in Syracuse, New York, in May of 1960 sent six thousand books to Kenya. Africa's new leaders can travel to New York in less time than it took Benjamin Franklin to journey from Philadelphia to Boston, or for that matter, often less time than they can travel to the more inaccessible regions of their own countries. Because men can and do move freely on our planet—from Accra to Moscow, Conakry to Peiping, from Abidjan to Paris, from Nairobi to Washington—absorbing words and ideas from a jumble of cultures and centuries, and because words and ideas can be transmitted even more rapidly than men, the leaders of Africa's new nations are constantly exposed to new ideas and philosophies. Through "Nommo [the word] man establishes his mastery over things. . . . The force, responsibility, and commitment of the word and the awareness that the word alone alters the world; these are the characteristics of African culture." [16]

Although new Africa receives literally and symbolically competing audio waves from Moscow and Peiping, from London, Washington, and Paris, and even from Accra and Cairo, there are at least some ideas and ways of behavior common to both West and East. A new role for women in African society is a case in point. The place of women in the political and social life of traditional Africa, with few exceptions, was a minor one and it was their lot to undertake the time-consuming chores of growing and preparing food and shelter, while the men, freed of domestic chores, consulted and made decisions for the community and gathered on occasion to settle disputes between clans and other constitutent groupings. Even in matrilineal societies like the Ashanti, the men dominated political life. But the role of women, along with that of youth, has been greatly affected by the sociation process that characterizes the African Revolution. The following excerpt from a letter to the District Commissioner in Bunyoro District, Uganda, is indicative:

"We would ask you to kindly inform us when Muruka Councils are to assemble so that we can prepare to attend. You know we the Bakyada [housewives] of Bunyoro are not considered much in councils of this district, men alone cannot save the country, we need to collaborate.[17]

Hardly a month goes by without an international conference of women, or of women's organizations. There have been conferences attended by

[16] Janheinz Jahn, *Muntu, The New African Culture*, translated by Marjorie Grene (New York: Grove Press, 1961), pp. 132-133.
[17] Letter from three women to the District Commissioner of Bunyoro (Jan. 26, 1955).

African women in the United States at least once every year since 1958. Mrs. Padmore, wife of the Liberian ambassador to the United States, recently wrote that the "story of women in Africa is really the story of women in Europe, or in America, or in fact anywhere. . . . We have one thing in common, we are the bearers of children. We are the custodians of the future." [18]

Community development and adult education—two powerful institutions whose impact throughout much of Africa is not sufficiently appreciated—particularly affect the lives and role of women.

THE AFRICANIZATION OF IDEOLOGY

The formation and growth of modernizing institutions in Africa has been accompanied by corresponding slogans of capitalism, socialism, democracy, Pan-Africanism, and so forth. Although Africa has yet to make its contribution to political theory, her spokesmen and leaders have not been content simply to borrow current systems and ideologies from the existing reservoir of Western philosophies. Unlike the newly emergent nations of Asia, political behavior in the newly independent African states has been particularly pragmatic. More often than not ideologies and systems are presented after the fact to dignify expedient behavior. At the same time there has been a sensitivity to too heavy a reliance on alien ideas and systems of government lest this dependence imply a racial or cultural inferiority. To avoid this interpretation some African countries have rewritten or invented aspects of their history to show an ancient knowledge of democracy. Thus, otherwise embarrassing deviations from the inherited Western systems of politics and government are justified as a movement toward consistency with indigenous democracy and policies. As Western democracy is peculiarly adapted to Western culture and history, it follows logically that independent African states, as they rediscover their long submerged personalities, will evolve democratic forms consistent with their own environment. Constitutions and multiple parties for example, are regarded not as elements basic to democracy itself but simply as peculiarly Western devices.

An important distinction is made between democratic values that the African spokesman insists are indigenous to Africa and systems of government which gave expression to those values. In an extraordinary political treatise defending his single-party proposals, President Nyerere of Tanganyika wrote that "people who are used to the two-party system cannot imagine democracy without it. They ask: 'How can one have democracy with a one-party system?' It will therefore sound to them like heresy when they are told that other peoples, who claim to be democrats, are now beginning to ask: 'How can you have democracy with a two-party

[18] Mai Padmore, "Some Misconceptions About Women in Africa," *Africa Report,* VI, No. 6 (June 1961), pp. 7-8.

system?' " [19] Western democracy, according to Nyerere and other African spokesmen, reflects the class division of Western societies and therefore naturally gave rise to a multiple-party system to give representation to the competing social classes. In the emergent African states, however, there is both a unity of purpose and a relative absence of social and economic class distinctions. To force a two-party system on an emerging African nation, therefore, tends to create undemocratic opposition where there is none. As the people will overwhelmingly support the revolutionary party, democracy cannot depend upon opposition within the single party. "Where there is one party, and that party is identified with the nation as a whole, the foundations of democracy can be firmer and the people can have more opportunity to exercise a real choice, than where you have two or more parties—each representing only a section of the community." [20]

Although there exists a tendency to justify and explain away inevitable deviations from the French or British political model, it is also evident that traditional beliefs and indigenous forms of socio-political behavior do in fact significantly temper the superimposed Western forms. It is evident to anyone who has studied traditional African societies, or for that matter the literature of the new African literary elite, that African society is not simple but rather rich in its metaphysics and in the unity of its constituent ethics, ideologies, and symbols. The power of traditional symbolism and cosmology to absorb and modify Western ideology possibly is most clearly demonstrated in the realm of religion.

Modern African history, unlike that of any other continent, is uniquely intertwined with the development of the Christian missionary movement of the nineteenth and twentieth centuries. It is only since World War II that men of the West have sought seriously and intensely to inculcate among the Africans over whom they ruled an understanding and appreciation of political democracy and a knowledge of Western political institutions. But nearly five hundred years ago and even before Columbus came to the Americas, Portugal established colonies in Southwest Africa. Since that time men of the West have sought, in the name of Christ, to save the soul of heathen Africa. But they have not had the missionary field to themselves, for the word of Mohammed traveled to the interior of Africa with the camel and slave caravans as they crossed the Sahara, and went ashore at Mombasa, Malindi, and Jibuti from Arab dhows as they caught the monsoons out of Persian and Arabian ports. Despite considerably larger investment in both human and physical resources, the influence of Christianity has been significantly restricted as a consequence of denominational competition and conflict. The Muslim faith, less subject to internal dissention, has sunk its roots deeper and probably

[19] President Nyerere, "Democracy and the Party System I," *Tanganyika Standard* (Jan. 16, 1963).
[20] *Ibid.*, Part IV, *Tanganyika Standard* (Jan. 21, 1963).

further afield in Africa. Unlike Christianity, which demands a complete break with indigenous beliefs and their sustaining social institutions, Mohammedanism may be embraced in easy stages and need not necessarily conflict with traditional values, and in fact may reinforce some that are threatened by Christianity. Although Christianity teaches that all are brothers in Christ, the African cannot help being aware of the subtle discrimination that often permeates even the mission station. The followers of Mohammed, in contrast to those of Christ, are relatively color blind. Given the powerful racial strain that flows through the African Revolution, the differing attitude toward race of the competing religions cannot be overemphasized as a major factor in the political evolution of the continent.

Catholic-Protestant competition during the early period of exploration and penetration in East and Central Africa has left a legacy of religious conflict and bitterness that dominates politics in not a few evolving territories to this day. The theology of the imported religion is often relatively unimportant, but the Church as a modern association possessed of collective identity and organized power is of considerable significance.

African philosophy nearly everywhere views events and human organization as a harmonious entity, incorporating politics, religion, and traditional associations. Thus, the Separatist Christian churches are playing an important role in the nation-building process, for they serve to integrate conflicting secular and religious forces.

Some of the main currents of an embryonic African political ideology can now be identified. The public sector in the new African nations is clearly dominant over the private, and with few exceptions Africa's nation-builders are constructing socialist states. Government is clearly evolving as the most powerful social institution, the fountainhead of modernization, and increasingly, the source of all authority. The modern African is fully aware of the egalitarian, public-service function of the socialist state and judges his leaders and governmental institutions more on how well they provide medical and health services, develop industry, and improve communications than on how effectively they guard individual liberties or freedom of speech.

Possibly one of the more important philosophical questions that the African Revolution may have to answer is whether a people can establish a socialist democracy before first experiencing a protracted period of limited "guardian" government, without sacrificing, in the process, individual liberties and freedom. "Can the new states," as Nkrumah has said, "afford to be liberal later?" Will they want to be?

Young men in a young Africa are rapidly acquiring the tools and ideas to transform their continent and to shape their destiny. The rapidity of the transformation reflects their determination to demonstrate their racial equality. Less visible but of equal importance, as this chapter has sought to show, is the internal revolution—the radical transformation and the evolution of corresponding associations. It is the young who must bridge the immense gap between the distant, but still recent, past and the trauma of the present by anchoring it to the past. An African ideology must evolve, it would seem, if the new African states are to find a national ethos other than that of racialism or anti-colonialism and one that is capable of giving expression and purpose to truly national life.

VI
The Enigma of Race

"The problem of the twentieth century is the problem
of the color line—the relation of the darker to the
lighter races of men in Asia and Africa, in America
and the islands of the sea."

W. E. B. Dubois, *Dusk at Dawn*.

BLACK AND WHITE

By chance or by design the earth's creatures, man not ex-
cluded, come in a variety of colors, dimensions, and shapes. As for the
creature man, his similarities are certainly more pronounced than his
differences. All colors, sizes, and shapes of man eat and drink a variety of
animal and vegetable substances. All have demonstrated at one time or
another a capacity to do violence to one another as well as an inclination
to love and to cooperate. All men are busy doing that which they must to
secure those things without which life is impossible, undesirable, or un-
pleasant. The process of birth, mating, and death, though varying slightly
in procedure and significance, is basically the same the world over.

Despite the similarities which characterize his species, man has preferred
to take particular notice of his differences. The contact of men of different
color or configuration is rarely characterized by the simple observation of
visual difference. Rather each attributes to the other, because he is black,
white, or brown, a number of other characteristics which from the point
of view of the beholder are deemed either good or bad, desirable or undesirable.

The laws of genetics and man's long relative immobility have distributed the various races of humanity over the planet in a distinctive
fashion. By and large white men are Euro-American, brown and yellow
men Asian and Oceanic, while black men are Africans. Thus, large segments of humanity are distinguished by color and at the same time by
major area of domicile. And quite different civilizations evolved within
these long isolated major segments of the planet. Even though the
human species may have had its origins in Africa, as Leakey would have
us believe, it was, until comparatively recently, a relatively unknown
region inhabited by black men of peculiar habits and beliefs—in short, by
strangers.[1]

[1] L. S. B. Leakey, *Adam's Ancestors* (New York: Harper Torchbooks, 1960).

79

The most important thing that happened to Africa and Africans during the latter half of the nineteenth and the first half of the twentieth century was its discovery and subsequent conquest by Europeans; the most important thing that has happened to Africa in this, the latter half of the twentieth century, is its rediscovery and reconquest by Africans. Both processes concern the interrelationship of black, brown, and white men.

We do not attempt here to cover comprehensively the relationship between Africans and the immigrant or transient Asian and European races, but to explore selected aspects of the issue, with the purpose of conveying to the reader a sense of the dimensions of the problem and of the implications of that problem for Africa's quest for order.[2]

EARLY CONTACTS

Contact between the peoples of Africa and those of Asia has existed for thousands of years. The commercial and cultural ties that once linked the Muslim civilizations and empires of the North African littoral with those in Central Africa have been well documented and described, as have early Arab and Portuguese settlements and penetration along the East African coast. Early in the nineteenth century, more than fifty years before European exploration gave rise to headlines in London and New York, Arab ivory hunters and slave raiders were permanent fixtures in the Upper Congo and along the great lakes of East and Central Africa. These early contacts are not without significance, but the period of major contact when large numbers of Europeans and Asians invaded, settled, and subsequently dominated the continent began much later.

Contact between Europeans and Africans reached substantial proportions in West Africa earlier than in East and Central Africa. West African harbors were needed to serve the rapidly expanding trade with the Far East. The proximity of the West African supply to the New World slave markets also encouraged relatively early contact. These factors, in conjunction with navigability of West African rivers, gave early impetus to commercial contact between European and African merchants. Interestingly enough there is little evidence of an inherent superior-inferior context to these early contacts. It was common, for example, for the garrison of the west coast port stations to take African wives. It is important to keep in mind that the technological gap, which in the nineteenth and twentieth centuries provided the immigrant races with an extraordinary advantage over the Africans, was not substantial during this period of initial contact. The European treated the black strangers with respect and the African was not overawed by the European's technology which was in some ways surprisingly similar to his own.[3]

---

[2] For a current and excellent treatment of this critical issue see Anthony H. Richmond, *The Colour Problem* (Baltimore, Md.: Penguin Books, Inc., 1961).

[3] Basil Davidson, *Black Mother* (London: Victor Gollancz, Ltd., and Boston: Little, Brown & Co., 1961).

Asian and European men came to Africa for many reasons and brought with them conflicting ideologies, skills, dreams, ambitions, and prejudices. The coincidence of the industrial and technological revolution in Europe with a religious revival was to have enormous consequences for Africa. While Manchester merchants were seeking new markets for the surplus of industrial plants, men of the cloth imbued with a renewed faith and fervor were determined to export the Christian Gospel to the heathen. Thus Africans soon found themselves a target for the aims of missionary and merchant alike.

INVASION AND ABSORPTION

A useful way of regarding early contacts with Africa is in terms of a softening-up operation. Initial European coastal settlements and exploitation, beginning with those of the Portuguese in the mid-fifteenth century, were in effect a preliminary reconnaissance of this enormous continent in anticipation of subsequent probes into the interior.

For many centuries, however, the continent effectively repulsed European and Asian attempts to penetrate its outer barriers and plunder its interior; with few exceptions alien influences were limited to the coastal towns. African reactions to these early contacts varied enormously. Along the coast and navigable rivers Africans traded food stuffs, ivory, and rare metals for guns, beads, and cloth.

In South Africa the coastal installations, although initially established to service the Indian trade routes, were quick to evolve into beachheads of permanent settlement. During the last quarter of the seventeenth century Dutch and German settlers along the Cape coast turned their backs on the sea and began to penetrate the interior. But while the Boer trekkers were moving their wagons and cattle northward into the veld, pushing aside or killing the relatively few Hottentot and Bushmen residing in the interior, a more powerful African people were driving their cattle southward. Within three years of the initial contact of Boer and Bantu these two virile peoples were at war. Violence and conflict have run like a thread through the relationship of European and African in South Africa from that time onward.

The relatively early date of large-scale European-African contact in South Africa must be appreciated if present relationships between the races in that region are to be understood. By 1837 there were more than five thousand Boers settled north of the Orange River.[4] The rest of Africa, however, was more successful in resisting penetration. While the Boer trekkers were giving birth to second generation Euro-Africans, European explorers had only just discovered the Niger. It was not until 1849 that Krapf first saw Mount Kenya, and until 1858 that Speke discovered Victoria Nyanza.

[4] L. H. Gann and P. Duigan, *White Settlers in Tropical Africa* (Baltimore, Md.: Penguin African Series, 1962).

Before considering the subsequent and more massive penetration of the heart of the continent by missionaries, governors, and settlers during the latter half of the nineteenth century, it is first necessary to review briefly the impact of the slave trade, which, along with the early peripheral settlements and explorations, effectively prepared the way for subsequent large-scale contact of Europeans and Africans.

THE LEGACY OF THE SLAVE TRADE

Massive migrations of people are frequently the watersheds of important historical epochs and eras. A relatively little documented migration, possibly the largest in human history, is the exodus of black men from Africa to the Americas, the regions of the Persian Gulf, and Southeast Asia. Arabs dominated slave trading and raiding along the east coast; Europeans, first the Portuguese, then the Dutch, and later the British and Americans, profited most from this human traffic in West Africa. It is impossible to calculate the suffering and enormous costs to Africa caused by the compulsory withdrawal, over a period of six and seven generations, of as many as fifteen million of her strongest, most promising men, women, and children.[5]

It is established that from 1680 to 1786 more than two million slaves were landed in North America and the West Indies. During the previous hundred years the Portuguese carried approximately one million slaves to Brazil. The peak years, however, were between 1835 and 1850 when the average number of Africans shipped in chains from the continent rarely fell below 136,000 per year. The real cost cannot be measured solely in terms of the exodus of millions of Africans. One must take into account the fact that 10 to 15 per cent of the slaves shipped from West Africa died before they reached the new world.[6]

According to Basil Davidson "So far as the Atlantic slave trade is concerned it appears reasonable to suggest that in one way or another, before and after embarkation, it cost Africa at least fifty million souls. This estimate may be about one-forth of black Africa's population today, and is certainly on the low side." [7]

The breakdown of traditional social and political systems in the wake of the slaughter and destruction accompanying the capture of slaves was enormous. The explorer Burton calculated that a slave raid to capture fifty-five women caused the destruction of "at least ten villages, each with a population of between a hundred and two hundred souls." [8] The significance of this extraordinary exodus is still to be fully measured. Destruction of the critical institutions, of organized and functioning societies in

[5] This estimate is taken from R. R. Kuczynski, *Population Movements* (1936), quoted in Basil Davidson, *op. cit.*, p. 87.

[6] For an excellent study of the slave trade see Daniel P. Mannix and Malcolm Cowley, *Black Cargoes* (New York: The Viking Press, Inc., 1962).

[7] Basil Davidson, *op. cit.*, p. 88.

[8] L. H. Gann and P. Duigan, *op. cit.*, p. 26.

much of tropical Africa, served effectively to soften up the interior of the continent, permitting relatively easy access and penetration of a subsequent generation of governors, settlers, and missionaries.

Slavery, it should be noted, was a monopoly of neither the Arabs in the East nor the Europeans in the West. The capture, transport to the coast, and subsequent export of an average of more than 100,000 Africans each year from 1800 to 1840, would not have been possible without the participation and cooperation of the Africans themselves. And black, white, and brown hands alike are forever stained by this sordid chapter in human history. True, the muskets, rum, and cloth were made available by Arabs and Europeans, but it was African chiefs and tribesmen who exchanged their captive neighbors for the weapons which they then used to capture and sell even more of their countrymen to the Europeans and Arabs.

Therefore, with the exception of the Boers in South Africa and permanent Arab settlements along the East Coast, the contact of large numbers of Africans with Europeans and Arabs during the seventeenth and eighteenth centuries occurred not in Africa but on the cotton plantations of Dixie, the sugar estates of Jamaica, or in the harems of the Persian Gulf sheikdoms. During the last two decades of the nineteenth century the nature of the contact between Africans, Europeans, and Asians underwent an important change. Prior to the scramble for Africa, Europeans and Asians, except for the few traders and explorers who had penetrated inland for slaves, ivory, and glory, were content to limit their relationship to Africa and Africans to the coastal ports and rivers, the occasional exploration, and, until its abolition in the 1870's, slave raiding and trading.

It is not our purpose here to describe in detail the wave of imperialistic conquests which characterize the foreign policy of the Western world from about 1870 to World War I. Our concern is to examine the manner in which this policy toward Africa affected the relationship of the Africans to intruding Europeans and Asians.

THE SCRAMBLE

The direction and pattern of invasion and occupation varies from region to region. In Central Africa alien penetration came largely from South Africa, where the discovery of diamonds and gold had attracted adventurous speculators from all over the Euro-American world. It was believed that the mineral wealth of Africa grew increasingly greater as one moved northward; this aspiration for sudden and great riches brought thousands of Europeans across the Limpopo into Southern Rhodesia and later into Northern Rhodesia. Cecil Rhodes, who dreamed simultaneously of a fortune in diamonds and of raising the Union Jack over an enormous state running from the Cape to Cairo, exemplifies the mixture of motives that led many Europeans to seek their destiny in Africa.

In Europe, new forms of production and styles of consumption required the extension of overseas markets and the procurement of additional sources of raw materials, while new religions and a revived Christian fervor gave a sense of urgency to Livingstone's and Stanley's plea that the Gospel be carried to African pagans. A third factor contributing to increased contact was the evolution in Europe of a new type of nationalism. The Third Republic sought to restore French grandeur; the newly unified German and Italian states were in search of their place in the imperial sun. Imperialists, missionaries, and merchants converged on a continent whose defenses had been breached by an earlier generation of explorers and merchants and whose interior has been rendered vulnerable by two centuries of strife and dislocation accompanying the slave trade.

In East Africa the missionaries followed the trails blazed by the early explorers. Stanley's visit with Mutesa, King of Buganda in 1875, led him to dispatch his famous letter to the *Daily Telegraph* requesting that European missionaries rush the Christian Gospel to Mutesa and his heathen subjects. The dramatic request fell on sympathetic ears, and within a year Protestant and Catholic missionaries arrived in Mutesa's kingdom bearing the Christian cross and the Bible, and causing Christian rivalry. A formidable task awaited these Christian pioneers. They were required to convert pagan souls and to contend with a firmly established Muslim religion. As he observed the maneuvering of his Mohammedan, Catholic, and Protestant teachers, Mutesa may well have been one of the first Africans to ponder and question the professed motivation of the immigrant missionaries. Although all preached peace and salvation, it was apparent that they regarded one another with something less than brotherly love. It was also apparent that the Anglican and Catholic missionaries looked to the United Kingdom and the French Republic, as well as to the heavenly kingdom, for their salvation and inspiration. The struggle between rival Christian missions, frequently erupting into violence, must be counted as a Christian legacy in East Africa along with the more positive contribution of education, Christian faith, and modern medicine.

As the tempo of European activities increased, Arab influence in East Africa and Zanzibar declined. In 1880 the Sultan of Zanzibar granted charters authorizing both the German East Africa Company and the Imperial British East Africa Company to administer and occupy portions of his ill-defined East African territories. By 1890 the situation in East Africa had become so complex that conflicting interests of the imperial powers ran the risk of collision. Under the pretext of rescuing the beleaguered Emin Pasha and his Egyptian troops in the Equatorial Region of the Sudan, the German explorer, Carl Peters, with a small detachment of German troops marched into the interior of Africa; at the same time, Stanley's Emin Pasha relief column was making its way toward the Lake Region of East Central Africa from the Congo. To further complicate matters a third company, under the command of Sir Frederick Jackson, was also presumably engaged in the rescue of Emin Pasha.

Peters and Jackson approached Buganda at about the same time, their arrival coinciding with a particularly violent episode in Buganda's religious conflict. After recapturing the kingdom from the Muslims, the Catholic and Protestant factions were themselves on the verge of civil war.

Although Stanley's relief column was the first to reach Emin Pasha, the beleaguered German, after reaching the Coast, preferred to join forces with his fellow countryman Peters. On his return to the coast, Peters paused long enough to sign a treaty placing Buganda under German protection, unaware that imperial rivalry in East and Central Africa had already led Bismarck and Lord Salisbury to demarcate spheres of influence (in the Heligoland Treaty) placing Buganda within the British sphere. Peters' agreement with the Kabaka of Buganda, much to his chagrin, therefore proved meaningless. In the meantime, Captain Lugard, in the service of the Imperial British East Africa Company, was busy establishing forts in the interior of present-day Kenya. Acting on company orders he proceeded to Buganda late in 1890 to find the kingdom teetering on the brink of another religious war. To keep peace Lugard completed a treaty with Mwanga, the new Kabaka, whereby the Company's authority over the kingdom was acknowledged. Despite this agreement a battle broke out between the rival Christian factions. Lugard re-established order in the interests of the Company and prepared to withdraw from Buganda. The Protestant mission, dependent on his support, was fearful that his departure would lead to renewed civil war. This fear in conjunction with an extraordinary expression of public and religious fervor over the Uganda issue in the United Kingdom led to a reconsideration of the decision.

In 1893 the British Government proclaimed a Protectorate over Uganda and in 1895 over much of what is now Kenya. The Imperial British East Africa Company gladly relinquished its unprofitable holdings to a British government that was not itself enthusiastic about assuming responsibility. This complex history of the extension of European influence and domination into a small portion of the interior of Africa is described at some length here because it illustrates the interrelationship (if not the confusion) of the roles and motives of missionaries, explorers, and imperialists.

The penetration of the inner reaches of the Congo followed a different pattern. Imperialistic competition in this region led to the Berlin Conference in 1885, which recognized Belgium's King Leopold as the sole ruler of the Congo Free State. In the Gold Coast (now Ghana) British penetration into the interior, after long contact with the coast, was hastened by conflict with the Ashanti Confederacy to the north. After a series of minor wars British troops finally moved into the interior in force, defeated the Ashanti, and occupied their country. In 1901 the coastal regions and Ashanti were declared British colonies.

With tongue in cheek, West Africans often speak of building a monument to the mosquito, for it was this malaria-carrying insect that determined the initial nature and scope of European-African relations in West Africa. Missionaries dispatched to the Gold Coast and other regions of West Africa never expected to return to their home countries. The fatality rate was extraordinary, and missionary influence was correspondingly less than in East Africa. In 1891, when nearly every Muganda was either Catholic, Protestant, or Muslim, less than 3 per cent of the people of the Gold Coast Colony had embraced a Christian faith.[9] Gustav Jahoda, who has intensively investigated the relationship of Europeans and Africans in Ghana, writes that "the primary fact to report about Europeans in the territory is that they were few and did not settle permanently." The average life span of a British soldier in the Gold Coast in the 1880's was less than one month and in 1900 one of every thirteen Europeans in the country died.[10] The European came to West Africa initially to trade and subsequently to proselytize and to govern. He regarded himself as a transient and looked forward to the day when he would return to France or England. In East and Central Africa, although he also initially came to preach and to profit and subsequently to rule, he often settled on the land and made his home there as well. It would be erroneous to conclude that the race issue is a problem only in those regions of Africa where white or brown settlement has been extensive; for unfortunately the problem of "race" and "color" permeates the entire continent. The African's legacy of a long history of alien domination and slavery and an embarrassing awareness of his present relative backwardness contribute to a racial self-consciousness that today seeks expression in African nationalism.

RACIALISM AND NATIONALISM

In most of Africa the boundaries of the new sovereign states were arbitrarily delineated at about the turn of the century by Europeans possessed of a knowledge of the balance of power and influence on their own continent but completely ignorant of the peoples of Africa and the configuration of their lands. We need add little about the manner in which African boundaries arbitrarily separate cultures, languages, and natural regions. This artificial delineation of what have since become sovereign states, when added to the small scale of indigenous traditional African cultures and societies, has reversed the orthodox process of nationalism whereby linguistic and cultural communities seek to win independent state status. In most of Africa, state status has been achieved prior to the existence of a sense of community coincident with the frontiers of the newly established sovereignty. Thus nation-building can be considered the conscious and deliberate effort by a multitude of cultural and lin-

[9] Gustav Jahoda, *White Man*, Institute of Race Relations (New York: Oxford University Press, Inc., 1961).
[10] *Ibid.*, p. 12.

guistic communities to create a sense of nationality corresponding to the inherited confines of their state.

If this is true, then what is the nature of the emotional force which drives African leaders to seek and to win independence for their artifical states? If it is not a compulsion to bring all men of like history, culture, and language under a single flag and set of laws, then what is it that compelled Kwame Nkrumah, Sékou Touré, Jomo Kenyatta, Joshua Nkoma, and others to risk imprisonment and in some cases even death? To cope with this question it is necessary to analyze the interrelationship of nationalism and racism.

To be treated with disrespect, to be a pauper on one's own land, to serve and not be served, to be ruled and never to rule—once an awareness exists that these things are not implicit in life but only in the lives of black men—is to be without dignity, a condition that no sane man can long tolerate. This awakening to the fact that to be black and an African is to be without dignity has coincided with the world-wide dissemination of philosophies proclaiming the equality of all men and the political dogma that equal men possess an inherent right to rule themselves.

Viewed in this light *uhuru* is the quest by millions of Africans for demonstrable proof of their equality. Black men are not equal to other men so long as they are ruled by men of an alien race. "Uhuru" means more than freedom; it is a symbol of equality and a sign of dignity.

Independence for his country is not alone sufficient to prove equality and dignity. Two other elements must also be present if there is to be no doubt of the equality of the African's race and thus of his dignity. First of all, every land where a majority of black men are ruled by a white minority must be liberated. There persists, even after independence for his own country has been won, the suspicion that he is backward and dominated because he is black. All Africa, from the Cape to Cairo, must be freed from white rule, for only then can the remaining pain be assuaged. This gnawing threat to the ego must be taken into account if we are to interpret correctly the fierce determination of Africa's leaders to rid the entire continent of every particle of white rule. To some observers the constant accusation and paranoid fear of neo-colonialism on the part of Africa's new leaders is only another indication of this attitude. The possibility that his newly acquired dignity as a citizen of an independent state may be bogus or second rate is a constant worry. The histories of struggles for independence of white and brown revolutionaries taught by European teachers and read in textbooks tell of war, supreme sacrifice, glory, bloodshed, and heroism—how extraordinary white men perform extraordinary deeds. But twentieth-century independence for African states was not achieved in this romantic fashion. Why not? "Is it because we are Africans?" "Is it because our independence is not real and has a string attached which we cannot see?" It is not surprising that histories of the struggle for independence of a number of the new African nations are being subtly reinterpreted with an emphasis on monuments and speeches dedicated to those who "gave their lives for freedom," for those who "died in the battle against imperialism."

A number of racially embarrassing questions persist. "If it is not because they are white and we are black, why were the Europeans able to rule us for so long? Why did we obey when they commanded? Were only black men slaves? Why has the alien Asian in our country dominated the economy and grown rich from our labor?" Having posed these vexing questions the African concludes that these things have occurred because the Europeans and Asians were in possession of certain tools and techniques which they deliberately withheld from Africans. Education is the magic key opening the door to knowledge and power. This logic underlies the thirst for education and the acquisition of diplomas and degrees that will signify to themselves and to the world that Africans too can obtain and employ knowledge.

A related factor is "modernity." The discrepancy in life style since the nineteenth century has long distinguished the ruler-white from the ruled-black. The European way, wherever brought to Africa, was modern whereas the universe of the African was backward. While white and brown men wore expensive clothes, Africans wore rags or went naked; while white and brown men drove big cars, Africans choked in their dust; while white and brown men lived in big houses and were well-fed, Africans slept in mud huts and went hungry. If he was not to attribute these differences to his race then it was imperative that the African prove to himself, and to the rest of the world, that his equality was genuine. Therefore he too must be "modern"! An independent but backward state is not truly free in African eyes for it has failed to provide dignity. Neither Ethiopia nor Liberia, for example, has played the predominant role in African affairs which a long history of independence would seem to have destined. Their failure, even though independent, to achieve a level of development comparable to even the poorest European country is embarrassing for it does not bear out the belief that African backwardness is a consequence of alien domination. The compulsion to develop rapidly, at almost any price, reflects not only the desire for a better life but the necessity of demonstrating racial equality.

African nationalism and the independence of the new African states cannot be fully understood without reference to the issue of race. What Africa's leaders and spokesmen are fundamentally seeking is not so much national independence as an end to the psychological suffering that indignity causes. Having achieved independence, Africa's leaders are quick to realize the necessity of creating "a nation." For only thus can they achieve modernity and the international respect without which their equality would remain in doubt.

It is difficult to be optimistic about the future relationship of black, brown, and white men in Africa. It is unlikely that the African revolution will be considered to have been won as long as a considerable differential exists between the races. At best the African, if he is to prove his equality beyond a shadow of doubt and lay to rest forever the question of his inferiority, will seek to discriminate against white and brown men as he himself was so long discriminated against. History is replete with the futile efforts of other minorities to win acceptance. The German Jew was discriminated against, forcibly exiled, and slaughtered, even though he spoke the same language and had the same color of skin as the Aryan.

THE DIMENSIONS OF THE PROBLEM

We can now examine the current situation in an attempt to foresee what the future relationship of the races might be in those territories of substantial European and Asian settlement. For it is in these territories that contact between black, white, and brown has demonstrated a capacity for both cooperation and conflict.

In ten countries in tropical Africa the non-African population exceeds 1 per cent of the total.[11] It is more than coincidental that the seven territories where 2 per cent or more of the population is non-African coincide exactly with those areas yet to achieve their independence.[12] In the order of their non-African population these seven countries include the Republic of South Africa, South-West Africa, Southern Rhodesia, Northern Rhodesia, Kenya, Angola, and Mozambique. The pattern of independence has been determined, in part, by the incidence of European settlement. Independence for tropical Africa came first to those territories where non-African settlement was minute. As a force it has moved from the northwest toward the southeast. Like an enormous floodlight its illumination has brought independence to one country after another. Independence for the territories of North and West tropical Africa has permitted a focusing and intensification of the struggle for independence in the remaining dependent territories. The current stage is characterized by an increasing intensification of the African's struggle for independence in conjunction with an increasing determination on the part of the remaining colonial powers and white minorities to maintain the status quo, a situation with a high potential for conflict and violence. That portion of Africa still to be "liberated" might well contribute the glory, violence, and bloodshed which some African leaders feel must accompany a true struggle for independence.

Few would challenge our prediction that by the end of 1965 an African majority will rule independent states everywhere on the continent except in the Republic of South Africa and possibly its satellite dependency, South-West Africa. The racial issue in South Africa is different in

[11] The Republic of South Africa, South-West Africa, Southern Rhodesia, Northern Rhodesia, Kenya, Angola, Mozambique, Tanganyika, Uganda, and the Congo.
[12] Except of course the Republic of South Africa, which as long as it is dominated by a white minority, is considered by the African leaders to be "unliberated."

kind from that elsewhere in tropical Africa because it differs so radically in scale. Nearly four of every five Europeans resident in tropical Africa live in the Republic of South Africa. The non-African portion of the population is approximately one-third of the total. About 20 per cent of its population is white and another 13 per cent either Asian or colored. Nowhere else in Africa south of the Sahara is there nearly the number of persons of European origin as in South Africa.[13] As one moves north from the Republic of South Africa, the proportion of Europeans to Africans grows progressively smaller. In Southern Rhodesia, where in 1962 a new constitution perpetuated white domination, only 6 per cent of the population is of European descent. In Northern Rhodesia, where elections in 1962 paved the way for an African-dominated government, the ratio falls to about 3 per cent. To the west lies Angola where the absence of constitutional change and elections led Africans to employ violence and bloodshed in an attempt to win their rights. Angola's whites constitute only 2.5 per cent of the population whereas in Mozambique, Portugal's other large African dependency, about one in every hundred persons is of European descent.[14] No constitution has been written or election held in Mozambique, and at first glance the absence of organized large-scale violence there would seem to contradict our theory that latent and manifest violence in Africa exists in direct proportion to the density of non-African settlement. A closer examination of the manner and timing of the rebellion in Angola, however, suggests that the serenity of Mozambique may only be the calm before the storm. Before the Congo achieved independence Angola was surrounded by European-dominated territories; it was relatively easy for Portugal, assisted by the Belgians, Euro-Rhodesians, and Afrikaners, to contain opposition. Independence for the Congo effectively removed this protective shield and was followed, almost immediately, by a savage conflict between Africans and Europeans. Independence for Tanganyika has removed the colonial shield from Mozambique's northern frontier, and it is not surprising that there is already discernible a quickening of nationalist agitation. Dar es Salaam is the headquarters of FRELIMO, the Mozambique National Liberation Movement. Dr. Eduardo Mondlane, brilliant president of the Liberation Front, left his academic career at Syracuse University in February 1963 to devote his entire energies to the liberation of his country. By the time these words reach the press Mozambique will be very much in the news, and unless Portuguese policy undergoes a radical change, there is a strong likelihood that racial violence will erupt there.

[13] Europeans make up about 10 per cent of the population of South-West Africa. The total is small, however, e.g., 1.7 per cent of all Europeans in tropical Africa.

[14] These appropriate ratios are based upon United Nations sources approximately three to four years old. In the case of Mozambique there is considerable evidence that the European population has been deliberately and significantly increased by large-scale immigration of Portuguese troops and settlers over the past two years.

A line connecting the northern frontiers of Portugal's two large dependent territories sharply separates independent from dependent Africa.[15]

Much to the embarrassment of its many sophisticated political leaders, Kenya until December 1963 remained a colonial enclave in independent Africa. Although every effort was made to attribute its continued colonial status to the dying gasps of British imperialism and the machination of the white settlers, Kenya politicians, in moments of candor, admitted that it largely was their own squabbling and failure to agree that delayed independence. Kenya is an area of considerable alien settlement, containing a larger non-African population than any other territory except South and South-West Africa and Southern Rhodesia. Yet this is somewhat misleading, for its large non-African population is primarily accounted for by its sizeable Asian population. Kenya's European population is but 1 per cent of the continent's total, proportionately less than any of the dependent territories to the south.[16] Kenya achieved its independence on December 12, 1963, while self-government for an African majority in Angola, Mozambique, Southern Rhodesia, South-West Africa, and the Republic of South Africa is still to be gained.

Race relations in areas of considerable white settlement can best be examined in terms of the frequency and intensity of the contact between the members of the various races. The intensity of the contact refers to the content of the relationship, with an intense contact characterized by a high level of mutual understanding of respective motives and actions. Any one of the four combinations of frequency and intensity (e.g., high frequency, high intensity; high frequency, low intensity; low frequency, high intensity; and low frequency, low intensity) provides a distinctive style of racial relationship. These relationships are shown below in outline form. In the remainder of this chapter we analyze the type and style of

TYPE AND STYLE OF RACE RELATIONS

Type	*Style*
High frequency–high intensity	Integration/violence
High frequency–low intensity	Segregation/conflict
Low frequency–high intensity	Cooperation/competition
Low Frequency–low intensity	Toleration/indifference

racial relationship as it affects the quest for order with particular reference to South Africa, the Central African Federation, and Kenya.

[15] The statement excludes Portuguese Guinea, a tiny enclave along the bend of the West Coast.

[16] Nearly 25 per cent of Africa's Asian population resides in Kenya.

THE FAILURE OF APARTHEID—SOUTH AFRICA

The larger the ratio of European and Asian to African the greater, in theory, is the likelihood of contact. More than a million coloreds in South Africa bear visual testimony to frequent and intense interaction between the early European settlers and indigenous African residents of the South African coastal region. The Zulu wars, however, demonstrate that frequent and intense contact of men of different hue, both determined to control the same pasture and water, can also lead to violence.

If a white minority of sizeable proportions wishes to prohibit a racial contact which is characterized by violence, as do the Europeans of South Africa, it is necessary that the frequency or intensity (or both) of the contact be altered. The racial history of contemporary South Africa is largely a record of the efforts of the governing white minority to do exactly this. Attempts to lower the frequency of contact however have been frustrated by the growing reliance of a rapidly expanding economy on an ever larger African labor force.

As early as 1913, with the Native's Land Act, the Afrikaners sought to compartmentalize the races in order to decrease frequency of contact. This act reserved 6 per cent of the land of the country (later increased to 13 per cent) for the native Bantu who constitute about three-fourths of the total population. The compulsory congestion that resulted had the opposite effect; it forced the Bantu to quit the crowded reserves to seek a livelihood within the towns. The European-dominated government responded to the influx of black men by requiring all Africans to carry a pass and to obey curfews. Permission to remain outside the reserves was granted only when the Bantu could prove he was gainfully employed. The constantly increasing number of Africans living outside the reserves was a perpetual source of anxiety to the Europeans and has given rise to periodic schemes and legislation designed to stem the flow and to return the Africans to their reserves.[17]

Up to about 1948, the policy of the South African government with respect to Africans, coloreds, and Asians vacillated, depending on the political fortunes of the various factions and parties. The relatively urban, English-speaking United Party faction, which had long controlled the government, ranged between the extremes of racial partnership and segregation. Although it received a majority of the popular vote, the 1948 elections toppled the United Party and replaced it with the predominantly Afrikaner, rural, agricultural Nationalist Party. The Nationalists, although themselves divided into extreme and moderate factions, put forth a platform of "apartheid"—a bold policy calculated to

---

[17] The Native Trust and Land Act of 1936; the Group Acts of 1950; the Expulsion Act of 1954, etc.

separate white from black in all but peripheral and absolutely necessary relationships.[18]

Political contact of black and white is certainly one of the most intense forms of racial relationship. Desiring neither integration nor violence the Nationalist-dominated government set out to segregate once and for all the political lives of whites and non-whites. The first session of the newly elected Nationalist legislature passed a bill making interracial marriage or sexual intercourse a criminal offense. It also required each person to carry a card documenting his racial pedigree. The passage of the Group Areas Act in 1954 sought to restrict all non-Europeans to designated racial residential areas. This was quickly followed by a bill directed at the Cape Coloreds, who had long possessed a status midway between European and African. As the Coloreds' political rights were protected by an entrenched clause of the South African constitution it was necessary to pack the Supreme Court before they could be shorn of representation and the vote. This was accomplished in 1954 when the Nationalist-controlled Assembly voted to double the Court's membership. The apportionment of seats in the upper house of the legislature was also altered, with the effect that its membership was similarly increased. As the constitution could be amended only by a two-thirds vote of the two houses sitting jointly, the enlarged upper house was needed to provide the Nationalists with the required extraordinary majority.

With the government firmly in their control the Nationalists proceeded to translate the principles of apartheid into action. From the Afrikaners' point of view this policy was both expedient and eminently just, for it was in conformity with Afrikaner culture and history. This righteous conviction is an important factor affecting the style of contact between black and white in South Africa. Important too is the Afrikaner's belief that, by and large, he is the native and the African, the alien immigrant. With this in mind it is worth noting that Dr. Verwoerd, the chief architect of apartheid, has defended the right of Africans to retrieve and rule their own country from those Europeans who had earlier expropriated their lands. "It is right that their land should now politically become their own." [19] In South Africa, however, it is by and large the European who is indigenous and the African, the would-be expropriator. Thus a policy of upholding the standards of white civilization and enterprise from the threat of submersion in an encroaching black sea is considered proper and honorable. And if principle is not sufficient to convince him of the propriety of his crusade, the Afrikaner has but to look

[18] Apartheid is a contraction of *aparte outwikkeling* meaning "separate development." Carried to its ideal end apartheid would lead to the complete segregation of Europeans and non-Europeans in separate states pursuing their separate development.

[19] "Live and Let Live," Fact Paper 91, South African Information Office (April, 1961), p. 21.

at the other side of the coin. For right or wrong the alternative to apartheid is his inevitable domination by a black majority. The South African High Commissioner to the United Kingdom summed up the situation in a speech delivered before the Rotary Club of London in 1953.

"To me there seems to be two possible lines of development; apartheid or partnership. Partnership means cooperation of the individual citizens with a single community, irrespective of race . . . demands that there shall be no discrimination whatsoever in trade or industry, in the professions and the Public Service. There, whether a man is black or a white African, must according to this policy be as irrelevant as whether in London a man is a Scotsman or an Englishman. I take it that partnership must also aim at the eventual disappearance of all social segregation based on race. . . . Need I say more to show that this policy of partnership in South Africa will only mean the eventual disappearance of the white South African nation? And will you be greatly surprised if I tell you that this white nation is not prepared to commit national suicide, not even by slow poisoning? . . . . The only alternative is the policy of apartheid, the policy of separate development. . . . Apartheid is the policy of self-preservation. We make no apology for possessing that very natural urge. But it is more than that. It is an attempt at self-preservation in a manner that will enable the Bantu to develop fully as a separate people.[20]

While the Afrikaner rationally concludes that segregation is the only correct policy, Nobel Prize Winner, ex-chief Luthuli maintains with equal conviction that "the solution to our problems will only be found in a multiracial South Africa through the efforts of all the people." [21]

South Africa's governing white minority is hardly apologetic, and adverse world opinion has done little to alter a determination to proceed with the implementation of apartheid. The Bantu Authority Act of 1953 pointed the direction that was to be followed. A powerful line was to be drawn between Africans and Europeans and, once the line had been demarcated, those found on the wrong side were to be "repatriated." Those Africans who were required of necessity to remain on the white side were to be treated politically as if they were on the black side of the line. Thus seats in the legislatures of the new Bantustans are provided for representatives of those Africans who, of necessity, reside in the white urban locations. All integrated education is forbidden, and African university students are permitted to attend only Fort Hare University for what one writer has aptly termed, "advanced tribal training." [22] On

[20] Press release of Union of South Africa Government Information Office (1953). Quoted in T. Walter Wallbank *Contemporary Africa* (Princeton, N.J.: D. Van Nostrand Co., Inc., 1956), p. 170.

[21] *New York Times* (Feb. 1, 1962).

[22] Donald L. Wiedner, *A History of Africa South of the Sahara* (New York: Random House, Inc., 1962), p. 519. Copyright © 1962 by Random House, Inc.

either side of the line, with the frequency and intensity of racial contact held to a requisite minimum, each race is to pursue its separate development according to its peculiar nature. The educational system for the Africans, for example, emphasizes the Bantu language, arts, and crafts and encourages loyalty to tribe. Political life is to be completely separate with the development in the African reserves of quasi-independent political entities (Bantustans) designed along traditional tribal lines. Thus, while tribal institutions are either disappearing or undergoing modernization elsewhere in Africa (see Chapter III), eighteenth- and nineteenth-century tribalism is being revived in South Africa with the hope that identification with their indigenous culture and polity will persuade Africans to give up their efforts either to integrate or to dominate European society and polity.

The long-range policy calls for the complete separation of black and white. All Africans, except the absolute minimum required to maintain the economy, are to be forcibly moved to the eight semiautonomous Bantustans. Retaining nearly 90 per cent of the territory, the Republic of South Africa is to become the home of the predominantly white population. More than one hundred thousand people have already been forced to leave their homes and take up life elsewhere, while more than half a million are slated for relocation.

The Afrikaner's passionate determination to implement apartheid is accompanied by an extraordinary lack of objectivity. In a sequel to the Tomlinson Report on the establishment of quasi-independent Bantustans, a government spokesman said that "the only form of political government that can function in our Bantu areas *during the next 150 years* is a modified aristocracy based largely on traditional chiefdoms. . . ." [23]

Ideally the Afrikaner hopes to reduce contact between himself and the other races to such a low frequency and intensity that each group will view the other with toleration or indifference. In theory this would appear to be a possible alternative to partnership or integration, but neither the realities of South African life nor the interests of the newly independent African states to the north will permit this solution. Nearly two million Africans live in the urban areas of the Republic, and many have been there for three or four generations; the culture of the urbanized black man is highly Westernized. About three million of South Africa's Bantu are salaried employees on European farms or mining enterprises. Of the remaining four and a half million residents in the rural tribal reserves only about half can be said to be living a tribal life.[24] These cosmopolitan city dwellers can no more return to the tribal womb than the Afrikaners can return to Holland or Germany.

[23] South African Information Office, White Paper 506 (Jan., 1957), p. 40. Italics is ours.

[24] Of the 1.8 million *literate* Bantu only about one-half million live in the reserves.

Apartheid, to the articulate mass of urbanized Africans, is regarded as an attempt to reconstruct their lives along completely alien lines. It is not surprising that as the Afrikaners accelerate the implementation of this policy, African resistance becomes more radical and violent. The situation is changing rapidly. A decade ago African resistance could be contained and isolated, but today the African National Congress and the more radical Pan-African Congress receive encouragement and support from a score of independent African countries. The tempo and brutality of violence is quickening. A series of racial conflicts has set in motion in the south, of Africa a force sufficiently powerful to overwhelm the leadership capacity of both races. The Sharpeville incident of early 1960, in which white police fired on a crowd and killed twelve African demonstrators, may have been the shock that dislocated the racial "gyroscope"; for South Africa more and more resembles an unguided rocket capable of wreaking havoc indiscriminately on black and white alike.

Both sides appear to have thrown caution to the wind; more frequent and violent attacks by Africans are met by increasingly restrictive legislation. The Bantu Laws Amendment Act denies Africans any right to reside permanently in South Africa anywhere except in the reserves and the Bantustans. Legislation has been passed providing the death penalty for anyone convicted of having been trained in sabotage outside of South Africa or anyone who advocates invasion of the country. More ominous is the legislation which allows the police to arrest and hold persons indefinitely without trial. This repressive legislation is defended on the basis of a rising tide of African violence and subversion. The proscribed Pan-Africanist Congress has gone underground and emerged as Poqo. The South African government maintains that Poqo is the same as the PAC and is therefore also proscribed. "Poqo," an Xhosa word meaning "to stand alone," is relatively more anti-white and tribally oriented than PAC. Its organizational and behavioral resemblance to Mau Mau is noted with fear by an increasing number of Europeans in South Africa. The police claim that Poqo planned a mass uprising and slaughter of Europeans to take place on April 1, 1963. A blood bath was barely averted, the South African spokesmen maintain, by the fortunate capture of Poqo plans and membership lists in a raid carried out by the British police in Basutoland. The South African police, in the last week in March, arrested one hundred and fifty Poqo leaders. By July 1963 Poqo arrests had reached more than three thousand. In May 1963, six Poqo leaders were hanged for murdering a native chief and more than two thousand suspected Poqo terrorists were arrested.

Subversion and rebellion from within are increasingly aided from without. The British-protected enclaves of Bechuanaland, Basutoland, and Swaziland provide a haven for political refugees and an important station on the underground railway to Tanganyika. In 1963 South Africa sought unsuccessfully to incorporate these enclaves into the Republic as semiautonomous "Bantustans," but now frontier posts are being built along the borders, and movement in and out of South Africa and the three enclaves is prohibited. Since nearly one half million Africans from the three British protectorates work in South Africa, the government's threat to deny them entry in retaliation for their assisting Poqo and the PAC is a powerful weapon. Prime Minister Macmillan, speaking in South Africa six weeks before Sharpeville, jolted his white audience when he told them that the United Kingdom was not only conscious of the winds of change blowing over Africa but was herself prepared to move with the current. He counseled his hosts that South Africa would be well advised to do the same. The Prime Minister's advice was disregarded, for early in 1961 the Nationalist Party received its first popular majority, which it immediately interpreted as a mandate for increased and more rapid apartheid. Thus while the West identifies more and more with the cause of African nationalism and racial equality, South Africa intensifies apartheid at the price of disassociating herself from the West. In May 1961, South Africa relinquished dominion status and declared herself a republic. At the subsequent Commonwealth Prime Ministers' meeting, the debate over Commonwealth approval of republican status was so bitter and the antagonism of the Afro-Asian member of the Commonwealth so strong that Prime Minister Verwoerd retaliated by leaving the meeting and by subsequently leading South Africa out of the Commonwealth. As outside pressure on South Africa increases there is a tendency for a closing of ranks among the European population. Verwoerd's apartheid government is receiving increasing support from the English-speaking and relatively liberal community.

More than two centuries have passed since the Afrikaner turned his back on the sea and trekked into the interior. Today the ancestors of the Boer Trekkers have made an equally momentous decision. They have turned their back on the principles of contemporary Western culture and have once again entered the wilderness. Not all the whites of South Africa are happy with this decision nor convinced that apartheid will secure the future. A considerable minority has long advocated "partnership" as a workable alternative. The failure of partnership in Central Africa to avert conflict and African domination has convinced the majority of Afrikaners that the future of their race in Africa depends on apartheid, whatever the cost.

THE FAILURE OF PARTNERSHIP—CENTRAL AFRICA

The rise and fall of the Central African Federation is a history of the white man's efforts to preserve a privileged position in the face of the African's growing capacity and determination to deny that privilege. Although apartheid has long had its supporters in Southern Rhodesia and even in Northern Rhodesia, the strategy of coping with African nationalism in Central Africa has been that of "partnership" and cooperation through the instrumentality of a federation of the two Rhodesias and Nyasaland. At first glance many thought the Federation to be a "natural" with the surplus labor of predominantly black Nyasaland combining with the capital and technological know-how of Southern Rhodesia to exploit the rich natural resources of Northern Rhodesia. Aside from the logic of the economic argument, the three territories are quite dissimilar. Southern Rhodesia's Europeans came primarily from the Union of South Africa. Conflict between black and white is a part of Southern Rhodesia's history; European land, by and large, was wrested from the Africans only after a number of short but violent wars. Nyasaland's relatively few Europeans, on the other hand, came to Central Africa either as Church of Scotland missionaries or as settlers from the United Kingdom. The Europeans who settled in the western part of Northern Rhodesia came largely from South Africa and Southern Rhodesia, whereas settlement in the eastern part of the country resembled that of Nyasaland. Despite these differing patterns of European settlement and indigenous African culture, the desire of joining the three territories has long existed and proposals to this end were advanced as early as 1915.[25] As a factor in the politics of federation, the African was largely ignored until after World War II. After extensive negotiations and assurance by Northern and Southern Rhodesian white politicians that federation would enshrine a policy of racial partnership, Great Britain gave its consent in 1953 and the Federation was officially concluded. Black hands neither held the pens that signed the instrument of federation nor toasted its long life. Although participating in the early Federation negotiations, the African leaders boycotted the ceremony despite contention that the Federation was to be built on a foundation of racial partnership.

The ideals of racial equality and cooperation are written into the preamble of the constitution.

> The association of the Colony (Southern Rhodesia) and Territories (Northern Rhodesia and Nyasaland) . . . in a federation . . . in particular would foster partnership and cooperation between the inhabitants. . . .[26]

The Federation was designed to bring about a partnership between 9,000,000 Africans and 220,000 whites. But few Africans or Europeans suffered any illusions as to what this partnership really meant. A statement released by a committee of the United Federal Party of Northern Rhodesia in 1953 is indicative.

[25] A. J. Hanna, *The Story of the Rhodesias and Nyasaland* (London: Faber & Faber, Ltd., 1960), pp. 243-270.
[26] Preamble to the Constitution of the Central African Federation.

Partnership does not mean equality between Europeans and the broad masses of the native population. It means . . . that the door to political advancement is not locked in the face of the Africans who may be able to conform to civilized standards.[27]

Welensky, the first and last Prime Minister of the Central African Federation, said, "When he [the African] shows his ability to contribute more to the general good . . . in *a hundred or two hundred years'* time [he] should be given more say in running his country." [28] Lest some Europeans fear losing control to the African majority in the year 2150, Welensky reassured them, "He [the African] can never hope to dominate partnership. He can achieve equal standing but not go beyond it." [29]

The prospect of being limited to equal status with one-quarter million Europeans after one or two centuries did little to endear the idea of partnership to the Federation's nine million Africans. As Harry Nkumbula, leader of Northern Rhodesia's African National Congress, stated, "Federation is a deliberate sabotage of the African's hope for self-government and independence within the British Commonwealth of Nations. . . . Federation was created to place both economic and political power in the hands of the European minorities." [30]

Thus the Federation has never been accepted by the African leaders. That African political parties should set out to destroy the Federation from the very moment of its birth was inevitable. By 1959, after six years of this lopsided partnership, the black men's patience began to wear thin.[31] Violence on a large scale, long smoldering beneath the surface, erupted early in 1959. In February an emergency was declared in Southern Rhodesia, and in a matter of hours the police arrested nearly five hundred leaders of the African National Congress. The emergency inspired a spate of restrictive legislation calculated to maintain order but which in effect contributed to a further hardening of race relations. The Unlawful Organizations Act permitted the government to proscribe any association as illegal, while the Preventive Detention Act enabled the government to arrest opposition leaders on the slightest pretext.

Across the border in Nyasaland the situation was even more ominous. There African political leaders concluded that violence alone would impress the dominant white minority with the fact that the African was determined to gain political influence consistent with his members. Large-

[27] Harry S. Albinski, "Concept of Partnership in the Central African Federation," *Review of Politics*, Vol. 19 (April, 1957), 196.

[28] Philip Mason, *Years of Decision* (London: Oxford University Press, 1960), p. 69. (Italics is ours.)

[29] *Ibid.*

[30] Ndabaningi Sithole, *African Nationalism: Capetown* (London: Oxford University Press, 1957), p. 42, as quoted from *Christian Science Monitor* (April 4, 1957).

[31] The principle of partnership did effectively lower the color bar, improve educational facilities for Africans, and provide limited political participation.

scale rioting began in mid-February, and within a week an emergency was declared. Troops from Southern Rhodesia were flown to Blantyre to cope with a rapidly deteriorating situation, and before order was restored more than fifty Africans had been killed.[32] Riots and near-riots dramatized the need for fundamental political change and gave rise to a series of constitutional negotiations and conferences. But the concessions made to African demands were too little and too late; by the summer of 1960 violence was again the order of the day. In July of that year police opened fire on demonstrators in Bulawayo, killing twelve Africans. This incident marked the doom of partnership; mutual confidence between the races, that one indispensable element, had been shattered.[33]

A year earlier the British Government had appointed a special commission to investigate the future of the Federation and to make appropriate recommendations. The Monckton Commission was, however, technically precluded by its terms of reference from dealing with the question of secession from the Federation. Prime Minister Macmillan admitted privately that the Commission could and probably should investigate the possibility of secession, but not officially.[34] By 1960 the future of the Federation and racial partnership were in desperate straits. It was apparent to most observers, including Prime Minister Macmillan, that the Federation would have to be radically overhauled or scrapped.

Britain, as her African wards frequently and vociferously remind her, is legally and morally committed to uphold the paramountcy of native interest in Northern Rhodesia and Nyasaland. Yet the Monckton Commission concluded that racial discrimination, though diminishing, remained one of the more important forces threatening the Federation. "The reference to partnership in the preamble in the 1953 constitution, led Africans to believe that discrimination would quickly disappear. The fact that it has not . . . has resulted in . . . disillusion." [35]

Under the fresh leadership of Ian Macleod, newly appointed Secretary of State for the Colonies, Britain took the lead in negotiations to improve relationships between black and white and to attempt to salvage the Federation. But at the very moment that Macmillan was speaking of the winds of change, and Macleod and Kenya's white and black political leaders were negotiating a liberal constitution, Welensky was thundering that "they can do what they want in Kenya . . . but we are not going to accept that here." [36]

[32] Philip Mason, *Year of Decision*, Institute of Race Relations (London: Oxford University Press, 1961), p. 212.
[33] David Cole, "Black States or Partnership," *Atlantic* (April, 1959), p. 75.
[34] Clyde Sanger, *Central African Emergency* (London: William Heinemann, Limited, 1960), p. 304.
[35] Report on the Advisory Commission of the Constitution of Rhodesia and Nyasaland, H.M.S.O. CMND, 1148 (Oct., 1960).
[36] *The New York Times* (March 11, 1960), p. 2.

In April 1960, Dr. Hastings Banda, imprisoned after the Nyasaland riots of 1959, was released and immediately flew to London to discuss Nyasaland's future with Ian Macleod. To the surprise and dismay of many he came back to his jubilant supporters with an agreement allowing for an African majority in the Nyasaland Legislative Council and the promise of internal self-government.

The Monckton Report was generally welcomed by Africans but viewed with alarm by Europeans. The federal Prime Minister Sir Roy Welensky rejected the recommendations and took particular issue with the Commission's majority opinion that secession from the Federation should be permitted. A series of conferences to hammer out new constitutions for Northern and Southern Rhodesia and to remodel and refurnish the Federation followed in the wake of the Monckton Commission's recommendations. Change was certainly needed, for after nine years the federal cabinet could boast but one African member and one African parliamentary secretary. The Southern Rhodesian Civil Service was still exclusively white. Although the color bar had been removed in public transportation, industry, and elsewhere, residential segregation and numerous other instances of discrimination still persisted. Nor was justice equitable. For example, Africans consistently received proportionately more convictions and longer sentences than Europeans for comparable offenses.[37] As late as 1960 twelve times as much money was being spent per pupil on white children as on black.[38] But most important, nothing had been done to face up to the two most intense areas of racial discrimination and antagonism—ownership of land and political rights.[39] As one of the author's students cogently remarked, "Africans could not understand why their voting qualifications should be so high while Indians voted by symbols and Nigerians threw pebbles into a bucket."

Negotiations for a revised constitution for Southern Rhodesia brought together Sir Edgar Whitehead and Joshua Nkomo. These two men, who had informally referred to one another by their Christian names for more than twenty years, now found themselves at opposite ends of the bargaining table with the Colonial Secretary, Ian Macleod, in the middle. Two men—one black and the other white—both mild and easygoing, both seriously wishing a partnership that would work, but both sincerely holding contradictory views as to what the term implied. Nkomo has said about Whitehead, "Sir Edgar might be a bit daft, a bit blind, a

[37] Thomas Franck, *Race and Nationalism,* for a well-documented study of justice within the Federation. Franck notes, for example, that 17 per cent of the Europeans tried for crimes were acquitted, whereas only 5 per cent of the Africans were so fortunate.

[38] James Lauderdale, "Scandals for Schools," *The Central African Examiner* (Jan., 1962), p. 9.

[39] This point is well made by N. M. Shamuyaura, "The Coming Showdown in Central Africa," *Foreign Affairs, XXXIX* (January, 1961), 292-293.

bit behind the time but he's not nearly as daft as Welensky." Sir Edgar's view of Nkomo bespeaks an earlier day—a day when reasonable men were looking forward to racial accommodation if not integration. "There is no harm in Josh." [40] Yet in October 1962 "old Edgar" found it necessary to outlaw "Josh's" party, send his old friend to restrictive custody, and permanently prohibit his participation in public life.

Nkomo and other Southern Rhodesian African leaders were prepared at one time during the 1961 negotiations to accept a white majority as long as they received approximately thirty of the sixty-five seats in the legislature, plus the acceptance of the principle of one man, one vote. Whitehead only offered fifteen seats and would not consider the principle of one man, one vote. Even then Nkomo was prepared to participate and cooperate.[41] His supporters repudiated the agreement, however, arguing that it failed to face up to the disproportionate allocation of land between Europeans and Africans. In July 1961, the predominantly white electorate overwhelmingly approved the new Southern Rhodesian constitution. The Africans, following Nkomo's instructions, demonstrated their hostility by boycotting the election.

Constitutional revision for Northern Rhodesia posed a somewhat different set of problems. Welensky, the federal Prime Minister, acted as the European spokesman and played a major role in hammering out a new constitution. He was acutely aware of what was at stake in the negotiations. If a constitution were to permit an African majority, Northern Rhodesia could destroy the Federation. Welensky was therefore as determined to prohibit the possibility of an African majority in the Northern Rhodesian government as Kenneth Kaunda was determined to see that the new constitution provided for such a majority. What resulted was a complicated system of double- and single-roll seats, requiring a successful candidate for the "National Seats" to obtain at least 10 per cent of the vote of both the upper (European) and the lower (African) rolls. Theoretically it was possible for the Africans to obtain a majority although the likelihood seemed slim indeed. Discussions over the new constitution bogged down, and the Africans became increasingly frustrated. Partnership seemed as dead in Northern as it was in Southern Rhodesia. To many, violence seemed the only solution, and in the summer of 1962 riots and arson broke out throughout Northern Rhodesia. In the face of this overwhelming African opposition Northern Rhodesian constitutional negotiations were reopened, with the result that changes in the electoral system were made and elections set for October.

But in Southern Rhodesia there was no compromise. In October 1962,

[40] *Kenya Daily Nation* (Oct. 9, 1962).
[41] Nkomo's moderation has cost him the leadership of the party (ZAPH). In July 1963 he was forced to give up the leadership to the more radical Rev. Sithole.

Joshua Nkomo's Zimbabwe African Peoples Union (ZAPU) was banned
and more than one hundred and fifty of its leaders arrested and held in
restriction. Joshua Nkomo pleaded with Great Britain to send troops to
restore order and to suspend the Southern Rhodesian constitution. "If
Britain fails to do so then she must accept full responsibility for our
peoples' blood. . . . The white man's true motive in banning ZAPU is
to remove opposition to his white supremacy constitution." [42]

Having first given the appearance that he was fleeing arrest Nkomo
returned to Salisbury where he was arrested and placed in restriction.
The tempo of violence increased; European farms were burned and
fields destroyed. The National Chairman of ZAPU, who had escaped
arrest, appealed to the United Nations Trusteeship Committee for an
end to the ban on ZAPU and for the release of Joshua Nkomo. In
prophetic words he warned the Committee that the days of compromise
and racial consultation had passed. "Bloody revolution is the next
phase." [43]

The conflict was brought to the United Nations in the fall of 1962,
and Sir Edgar Whitehead dramatically flew to New York to defend the
Southern Rhodesian constitution, the European minority, partnership,
and the maintenance of the Federation. "We have a permanent place in
Africa. We cannot feel because once upon a time we lived in England
therefore our main ties are with Europe. . . . Africans will have a
majority within fifteen years," he pleaded. "This will seem a very long
time to this Assembly, but it is a very short time in the life of a nation
—a very short time to train administrators." [44] His dramatic plea was
received with little sympathy. The African states subsequently steam-
rollered their motion through the General Assembly, demanding the
suspension of the Southern Rhodesian constitution. Testimony favorable was precluded or cut short. One day after the new Southern Rhodesian constitution took effect, the General Assembly, meeting on short
notice, adopted by 81 to 2 a resolution calling on Great Britain to take
the "necessary" measures to secure suspension of the constitution and
cancellation of the elections scheduled for December.[45] The security
council bowing to the demands of the thirty-two strong African bloc met
on September 8, 1962 to consider the rapidly deteriorating situation in
Southern Rhodesia.

The winds of change have indeed brought a new climate to Central
Africa. Whereas Nkomo and Whitehead spoke of each other respectfully
in 1960, Apollo Kironde, Uganda's representative to the United Nations,

[42] Joshua Nkomo at a Lusaka Press Conference (Oct., 1962).
[43] *East African Standard* (Oct. 11, 1962).
[44] *Tanganyika Standard* (Nov. 1, 1962).
[45] *Uganda Argus* (Nov. 2, 1962).

referred publicly to Sir Edgar as "a self-complacent old man who must
not be taken seriously." Sir Edgar was being "used as a cat's paw," who
would be "thrown aside by the racists in South Africa if he was to win
the election." [46]

In Northern Rhodesia the October 1962 elections proved as inconclusive as many observers had predicted and, some say, as Ian Macleod
had intended. A Legislative Assembly of forty-five seats was to be elected
—fifteen from a lower roll of 92,000 voters (African); fifteen from an
upper roll of 3,700 voters (European); fourteen seats requiring the winning candidate to obtain 10 per cent of the total vote of each roll; and
one reserved seat for the Asian community. Only four of the fourteen
national seats requiring racial cross-voting were filled, for none of the
other candidates was able to poll even 10 per cent of the vote of both races.
Kenneth Kaunda's United National Independence Party (UNIP) won
twelve of the fifteen seats in the lower roll, with the African National
Congress (ANC) led by Harry Nkumbula winning the remaining three
seats. All fifteen upper roll seats went to Welensky's United Federal Party.
The Liberal Party, representing those Europeans favoring a non-racial
approach and an African government in the near future, failed to capture
a single seat and polled so few votes from either race that its leaders
decided to disband the party with the plea that its few supporters join
the UNIP.[47] The election demonstrated a further hardening of racial
lines. In 1960 Progressive and Liberal candidates had fared well, whereas
in 1962 the Liberal candidates did so poorly that they all forfeited their
deposits.

Sir Roy Welensky's party prematurely viewed the election with opti-
mism for it seemed that they had successfully precluded the Africans
from obtaining a majority in the Northern Rhodesian Legislative Assembly.[48] Kenneth Kaunda warned his European countrymen: "We are
ready to meet violence with violence. . . . There are limits to what a
man can support, even if your skin is black." [49] Just before returning to
Southern Rhodesia to be arrested and placed under restriction Joshua
Nkomo gave notice, "We are determined to fight the constitution. . . .
No man is fit to live if he fails to fight against a document that robs him
of his birthright and his human dignity.[50]

[46] *Ibid.*
[47] *Tanganyika Standard* (Nov. 6, 1962).
[48] The *Kenya Daily Nation* reporter in Lusaka reported that "there can be no doubt
that racial attitudes have hardened in Northern Rhodesia and that when the Africans
inevitably get power they will show less sympathy to the European minority which
has slapped them so severely in the face this week." Richard Hall, *Kenya Daily Nation*
(Nov. 6, 1962).
[49] *Kenya Daily Nation* (Nov. 7, 1962).
[50] *Tanganyika Standard* (Oct. 20, 1962).

But violence was forestalled, for the time being at least, when as tumultous 1962 drew to a close, the Federation was dealt a series of fatal blows. In November, Dr. Hastings Banda made another journey to London prepared to demand self-government for Nyasaland. His party had won twenty-three of the twenty-eight Legislative Council seats in the August 1961 election. He said that he had gone to the London Constitutional Conference in 1960 in the spirit of "give and take" but "this time I have come in the spirit of take, to take what is mine by conquest at the ballot box and also by a successful and practical performance in office." [51] And take he did, for he returned in triumph carrying with him an agreement that self-government would be granted early in 1963. And on February 1, 1963, Dr. Banda took office as first Prime Minister of Nyasaland (soon to be restyled Malawi). Even more important was the British agreement that independence would follow later in 1963 and that Nyasaland would be permitted to secede from the Federation. Prime Minister Banda's first speech sounded the death knell of the Federation and of white domination in Central Africa, "a great and momentous occasion—the birth of the state of Malawi. . . . This is now . . . a black man's country in a black man's continent. . . . We are seceding, and our independence will start a chain of reaction in Africa no matter what anybody on the other side of the Zambesi may think or say about it." [52]

While African nationalism dealt the Federation and partnership a shattering blow in Nyasaland, the rejection of partnership by Southern Rhodesia's dominant white minority added still another. If there was ever any doubt that the relations between the races were hardening it was quickly removed by the 1962 electoral defeat of Sir Edgar Whitehead's United Federal Party by the white supremacist Rhodesian Front. The rejection of Sir Edgar Whitehead's philosophy of moderate partnership is reminiscent of South Africa's 1945 rejection of the liberal party and the victory of the Nationalists. For the march toward apartheid in South Africa can be dated from that crucial election. What now for Southern Rhodesia's 220,000 whites? To many, the election finally paved the way for unity with South Africa—possibly as the Republic's fifth province. To everyone, including even Sir Roy Welensky, it was now evident that the Federation was dead. For the white nationalists of Southern Rhodesia are not inclined to support union with an African-dominated Nyasaland and Northern Rhodesia. North of the Zambesi an uneasy alliance between Kenneth Kaunda's United National Independence Party and Harry Nkumbula's African National Congress has given Northern Rhodesia its first African government. Internal self-government is scheduled

[51] *Tanganyika Standard* (Nov. 13, 1962).
[52] *East African Standard* (Feb. 2, 1963).

for early 1964. At the first session of the African-dominated legislature, the coalition government introduced a motion calling on Great Britain to allow the mineral rich territory to secede from the Federation, and in March 1963, the British Government granted Northern Rhodesia the right to withdraw. The following month, Sir Roy Welensky's United Federal Party held its last executive meeting, while a series of conferences were scheduled for London to plan the painful process of defederation. The demise of the Federation and the rapid acquisition of political power by the Africans in Northern Rhodesia contributed to a further hardening of race relations in Southern Rhodesia.

Nkomo was released from detention in January 1963, but was arrested again the following month and in April was sentenced to six months' imprisonment. With its political link to the north shattered, and faced with the necessity of doing it alone, the white-dominated government of Winston Field began to agitate for complete independence and once again looked to the south for assistance.

In July 1963 representatives of Nyasaland, Southern and Northern Rhodesia, and Great Britain met at Victoria Falls to plan the dismantlement of the Federation. A committee was established to arrange the transfer of federal powers to the separate territories. The problems of defederation are as complex and as perilous as those of federation. In addition to the dismantlement of the organization and functions of the federal ministeries arrangements for such statutory bodies as the Central African Airways, Rhodesian Railways, and the Federal Power Board which controls the enormous hydroelectric developments at Karibam, must be made. Major issues of contention revolve about the disposition of the Federation armed forces—and particularly its substantial air force and the allocation of the Federation's three hundred million-pound debt. The dismantlement was concluded on December 31, 1963. Arrangements were reportedly concluded for a five million-pound loan from South Africa to Southern Rhodesia. Rumors of secret agreements and proposed military alliances swept the continent and were a dominant subject of conversation at the May 1963 Addis Ababa African Summit Conference.

The racial lines in Central Africa are no longer blurred by professions of partnership, and the Zambesi now sharply separates white- from black-dominated Africa. Few areas or issues capable of comprise remain. But it is in the interests of all men that the conflict between the two races in Central and South Africa be reconciled before the Zambesi runs red with the blood of white and black alike.

THE FAILURE OF MULTIRACIALISM—KENYA

If which race is to dominate is still to be decided in Southern Rhodesia, the die has already been cast in Kenya. Long regarded as the white man's colony, Kenya achieved its independence on December 12, 1963. The current issue affecting the relationship of black, brown, and white men in Kenya is not therefore the struggle by European or Asian to win or to preserve political power, as it is in Central Africa. The dominant position of the African in Kenya has been determined, but the place of the European and Asian is still much in doubt. The question uppermost in the minds of Europeans and Asians is "What is to be our future in a new Kenya dominated by an African majority?" Kenya's race relations and politics are anxiously studied by Europeans in Southern and Northern Rhodesia. It is in Kenya that the real test of whether a sizeable European and Asian minority can exist under an African government is to be made.

Unfortunately, the history of the relationship of black and white in Kenya does little to promote an optimistic view of the future. Large-scale European plantation agriculture over extensive and contiguous areas has effectively isolated the white settlers from the great mass of their African countrymen.[53]

As Susan Wood has written, "There remains . . . a legacy of mental isolation which leaves Europeans in general out of touch with the ferment of ideas. . . . They are living in a small and fragile glass house, out of touch with the forces prevailing outside. The interchange between human beings in normal life hardly exists between them and the other races except at a very simple master-servant level."[54]

A failure on the part of the settlers to comprehend the likely consequences of their segregated and restrictive land and education policy for the rapidly expanding Kikuyu population contributed significantly to the racial frustrations and bitterness which in 1952 erupted into the infamous Mau Mau rebellion. Although directed against European political domination and land control, the three-year struggle was in effect a civil war among the Kikuyu people. Although many European farms were burned, crops destroyed, and cattle slaughtered, only thirty-two European settlers were killed by Mau Mau terrorists, whereas 2,000 African peasants met death in this manner.[55]

The Mau Mau rebellion demonstrated the necessity for immediate political reform and set off a series of constitutional conferences and

[53] Unlike Tanganyika where European settlement is relatively scattered, Kenya's white settlers are nearly all resident in the White Highlands, covering about 17,000 of the country's 224,000 square miles and stretching generally in a contiguous belt from Nairobi to the Uganda border. Although their contact with their many employees was of high-frequency/low-intensity their over-all range of contacts was circumscribed.

[54] Susan Wood, Kenya—Tensions and Progress, Institute of Race Relations (London: Oxford University Press, 1961), pp. 11, 14.

[55] An additional 63 Europeans and 524 Africans were killed while serving in the military forces.

108 THE ENIGMA OF RACE

changes designed generally to increase African participation in the government of the territory. Africans participated in elections to the Legislative Council for the first time in 1957, and the post-Mau Mau Lyttelton Constitution heralded innovations to come by increasing African representation to the point where a white majority of elected seats was no longer possible.[56]

In October 1959, the multiracial Kenya government announced that future policy would open the formerly racially exclusive White Highlands to all races. It was further stated that racial discrimination in educational institutions was to be abolished. This struck at the very foundation of two of the three most vital pillars of European domination—exclusive control of the White Highlands and segregated education. The third element—preponderant political power—was the next to topple. The 1960 Lancaster House Conference to revise the Kenya constitution provided for four African ministers, a sixty-five member Legislative Council with an African majority, and reduction of European representation to only ten reserved seats. Group Captain Briggs termed the new Kenya constitution a victory for Mau Mau.[57] On his return to Nairobi from the London negotiations, Michael Blundell was met at the airport by twelve Europeans, one of whom, as he threw thirty pieces of silver at his feet, shouted "Judas Blundell, you have betrayed your people." [58]

The Europeans generally are divided between those willing to try to find a place for themselves in the new Kenya and those prepared to leave. Property values have tumbled; some farms were deserted while many others are being operated on a maintenance basis; capital has fled the country in unprecedented and dangerous quantities; unemployment, long a problem, has reached endemic proportions. In the Kitale Region of the White Highlands, European farmers formed a Pioneering Society to investigate the possibility of emigration and resettlement elsewhere. In March 1963, sixty Kenya farmers and their wives flew to Brazil to examine the possibility of settlement. Other Latin American countries have also been approached and have indicated an interest in obtaining the skills and capital of embittered European farmers, many of whom are second and third generation East Africans. The South African government is seeking to entice Kenya settlers by promising transportation costs and by providing financial assistance to help in their resettlement. During 1961 more than six thousand Europeans and two and one-half thousand

---

[56] The Lyttelton Constitution provided for thirty-six elected constituency seats of which fourteen were reserved for Europeans, fourteen for Africans, and eight for Asians.
[57] George Bennett and Carl Rosberg, *The Kenyatta Election* (New York: Oxford University Press, 1961), p. 22.
[58] Susan Wood, *op. cit.*, p. 73.

Asians permanently emigrated from Kenya. In 1962 more than ten thousand residents, of whom more than eight thousand were Europeans, packed up and left. Over this two-year period more than fourteen thousand, or one in every five Europeans, left Kenya.[59]

The release in August 1961 of Jomo Kenyatta, convicted leader of the Mau Mau rebellion, heralded to many European settlers the beginning of the end. But with domination over the Europeans within grasp and independence within sight, Kenya's African leaders and tribes lost their unity and began to fight among themselves. The two major parties, KANU and KADU, are split along tribal lines with the former eliciting the nearby unanimous support of the Kikuyu and Luo—the two largest tribes. Fearing Kikuyu and Luo domination and suspicious of the radical and authoritarian political style of KANU, most of the remaining smaller tribes support KADU. Neither party is itself strongly united. The conflict within KANU, for example, between the radical faction led by Oginga Odinga and the more moderate element represented by Tom Mboya, with Jomo Kenyatta in the unlikely role of peacemaker, is a constant threat to political stability. Factionalism, when added to inter-party competition, creates a climate of increasing racial uneasiness, tension, and insecurity. During the 1963 election campaign rival leaders, factions, and parties in competition for mass support rivaled one another in anti-European and Asian threats and diatribes. Ambitious leaders and would-be leaders are quick to accuse the opposition of being "soft on Europeans." The more responsible and knowledgeable politicians are in an uncomfortable position. Their own political future sometimes requires them to play the racist game whereas their knowledge of the economic conditions of the country and of the absolute necessity of retaining European farmers and administrators leads them to try to convince the Europeans and Asians that they should neither desert the country nor export their capital.

Never far beneath the surface in Kenya, violence early in 1962 threatened to break out anew in the Rift Valley area, where the secret Land Freedom Army, in a style reminiscent of Mau Mau, revived covert oaths and meetings. Composed almost solely of Kikuyu people, the Land Freedom Army has declared its intent of taking over the White Highlands after independence. The struggle for political power between KANU and KADU is of direct relevance to Kenya's non-Africans. Although it received a majority of the seats in the 1960 elections KANU refused to accept ministries until Kenyatta was set free. The impasse was temporarily solved when KADU, although winning a minority of the seats, agreed to

---

[59] *Kenya Daily Nation* (Feb. 19, 1963). *East African Standard* (July 1, 1963). This does not take into account immigration of Europeans which totaled nearly four thousand in 1962.

form a government. The release of Jomo Kenyatta in August 1961 opened the way for the participation of KANU in the government. Kenyatta's liberation, the rule of the minority KADU party, and general agitation for the next constitutional step toward independence led in February 1962 to the second Lancaster House Conference. At this juncture the basic divisions between KANU and KADU came to the fore. KADU proposed a federal constitution with reserved powers for tribal regions. The KADU leaders maintained this to be necessary to safeguard the minority tribes against domination by the Luo and the Kikuyu. KANU, on the other hand, supported a highly centralized unitary state, capable of rapidly developing the country. Also at issue were constitutional safeguards for minority rights and properties.

The Lancaster House compromise provides for a modified federal form of government, with a 117-member lower house based on population, an upper house representing the constituent districts and nine regional governments. Most European settlers supported KADU but not too loudly or too overtly, since they too, like many small African tribes, seek minority protection through the constitutional separation and distribution of powers.[60] Until elections could be held to determine which party should govern, it was agreed that the two parties would share ministerial responsibility. Ronald Ngala became Minister of State for Constitutional Affairs and Economic Planning.

Evidence of increased racialism accompanied the showdown between KANU and KADU. The leaders of KANU sought to discredit KADU by linking it with the Europeans. Kenyatta's words are typical: "The time is now ripe for us to tell KADU men, who are the settlers' bootlickers, that we are fed up with them." [61]

On the other hand, in an apparent bid to entice some Europeans and many Asians to hurry aboard the KANU bandwagon, Kenyatta announced on October 20, 1962 ("Kenyatta Day") that KANU membership would henceforth be open to Europeans and Asians. But he reminded would-be white and brown KANU members that the party was an African institution. "Those who want to be called Bwana and Memsahib should go back to their own country." [62] Elections were held in May 1963; KANU won a majority of the crucial lower house seats and surprised many observers by capturing more of the upper house seats than the rival KADU-APP Alliance. Jomo Kenyatta, who less than two years ago was still in detention, has become independent Kenya's first Prime

[60] Constitutional amendments require an extraordinary majority of the upper house, while the electoral system is designed to insure the election of an upper house reflecting the views of smaller tribes.
[61] Jomo Kenyatta at Nairobi stadium on October 20, quoted in *East African Reporter* (Oct. 27, 1962), p. 10.
[62] *Ibid.*

Minister. However, to the surprise of many, Kenyatta's government has demonstrated considerable tolerance toward the European community. It is difficult to come to any conclusion but that the trend in the relationship between the races in Africa is toward increased violence and conflict. This is not to say that one cannot find instances of integration and cooperation. Possibly the next generation of white, brown, and black Africans will be less blinded by color and by a legacy of racial superiority and inferiority. Schools in Kenya and Tanganyika are legally integrated although relatively high fees in the formerly European institutions continue to perpetuate segregation. Universities and colleges for the time being present a better opportunity for racial contact and thereby contribute to cooperation which might carry over into the future.

The trade unions also provide an institutional arrangement of increased frequency and intensity of racial contact. It is important to recall, however, that competition and violence are also a possible concomitant of increased racial contact. In South Africa and in the Rhodesias the presence of a sizeable European labor force has contributed to racial competition and violence. Color has long determined personal status and salary while European labor unions have given significant support to racially discriminatory policies. Racialism in the labor movement cuts both directions. In Tanganyika the all-black Tanganyika Railway African Union (TRAU) refused the Tanganyika Federation of Labors (TFL) orders to integrate with the Asian Railway Workers Union.

Among the members of all races a small minority of men of extraordinary goodwill have gained mutual understanding and respect. These non-racial persons play a critical role in keeping open the channels of communication between the races by interpreting the one to the other and thereby lessening the likelihood of violence and conflict. By and large the Europeans who have chosen to remain in East and Central Africa are those who have come to know, understand, and respect their black countrymen.

The racial integration of a wide variety of institutions, including local and central government, professional associations, recreational clubs—in short, the movement toward multiracial association—is not without its positive consequences. The separate European clubs which characterized and dramatized segregation of black, white, and brown settlers in Africa are being replaced by the nonracial clubs bearing simply the name of the town or region. Although such instances of integration and cooperation are numerous, they are difficult to document. Still, their cumulative effect is to help balance the much better publicized racial incidents. As Africans flex their newly acquired racial and political muscles, the headlines feature such events as the expulsion of the Anglican Archbishop from Ghana, the forced emigration of a number of Europeans from Tanganyika and Uganda, the withdrawal of visitor permits from eminent journalists in Sierra Leone, the expulsion from Nyasaland of a woman because of the name she gave to her dog, and similar instances.

RACE—A HUMAN ENIGMA

Even though the future of black and white in Africa is uncertain, some aspects of the relationship can be predicted. It seems inevitable that interracial contacts will increase both in frequency and intensity. For communications technology has liberated mankind from his spatial parochialism and is sweeping away the myths of racial, ethnic, and nationalist exclusiveness and superiority. The twentieth-century diffusion of ideologies and knowledge is narrowing the dimensions of "strangeness," which have for so long dominated the manner in which men of differing races perceived one another. At the same time that empirical knowledge and universal ideologies of equality and dignity are breaking down emotional barriers to contact; the African, himself imbued with the new knowledge and ideology, is demanding that he be accepted and regarded as equal.

Formerly it was the European and Asian who came to Africa and the African's relationship to European and Asians outside the African continent was almost solely limited to that of slave and master. But World War II destroyed forever this one-way avenue of racial contact. Thousands of young Africans were recruited, trained, and equipped with weapons, and subsequently sent to the far corners of the planet where they came into daily contact with peoples of other races and nationalities. In the process the African soldier learned that the European was vulnerable—that rifles and large-scale organization were extraordinary equalizers and that Asian peasants in many instances were even poorer than Africans. These legacies of World War II were carried back to Africa and the relationship of white, black, and brown men was never to be the same again. As surely as the Four Freedoms contributed to a weakening of colonial bonds, the war-time experience of thousands of African youth created a mentality that black men should and could sever these bonds.

Contact of black, brown, and white men in a non-African environment has been rapidly accelerated. One has only to visit the campus of any large university in the United States, the United Kingdom, France, Belgium, Israel, India or the Soviet Union to be aware of the extraordinary number of young Africans currently living their lives abroad.[63]

The changes in the manner of racial contact, as a consequence of the initiative now assumed by Africans, by increased frequency and intensity, and by the extension of the relationship to every continent, are fundamentally altering the traditional style of African-European-Asian relations. This is proving to be a heady wine, and like the younger brother who has

[63] For example, approximately 8,000 Nigerian students are in residence in the United Kingdom alone.

just discovered that he is as strong as his elder, the African is inclined to take advantage of every opportunity to demonstrate this new-found equality.

The newly acquired freedom of the African to define his relationship with other people has not, as some direly predicted, led to a wholesale casting out from Africa of all Europeans, or even to a closing of African doors to Europeans and Asians. More important than the exodus of European settlers is the arrival of a new type of white man. Thus, while there is a basic continuity in the relationship of black and white on the African continent, the style of that relationship is undergoing a basic change as the African gains the capacity to determine who should come to Africa, for what purpose, and for how long. As settlers and governors leave, Peace Corps engineers and teachers, United Nations technicians, Japanese traders, Swiss investors, Polish diplomats, European university lecturers, and countless others arrive daily in Africa—but they do so at the invitation of Africans.

World War II will almost surely serve tomorrow's historian as an episode dividing one important era of human history from another. The second half of the century marks the beginning of a new world—a world dominated by a fear of its capacity for self-destruction and by the end of the monopoly of white domination. The two factors are not unrelated. As a continent of dependent territories, Africa long provided the West with a degree of international flexibility. Territories could be exchanged, rights of trade granted, boundaries altered, lands alienated for settlers. Africa's natural and human resources have long contributed to the maintenance of European domination of the planet, but Africa no longer contributes to European hegemony or international flexibility.

It is more and more evident that the precarious existence of mankind is to be increasingly determined by the nature of the relationship of men of different color. A fragile planet can no longer tolerate the blows of ethnic, racial, or national struggle. But until the entire continent is "liberated" the African's irrational, but nonetheless powerful, suspicion of inferiority will persist. The relatively easy battles have all been won; the remaining bastions of European domination might well have to be taken by storm.

Large-scale warfare in the south of Africa pitting the armed forces of independent African states against the white troops of Southern Rhodesia and the Republic of South Africa could hardly be restricted to the African continent. The independent African states cannot rest until the rule of the Portuguese, white Rhodesians, and Afrikaners has been replaced by that of black Africans, and the world will know neither security nor peace until that goal is won. Today Africa and Africans are a force to be reckoned with, the likelihood of the African people's contributing to world stability and unity until they have firmly established their equality and dignity is small, while their capacity to contribute to global insecurity, in the meantime, is great indeed. Or, better still, as Kwame Nkrumah himself has said, "As long as a single foot of African soil remains under foreign domination, the world will know no peace." [64]

[64] Before the United Nations General Assembly, Fifteenth Session, Sept. 23, 1960.

VII
African Unity and Disunity

The quest for a new order of modernity and racial dignity has led Africa's independent states into the complex and dangerous universe of international politics. The interstate relationships of the new nations of Africa seem, to the relatively staid and orthodox observer from the West, hopelessly confused, irrational, and irresponsible. A closer examination of interstate politics on the African continent reveals that there is a logic to the often confusing machinations of these recently sovereign states. With a singleness of purpose, not unlike that of the United States in its formative years, the new nations are concerned (collectively and individually) with the enhancement of their own power and dignity and with rapid economic and social development of their respective territories.

Given their extraordinary number and the critical role of international organizations in which the rule of numbers prevails, all within the context of a competitive cold war, the African states are finding the international arena most effective for the furtherance of their quest. It is here that they compete with one another and with the developing states of Latin America and Asia for a redistribution of the planet's resources requisite to their modernization. And as we shall see, the assembly halls at the United Nations, Addis Ababa, Casablanca, and Monrovia provide an extraordinary opportunity for young men and young nations, long denied a voice, to exercise power and influence.

Because the international arena is so critical to Africa's quest for order, this subject is dealt with in two chapters. The politics of African Federation and other forms of interstate association, relationships with the former metropolitan powers, and the movement toward Pan-Africa with its accompanying philosophy of Négritude are covered in this chapter. The concluding chapter deals with a fourth aspect, the involvement of the emergent African sovereignties in the bipolar currents of the cold war and, finally, with the most extensive level of international politics—the immersion of the new African states in the politics of international organization and particularly with their participation in the programs, agencies, and politics of the United Nations.

INTEGRATION

Interterritorial unity is not a novel idea in Africa; the colonial powers found that linking their overseas dependencies frequently eased the financial and administrative burdens of imperialism. The French West and Equatorial states, for example, were launched into the world of independent sovereignties as integral parts of the French Union. In East Africa—Uganda, Kenya, and Tanganyika are striving to preserve an inherited economic union and to build an even larger political federation. And even the now defunct Federation of Central Africa can be seen as an attempt, on the part of the Colonial Office and European settlers, to establish a union in which the riches of one region (Northern Rhodesia) would support another (Southern Rhodesia), while preserving white dominance in still a third (Nyasaland). In British West Africa too, federation was an early feature of political transition. One of the preconditions of Nigerian independence was the establishment of a visible federal arrangement.

Federation as a form of economic and political unity is becoming increasingly attractive to Africa's new states. At no time have territorial frontiers in Africa attained the emotional rigidity characteristic of Europe. Even before European hegemony the frontiers separating linguistic or cultural groupings (tribal) were constantly being altered; traditional Africa was, above all, a continent in motion. The territorial jurisdictions of even the relatively large and powerful African kingdoms were not precisely demarcated. These kingdoms were themselves amalgamations and alliances of formerly independent or quasi-independent territories and peoples.

The purposes as well as the terms of cooperation among the federating states differ widely. Ghana, for example, has loudly proclaimed a willingness to surrender its sovereignty, initially to a West African union, and ultimately to a powerful highly centralized continental federation. But where federation has worked in practice as in Nigeria, or is being seriously approached, as in East Africa, more emphasis is usually placed upon the prerogatives of the constituent states rather than upon the powers of the center.

Federations and interstate associations emerge in a variety of ways in Africa. We are here primarily concerned with forces favorable to unity. As we shall see, some federations are inspired by defensive requirements, others by the politics of aggrandizement, and still others by economic advantages.

Inherited from the period of colonial rule is a tendency for international cooperation in the allocation of resources and manpower. France's development of the less well-endowed territories of French Africa, such as Soudan and Mauritania, was long subsidized by the relatively rich Ivory Coast. And a sense of obligation to subsidize one's poorer neighbors persists within the French community of independent republics. President Senghor of Senegal, for example, envisaged his newly independent country as assuming a benevolent leadership over the more backward countries of French West Africa. The Ivory Coast, however, under the leadership of President Houphouet-Boigny, interpreted the maneuverings of Senegal as a threat to its potential leadership of the French West African states. Senegal's President Léopold Senghor originally conceived of the five federating states (Senegal, Soudan, Niger, Upper Volta, and Dahomey) as "complementary" territories needing to join together for economic and political viability. To promote federation of these five territories, Senghor made use of both the carrot and the stick. The proffered carrot was to be a sharing of the wealth resulting from a common market and from massive assistance from France in recognition of the Federation's continued membership in the French community. Associate membership in the European Common Market, with its substantial African Development Fund, and relative freedom from the anxieties of balancing cold war aid from America and the Communist bloc were seen as an additional bonus for the proposed Federation.[1]

The stick that Senghor flourished was a reminder of the latent fear in Niger and Dahomey of their larger and wealthier neighbors, Ghana and Nigeria. In his address to the party of African federation in June 1959, he warned that "war is being waged, not only between East and West, but also secretly between the members of NATO." He then speculated that the British Foreign Office was not displeased with the recent union of Ghana and Guinea.

But neither the stick nor the carrot was successful, for Niger, Dahomey, and Upper Volta began to turn away from Senegal and to look toward the Ivory Coast for assistance and leadership. Aware of the conservative, pro-French attitude of the leaders of Dahomey, Niger, and Upper Volta and of their suspicion of Soudan's militant socialism, Houphouet-Boigny successfully enticed these states away from the projected union, thereby restricting the proposed grand Federation to an uncomfortable union of Senegal and Soudan. The resulting Mali Federation was probably doomed to failure from the moment of its birth. Without the conservative influence of Dahomey, Niger, and Upper Volta to help dilute the political militancy of Soudan, Senegal quickly discovered that its union with

---

[1] The European Economic Community and its eighteen African associates in December 1962 signed a five-year trade and aid agreement. Of particular interest is the fact that the treaty permits the African associates to join with other African states in customer unions or other interstate associations. The treaty also made provision for associate membership for the former British dependencies, of which only Sierra Leone has demonstrated a willingness to accept. The agreement provides for the provision of about eighty million dollars in grants and low interest loans over the next five years. The treaty also anticipates the establishment of a Council of Ministers, a Committee of Permanent Representatives, a Parliamentary Assembly, and a Court of Arbitration.

Soudan in the Mali Federation would work to its economic disadvantage and against its political interests. The internal political system of Soudan (now the Mali Republic) had much more in common with militant, highly centralized Guinea than it did with Senegal's laissez-faire party system and humanistic socialism. Modibo Keita, leader of the highly centralized and disciplined mass *Union Soudanaise,* had envisaged not so much a flexible economic association as a mystic union of the Mali peoples under a strong central party state which would one day attain the greatness of the legendary thirteenth- and fourteenth-century Mali Empire.

Differences in political philosophy and competition for power between rival centers and leaders was more than the ill-fated union could sustain, and in August of 1960 Senegal reluctantly withdrew from the Federation. Soudan, neither very surprised nor displeased, retained the name "Mali."

The two states could hardly be less alike, even though they share a legacy of French administration and institutions as well as a common frontier. Senegal was the first French colony in Africa; its ties to France and French culture stretch over three hundred years, and Senegalese, in the coastal towns, have long possessed the status of French citizens. Dakar, Senegal's capital city, often referred to as the Paris of Africa, was the administrative headquarters of France's West African Empire. Mali, on the other hand, is linked with the sea only through the railroad running from its capital city of Bamako to Dakar—a railroad which was cut at the time of the disintegration of the Federation. Its ties to France have been shorter and less extensive. In December 1960 less than four months after the disintegration of the short-lived Federation, Mali joined the Guinea-Ghana union and subsequently played an important role in the establishment of the "Casablanca" bloc of militant African states. Writing about the disintegration of the Mali Federation, Mamadou Dia, the eminent Senegalese statesman, addressed his post-mortem to all of Africa's Federalists and Pan-Africanists, "Our error has been that in our fight against Balkanization, we failed to consider the precolonial fact that is territorialism. Our mistake has been our failure to pay sufficient attention . . . to this phenomenon, a fruit of colonialism and socio-political fact that a theory of unity—no matter how praiseworthy or attractive— cannot abolish." [2]

A still more powerful force conducive to federation and other forms of interstate linkage, is the likelihood that union will considerably enhance the political power of the new states, not only within the international sphere generally, but vis-à-vis other African states or power blocs.

These political forces and interests give rise to new regional alignments on the continent which would have been inconceivable a few short years ago. Muslim, white North Africa, for example, is now politically closer

[2] Mamadou Dia, *The African Nations and World Solidarity* (New York: Frederick A. Praeger, Inc., 1961), p. 140.

to parts of West Africa than are many East or Central African states. The Sahara, which centuries ago linked tropical and North Africa, may possibly be destined once again to bring peoples and cultures long-separated into close proximity. But what do Ghana, the United Arab Republic, and Guinea, for example, have in common? Certainly they have neither a contiguous territory nor a common colonial culture and language; not even complementary economies. While most Ghanaians and Egyptians speak English, the leaders of Guinea, Morocco, Mali, and Algeria converse in French. These four along with Egypt are predominantly Muslim countries, but then Ghana is not. Guinea and Mali share a common frontier, but Ghana and the United Arab Republic are contiguous to none. Despite these obvious differences, a number of political forces, some purely African and others international, brought the sub-Saharan states of Mali, Guinea, and Ghana into alliance with the Mediterranean and Arab states of Morocco, the United Arab Republic, and Algeria.

The Ghana and Guinea union was initially planned in 1958, but the only specific and important measures taken to implement the Federation were the abolishing of visas and the exchange of resident ministers in place of ambassadors. Neither nation has been prepared to accept a unified currency or to develop a common market and trade organization. In April of 1961 this paper union was enlarged with the inclusion of Mali and the proclamation of the formation of a Union of African States (UAS). While no important common institutions have been established, this union was not without significance for it formalized the growing alienation of its three-member nations from the less militant West African states. Immediately after its formation the UAS sought to test its power by maneuvering to force the postponement of a conference of African states scheduled to be held in Liberia's capital city of Monrovia. Guinea, Ghana, and Mali's refusal to attend did not wreck the conference as planned, but it did give birth to a counter organization—the Monrovia bloc—composed of the twenty states that did attend.

The charter of the Union of African States, signed in April 1961, had been under consideration as early as December 1960. In the following January the UAS powers met with Morocco, the United Arab Republic, and the Algerian Provisional government at a historic meeting in Casablanca. At this meeting the six states signed a charter proclaiming their support of Lumumba and the unification of the Congo, and made the first of many subsequent condemnations of Western imperialism.[3] Another outcome of the meeting, which contributed to a growing alienation of the Casablanca powers from the rest of Africa, was a decision to establish an aggressive all-African Trade Union Federation as a step

[3] For a concise but excellent survey of the differences between the Casablanca and Monrovia factions, see John Marcum, "How Wide is the Gap Between Casablanca and Monrovia?" *Africa Report* (Jan. 1962).

toward Pan-African Union. The Casablanca powers demanded that their sister African states sever all ties with the "Western dominated" International Confederation of Free Trade Unions (ICFTU). The Casablanca bloc pledged financial and organizational assistance to those African trade union movements willing to cooperate and explicitly determined to undermine and destroy those that would not.

It would be an oversimplification to conclude that exclusive alignments have developed in Africa. As John Marcum has significantly pointed out, the United Arab Republic declined an invitation to join the UAS; Ghana has signed trade agreements with Dahomey, agreed with Upper Volta to abolish customs barriers, and has remained in the Commonwealth along with Sierra Leone and Nigeria; Mali is an associate member of the European Common Market along with her more conservative French Community neighbors; both Senegal and Guinea have crossed blocs in their trade agreements; the United Arab Republic and Morocco share membership in the Arab League with Libya; and both Libya and Tunisia attended the Monrovia Conference while the Sudan stayed away out of deference to the United Arab Republic.[4]

A third set of forces tending toward the formation of new alliances and federations is a concern on the part of both the Monrovia powers and the remaining European-dominated states with the defense of their respective systems against an extension of the militant philosophy and influence of the Casablanca powers. Thus the power tropism of the militant Casablanca states in their attempts to unify Africa served as a catalyst in the formation or attempted formation of other alliances and federations (1) among the North African states, (2) between less militant French West and Equatorial African states initially in the Conseil d'Entente, then in the Brazzaville Twelve, and most recently in the Union of African and Malagasy States (UAMS), (3) among all independent African states not part of the Casablanca group, (4) between South Africa, Southern Rhodesia, Mozambique, and Algeria, (5) and most recently (May 1963), a union of all non-European-dominated African states into the Organization of African Unity.

The Entente states have achieved relatively more real unification than the UAS, are all governed by sections of the old RDA (Rassemblement Démocratique Africaine) Party, have adopted very similar constitutions, and some even share embassies abroad.[5]

The Entente, along with the four former French Equatorial States (Tchad, Central African Republic, Gabon, and the Republic of the Congo) which themselves have retained and created additional common institutions, together with the Cameroon Republic, Mauritania, Senegal,

[4] Ibid.
[5] In February 1963, the Union of Africa and Malagasy States established a secretariat in New York to coordinate United Nations policies.

and the Malagasy Republic held a series of conferences in 1960 and 1961. These meetings, initiated by Houphouet-Boigny, sought a compromise solution to the French and Algerian conflict before it forced the former French territories to choose between African nationalism and France and thereby lead to the complete disintegration of the emergent union.

The meetings of the Brazzaville Twelve—subsequently the Union of African and Malagasy States (UAMS)—have led to a remarkable degree of unity on a number of political points, as well as to the establishment of common economic and communications institutions and to an agreement on collective defense. The Twelve (subsequently thirteen) put pressure on France to settle the Algerian conflict in 1961, threatening that their continued neutrality depended on a rapid solution to the issue. In 1962, at its third meeting, the UAMS laid plans for a common development bank, a joint shipping and airline company (Air Afrique), and agreed on a unified policy in the United Nations and the European Common Market. Organizational activities of the UAMS are deliberately divided among the member states: the political secretariat is located in Cotonou (Dahomey); a military coordinating committee has its headquarters in Ouagadougou (Upper Volta); the postal and telecommunications unions is based in Brazzaville (Congo).

Soon after the Brazzaville agreements the Casablanca powers met and took opposing positions on nearly every issue. Growing antagonism between the two blocs contributed to the calling of the Monrovia Conference in May 1961. Liberia's President Tubman hoped that the initiation of such a conference by an African state aligned with neither bloc would make it possible for all African nations to cooperate in a reconciliation of the differences separating the Casablanca and Brazzaville groups. But as the Casablanca powers boycotted the meeting it did little more than dramatize the gulf separating the two blocs. As we have noted, the Conference attracted twenty states, including in addition to the Brazzaville Twelve and Liberia—Nigeria, Ethiopia, Tunisia, Libya, Togo, Somalia, and Sierra Leone.

With Nigeria playing a dominant leadership role for the first time, the Conference came out in favor of the maintenance of national sovereignty while working toward economic unity and political cooperation. The Conference deliberately left the door open to reconciliation with the Casablanca powers in the process of making plans for subsequent meetings. Possibly the most severe blow to Casablanca solidarity is the growing alienation of Guinea and Ghana—the charter members of the UAS. It will be recalled that in 1958, embittered by De Gaulle's abrupt and hostile behavior because of its vote for complete independence, Guinea took a sharp turn to the left. Mutual aid agreements were signed with the Soviet Union and with other Iron Curtain countries. Russian and East European technicians flocked to Guinea in unprecedented numbers. To many observers Guinea was in effect a Soviet satellite. Possibly the Russians assumed as much. In 1961 their interference in domestic politics led President Touré to demand the recall of the Soviet ambassador, restrict Communist activity, and begin to rebuild his ties with the French Community and the West. At the same time Sékou Touré watched with anxiety the growing interference of Ghana in the internal affairs of Togoland and other neighboring West African states. The assassination of Sylvanus Olympio, Togoland's President, in January 1963 may have signaled the end of the UAS. The Guinean President, in a major speech delivered immediately after the assassination, said that there was definite proof that the assassination was "the tragic result of an odious plot, knowingly organized outside the country." [6]

Since the May 1963 Addis Ababa Conference and the establishment of the Organization of African Unity, the sharp distinction between the Casablanca and Monrovian blocs has rapidly disintegrated. The first foreign ministers' meeting of the new organization was held in Dakar in August 1963. A major purpose of the meeting was to discuss the dismantlement of the regional blocs. However, at a meeting in Dahomey at about the same time the fourteen former French and Belgian territories resisted pressures to dissolve the UAMS. The UAMS states voted instead to cooperate with the newer and larger organization and to move only gradually into complete union with the OAU.

As the Central African Federation is dismantled, there is a growing possibility for closer union between the four remaining white-dominated territories in the south of Africa. The defeat of Sir Edgar Whitehead's moderate United Federal Party on December 14, 1962, in Southern Rhodesia and victory for the white supremacy Rhodesian Front—coming on the heels of the formation of the first African government in Northern Rhodesia—could drive Southern Rhodesia into the arms of a receptive South Africa. There is ample precedent for such a union inasmuch as proposals and plans for federation between South Africa and Southern Rhodesia have a long history. The arguments for defensive cooperation and unity between South Africa, Southern Rhodesia, and the two Portuguese territories grow louder and more compelling in direct proportion to the southward spread of African domination and influence. A mitigating factor is the Afrikaner's fear that union with Southern Rhodesia would so increase the English portion of the population as to threaten the Nationalist Party's control of the government.

A fourth factor promoting federation which frequently combines with economic, defensive, and political reasons is the force of cultural and historical "irredentism" and its handmaiden "secessionism." Federation with its myriad meanings has evolved as one answer to this quandary. Eritrea, which won postwar autonomy from both Ethiopia and Italy

[6] *Tanganyika Standard* (Jan. 25, 1963).

following a United Nations plebiscite, in 1952 federated with Ethiopia.[7] On the other hand, Ethiopian unity is threatened by Somali irredentism in the former's Ogaden Province. A frequently suggested solution to Somali irredentism is the formation of a federal union to include the Somali people now resident in the tiny French enclave, those in Kenya's Northern Frontier District, and, of course, the Swahili-speaking people of Ethiopia's Ogaden Province. Although many of Kenya's political party leaders have never been in their country's northern frontier area, to a man they have passionately stated that if necessary they will go to war to retain this remote region in Kenya. Kenya's approaching independence has sharpened this conflict and the Somali Separatist Protest has become increasingly violent. Anglo-Somali talks in September 1963 reached no conclusion. It is now evident that a solution to this highly charged border dispute will depend upon future negotiations between an independent Kenya and Somalia. Another suggested remedy to Somali irredentism proposed by those East Africans already committed to the idea of federation is that Somalia join a federal union with Tanganyika and Uganda. It is further argued that an East African Federation could solve other irredentist or secessionist problems. Thousands of Masai pastoral people herd their cattle along both sides of the Kenya-Tanganyika border but have developed little loyalty to either state. Although the demand for Masai unity within a single state has not yet undermined the stability of East Africa, it remains a latent threat. Irredentist conflict, in view of the radically divergent evolution of the respective Tanganyikan and Kenyan political systems, is a growing possibility. Whereas multiparty Kenya received its independence in late 1963 as a quasi-federal state with significant powers reserved to seven predominantly tribally oriented regional governments, Tanganyika is rapidly becoming a highly centralized single-party state. The Tanganyika African National Union (TANU) has effectively established an organizational monopoly over the entire country; opposition parties are proscribed and deportation is employed to ensure single-party, centralized domination.

As these illustrations seek to demonstrate, federation is attractive to many of Africa's new leaders because it promises to dilute dangerous and divisive tribal and parochial conflicts. A large East and Central African Federation, as proposed by PAFMECSA,[8] for example, conceivably would reduce the irredentist tensions within and between Kenya and Somalia. It might mitigate the problems that the powerful Buganda Kingdom poses for recently independent Uganda. If Nyasaland, Burundi, Rwanda, and Northern Rhodesia were also included, as some PAFMECSA spokesmen advocated, a number of other potentially disrupted problems would be correspondingly diluted.

[7] Later in November of that year, Eritrea voted to abandon its federal status and merge with Ethiopia.

[8] The Pan-African Freedom Movement of East, Central, and South Africa.

The most recent attempt at federation that has clearly demonstrated economic, political, and defensive aspects is, of course, the forcible federal unification of the Congo. Katanga's Tshombe with entraordinary skill was able to maintain the separate independence of the Congo's far eastern mineral-rich province through 1962. The new year, however, brought an end to Katangan independence and that unhappy country's long sought reunification into a federated Congo state, in general conformity with a plan prepared by Secretary-General U Thant. It is somewhat ironic that the newly independent African states, which so recently demanded for themselves the right of self-determination, were prepared to employ their influence in the United Nations and their armed forces to deny forcibly an identical right to the people of Katanga. The similarity, at least from the point of view of most African leaders, is, however, more apparent than real. A Balkanized Congo, it is firmly believed, would provide easy pickings for the neo-colonialists, as Katanga had clearly demonstrated. Viewed in this light the willingness to use force to unify the Congo makes sense and is not inconsistent with Africa's quest for order.

A preoccupation with the inter-African and international aspects of the Congo crisis have tended to obscure disruptive problems of tribal irredentism. The large Bakongo tribe that provides President Kasavubu's Abako Party with its primary support spills over into the Congo Republic (Brazzaville), where it also supplies the major backing for former President Fulbert Youlou. The same people inhabit Northern Angola, where their war against a Portuguese Army is considerably assisted through the sanctuary the Congolese provide their fellow tribesmen.

DISINTEGRATION

Although the promise of regional alliances and federal unions obviously has great appeal to the statesmen of new Africa, there are three powerful reasons why federal arrangements have failed to evolve or to be as durable as many had anticipated.

The new African states are in the advantageous position of being able to bring their many plates to what might be termed the international smorgasbord, where they are free to select and compete for the choicest and largest morsels. Would a federation of Uganda, Kenya, Tanganyika, Zanzibar, Northern Rhodesia, Nyasaland, Burundi, and Rwanda, for example, receive from Western Europe, the United States, and the Communist bloc assistance comparable to the total they could receive individually? As long as foreign aid is determined, in large part, by the cold war strategy of winning the support or neutrality of new nations it is conceivable that small, relatively poor states might fare better by continuing to carry their own plates to the smorgasbord than by relying upon the distribution of development aid by a federal authority.

An even more powerful but related factor discouraging amalgamation of existing small independent states into large federations is that the process would seriously weaken the over-all bargaining position of the African states in the United Nations. The United Nations is an extraordinary equalizer wherein small and poor but nonetheless independent states speak on the same rostrum as the mighty, and where the votes of Togo and Tchad are counted with those of the United States and the Soviet Union. The importance of the United Nations to the newly independent African nations can hardly be overemphasized.

Africa's new leaders have sacrificed a great deal over many years to win independence for their respective countries. The amalgamation of a number of independent states into an effective federation requires the downgrading of these hard-won positions of influence and power; it means relegating a long sought and recently won independence to the status of a constituent federal state. It is not difficult to understand why even the most militant states, which have loudly proclaimed a willingness and intent to submerge their sovereignties to the goal of African unity, have been careful to avoid actually doing so.

A third force opposing federation is the problem of constructing even larger collective identities. Without exception African leaders are struggling with the task of building a sense of nationality and identity within the confines of the recently established independent state. Faced with traditional and long-standing antagonisms between rival tribal factions, Africa's nationalist leaders are reluctant to attempt the creation of an even more distant sense of nationhood.

As the first African territory to win independence after World War II, Ghana long enjoyed a virtual monopoly as spokesman for the African Revolution. President Nkrumah's Pan-African vision contributed to this monopoly and at the same time enhanced his capacity to juggle profitably the rival enticements and threats of Moscow and Washington. But Nkrumah's reluctance to relinquish the mantle of Pan-African spokesman and leader is running headlong into the rapidly growing influence of Nigeria, the Union of African and Malagasy States, and the newly independent countries of East Africa. An important aspect of the pattern of interstate relations, at this particular juncture in the African Revolution, is the maneuvering for regional and continental leadership. While Ghana's assistance and involvement in the independence movements of Nigeria, Tanganyika, and other recently independent states was certainly welcomed, a continued interest and involvement in the internal affairs of the now sovereign nations of Africa has led to considerable opposition to Ghana and to her dynamic President.

The hardening of relations between Ghana and Nigeria is of particular importance. The philosophy of the Nigerian federal government and of two of the three regional governments is more sympathetic with the Monrovia than with the Casablanca powers. There is within Nigeria, however, a sizeable opinion favoring alliance with Ghana and Guinea and a more militant and radical approach to internal and external affairs. Receiving encouragement from Ghana, this faction—particularly strong in the Western Region—in 1962 seriously threatened the stability of the continent's most populous state. In May of that year the federal authorities suspended the government of the Western Region, arresting Obafemi Awolowo, former Western Region Premier and leader of the federal opposition Action Party, and many others. Subsequent police raids unearthed caches of arms and ammunition which were claimed to have come from Ghana. In December of 1962 Awolowo and twenty-six other Action Group leaders were charged with treason and with an attempt to overthrow the government by force. Awolowo was accused of leading the proposed coup, of arranging for the training of guerilla forces and the procurement of weapons and other assistance from Ghana. Witnesses told of plans for a September 1962 coup d'état and how, under Awolowo's instructions, they had traveled to Ghana where they received personal assistance from President Nkrumah in obtaining the necessary weapons and ammunition.

Relations between Ghana and Nigeria have hardened as accusation and counteraccusation have been made. In New York in October 1962 the Nigerian Foreign Minister, J. A. Wachuku made a faintly veiled reference to Ghana's activities as "black imperialism" and firmly stated that Nigeria would not tolerate "any attempt by any African country . . . to bully another. . . ." [9]

Political opposition groups often coincide with tribal and regional factions, and often spill over into neighboring countries as well. Rival states and blocs provide refuge for proscribed opposition parties and leaders. Plot and counterplot to overthrow existing regimes are hatched by exiled oppositions often aided and abetted by the political leaders of the host countries.

Political opposition in Ghana in 1961 and 1962 resulted in the flight of a number of former CPP Ministers, important journalists, and members of Parliament. Many fled to Togo where the irredentist movement of the large Ewe tribe, spreading across the Ghana-Togo border, provided a sympathetic haven. Exiled Togo leaders are active in Ghana; dissident Nigerian agitators for political reform are also active within Ghana. The latent explosive potential of such a situation was manifested in January 1963, when immediately after an interchange of a series of notes between Ghana and Togo protesting the interference and connivance of each another in internal affairs, the President of Togo, Sylvanus Olympio, was assassinated on the threshold of the American Embassy where he had fled for safety.[10] Within a matter of hours opposition leaders exiled in Ghana and Dahomey returned to Togo to consolidate the coup while the Nigerian and Ivory Coast governments anxiously prepared to resist any

[9] *East African Standard* (Oct. 17, 1962).
[10] This is not to imply that Ghana was responsible for Olympio's assassination.

attempt to annex Togo. The Togo leaders who managed to escape have surely sought sanctuary in sympathetic neighboring countries where in turn they will seek to plan a counter coup.

The initial disputes over Ethiopia's contested Ogaden Province, between that country and Somalia, is another illustration of the manner in which irredentist movements tend to structure the relationship between newly emerging states. In September 1962 the Somalia Minister of Information claimed that relations had reached such a state that Ethiopia was plotting to assassinate the President of Somalia, which elicited a strong denial from Emperor Haille Selassie.

Nor has Uganda, one of Africa's newest states, been spared the anxiety accompanying neighboring irredentist movements. Sharing frontiers with the troubled areas of the Congo, Rwanda, Burundi, and the Sudan, this new nation has already been faced with an extraordinary number of explosive interstate incidents. The flow of Watutsi refugees from Rwanda has been further complicated by the tendency of these refugees to organize raids into their country from the security of Ugandan soil. Border friction and incidents with the chaotic Congo are common. More serious still is the problem created by the flow of refugees from the Southern Sudan into Northern Uganda. The African minority resident in the Sudan's southern provinces has long resisted domination by Arab administrators, teachers, and governors sent from the Arab north. In August 1955 a short but bloody uprising occurred as African non-commissioned officers and troops mutinied against their Arab officers. The uprising was suppressed but the Africans, many of them members of Uganda tribes, have continued to resist the forceful extension of Arab culture, the Muslim religion, and northern domination. Given sanctuary by their fellow tribesmen in Northern Uganda, hundreds of Southern Sudanese have sought to form a liberation army to free their fellow southerners from Arab domination. Even though the bulk of sympathy in Uganda lies with their persecuted fellow Africans, Uganda's armed forces have acted to break up raids into the Sudan.

This situation also has some internal implications, for if the government coalition (UPC-KY) jeopardizes the support it now receives from the tribes in Northern Uganda, who are emotionally involved in the struggle, it conceivably might risk its majority position. The risk of internal disaffection must be weighed in every case of this sort against that of interstate conflict.

Even those territories which have not yet won their freedom are affected by irredentist forces as well as by the remnants of the Casablanca-Monrovia split. The revolutionary movements in Angola and Mozambique, for example, are divided on the one hand between those favoring and consequently assisted by Ghana, and on the other by those allied more closely with the Monrovia powers. The Peoples Movement for the Liberation of Angola (PMLA) faction, led by Agostino Neto, operates out of Ghana and Guinea, while Roberto Holden's Union of Angolan People (UAP) is more closely associated with the Congolese Central government and with the leaders of the Monrovia bloc. Friction between the rival factions has reached the stage where not all the fighting in Angola has been directed against the Portuguese.

In East Africa, Dar es Salaam has become the headquarters of exiled revolutionary factions and parties from South Africa, Mozambique, Southern Rhodesia, and South-West Africa. Many East African nationalist leaders are well known to one another; a reunion of the early graduating classes of Makerere College would bring together an extraordinary number of the leaders and administrators of the three territories. A long history of economic association and cooperation during their respective struggles for independence has established a pattern of mutual involvement in one another's affairs. There is considerable evidence, however, that whereas this cooperation and involvement was welcomed during the struggle it is considered to be undesirable and meddlesome after self-government is, or is about to be achieved. Uganda's Prime Minister, Milton Obote, in 1962 was heatedly accused by Kenya's Minister of State for Constitutional Affairs, Ronald Ngala, of meddling in Kenyan affairs and of attempting to further the cause of KANU to the detriment of KADU. The support of one party over another in the domestic politics of a neighboring state is not, however, without its long-run implications. If an electoral victory for KADU in the May 1963 elections had materialized, the support of KANU by the majority parties in Tanganyika (TANU) and Uganda (UPC) could have sealed the doom of an East African Federation and might have substituted hostility for a long history of cooperation.

Ghana's involvement in African politics is not restricted to West Africa, but is much in evidence in Kenya and Uganda as well. The General Secretary of the Kenya Democratic Union, commenting on Olympio's assassination in January 1963, condemned the interference of African states in the domestic politics of their neighbors. He primarily and firmly criticized the "reported Ghana financial assistance to KANU and warned that 'what happened in Togo might happen in Kenya if the outside financial influence continues.' " [11]

Tanganyika's statutory single party, TANU, has been heavily involved in the frequently violent factional and racial disputes that have rent Zanzibar since 1959. TANU has played an important role in the inter-party and factional struggles of the Mozambique Liberation Front and has made its influence felt in the contest for power between the two major Northern Rhodesian African political parties.

In short, the affairs of the new African states are extraordinarily inter-related as a consequence of overlapping tribes, a history of mutual

[11] *Tanganyika Standard* (Jan. 19, 1963).

involvement in each other's liberation movements, a genuine desire to replace new nationalism with Pan-Africanism, and the emergence of two contradictory competing political philosophies. Pan-Africanism and strong continental unity are the ultimate goals, but in the meantime the world may witness many strange federations and unions formed under the aegis of African "federation and solidarity."

NEW NATIONS AND OLD COLONIZERS

Obviously the postindependence relations between African nations and metropolitan colonizers are varied in emotional and substantive content. A distinction cannot merely be drawn between France and her former dependents and Britain and her African ties. African attitudes toward the French metropole run the gamut from truculence to friendly identification. A strategic factor determining the relationship between the European power and its former colonies has been the timing and the nature of the nationalist movement relative to the achievement of independence.

France and the Communauté: With a boldness that has since become his trademark, President De Gaulle in 1958 offered France's sub-Saharan dependencies a choice of complete independence or continued association with the metropole in a French *Communauté*.[12] The *Communauté* provided for republican status for its members, their Prime Ministers composing an executive council presided over by President De Gaulle. Of the thirteen French African territories only Guinea resisted the temptation of continued security and economic advantage inherent in economic and political association with France and voted for complete independence. But after Guinea set the precedent the *Communauté* disintegrated. The break-up of the Mali Federation spelled the death warrant for the *Communauté*, enabling Mali, without resort to a referendum and without reference to France, to proclaim herself outside the *Communauté*— which in turn made it necessary for France to grant Senegal independent status. The disintegration of the Mali Federation in 1960 set the rest of French West Africa in a turmoil. All of the states sought new arrangements with France which would permit them to preserve the economic benefits of the colonial liaison and at the same time enable them to keep up with their neighbors in the race for international status and prestige.

The *Communauté* institutions—the Senate, Council of Prime Ministers, and Secretariat—ceased to function as each country or group of countries negotiated independence. In face of the inevitable, De Gaulle agreed to grant independence to the Entente states of Ivory Coast, Upper Volta, Dahomey, and Niger and to the five Central African States and Mauritania as well. The Constitution of the *Communauté* was subsequently

---

[12] This was to replace the French Union under which the African territories in 1949 had been granted a degree of internal autonomy and representation in the French Assembly.

altered so that independence did not necessarily mean loss of membership. The five Central African States and Mauritania, for example, still consider themselves members. But within two years of its founding every member Republic had requested, and was granted, complete independence. Constitutional relationships however are less significant than the actual degree of interdependence existing between France and her former territories. With the exception of Guinea and Mali—and even here the situation is changing—a close relationship and dependence has persisted.

Two elderly men, one black, the other white, both long in public service and both "Frenchmen," are primarily responsible for the perpetuation of French influence and for the support that the West African and Equatorial African States have provided France in the international sphere. President Houphouet-Boigny, at 58, is one of the older African nationalist leaders and shares much of the paternalism and pragmatism that characterize De Gaulle's outlook on Africa. Not bothered by Nkrumah's phobia about economic independence and neo-colonialism, Houphouet-Boigny openly acknowledges that he has asked France to continue to supervise the economic and technical progress of his country until the Ivory Coast has itself developed requisite internal capacity. French assistance to her former African wards is consistent with this trust. In 1961 France delivered fifty million dollars in technical assistance, financial aid, and market subsidies—more than twice as much as total United States aid to sub-Saharan Africa during that year.

The extent of economic dependence is suggested by France's monopoly of trade. Between 60 and 70 per cent of Ivory Coast trade in 1962, for example, was in the franc zone. Because the country is pro-French and has been relatively stable, French investors have flocked to build factories, and an unusually large number of French nationals from Algeria and the mainland have immigrated to or have remained in the Ivory Coast.

Although risking accusations of neo-colonialism, Houphouet-Boigny has received grudging respect from the leaders of the more radically independent states. Until 1963 he managed to keep internal opposition to a remarkable minimum by rapidly Africanizing the administration, by "promoting" potential dissenters to responsible governmental positions, and by effectively utilizing French assistance to deliver the goods of "modernization." Nearly half of all school-age children in the Ivory Coast are in school—one of the highest percentages in sub-Saharan Africa. Nonetheless, in January 1963, within a few days of the assassination of Togo's Sylvanus Olympio, Houphouet-Boigny was himself faced with considerable opposition. In the ensuing crisis three Ministers were required to resign, and a state security court was established providing for two months' detention. Even the Ivory Coast was not to be exempt from the weighty problems of reconciling democracy with the matters of internal security of the state.

Although economic interdependence has always been a major factor

holding France and he   ritories together, one must not ignore
the unusual appreciat'   athy for French problems and culture
that is shared by former Frenc.. African leaders. Even Guinea's Sékou
Touré notes that the first diplomatic envoy independent Guinea named
was the representative to France, and had De Gaulle been able to over-
come his pique over Guinea's option for independence, France might
have maintained both her national pride and friendly relations with the
first sovereign state of French West Africa. Senegal's Léopold Senghor
demonstrated a more sophisticated reaction when he observed in 1959 that
France needed ties with black Africa psychologically even more than she
did economically.

Another illustration of a sympathetic concern for France was the
sincere efforts of the independent French African states (excluding
Guinea, Mali, and Morocco) to mediate the French Algerian War. They
consistently offered compromise plans and refused to condemn France
outright for her oppressive role in Algeria.

Britain and the Commonwealth. Much has been written about the
different philosophies of colonial rule of France and Great Britain, the
two major imperial powers. What seems more important, particularly
with reference to the future, is the surprising difference in their respective
relations with their former dependencies.

The rejuvenation of France and her return to a leading role in Africa
is certainly one of the more remarkable performances of the postwar era.
Firmly entrenched at the hub of the European Common Market, France
has been able to employ the political and economic revolution under way
in Europe to complement her capacity to cope with the African Revolution. The former French African territories, in many respects, are more
closely linked to France as independent states than they were as dependent
territories. Through the agency of France they have all become associate
members in the European Common Market.

Although in contrast to France there was never any doubt as to Britain's
ultimate aim of granting complete independence to her African wards—
hopefully within the Commonwealth—demands for independence have
seemed invariably to outrun British willingness to disengage. Pragmatic,
piecemeal, often vacillating, British disengagement policy has lacked the
imagination and boldness of France. Whereas France has won the respect
and cooperation of her former dependencies, Britain has more often
reaped hostility and bitterness. The reasons for this ironic but important
difference in the posture taken by former dependencies to the two major
colonial powers are complex and even obscure, but by and large reflect
diverse colonial legacies and distinctive disengagement policies. The
formalism and the detached attitude of British colonial rule, in contrast
to that of France, is exemplified by an emphasis on treaties, charters, and
agreements.

The philosophy of indirect rule, which served to minimize contact between ruler and ruled, contributed to the extraordinary success of British imperial rule over the centuries, but though this policy may have won the respect and even the awe of subject peoples it rarely engendered a sense of equality, affection, or comradeship. British institutions brought to Africa were marked "For Europeans Only" or were explicitly tailored for the African environment. It is inconceivable, for example, that a Kenyan or a Ghanaian should sit in the British House of Commons. But African faces in the Chamber of Deputies were considered normal and proper. A Nigerian member of the British Cabinet is an incongruous idea, whereas French African citizens have upon occasion served as ministers in the French Government. Although France failed in her grandiose dream of absorbing her overseas territories into a greater cultural and political union, the institutional manifestations of that philosophy have left a legacy of understanding and an inclination to cooperate for mutual advantage that is conspicuously missing among the former British territories.

Whereas the mystique of French involvement in Africa arrogantly assumed a superiority of French culture that would naturally absorb indigenous systems, Britain's colonial rule has been uncomfortably self-conscious. French commitment of men and resources was regarded as an investment in a community; Britain's involvement has been perceived either in terms of a return on an investment or, in the postwar period, as an atonement for a long period of self-conscious colonial rule and exploitation. The point is not the difference in attitude and policy per se, but rather the frame of reference within which the former African subjects consequently view their old masters. Mamadou Dia, former Prime Minister of Senegal, in his important work, *African Nations and World Solidarity,* makes this point well. Referring to the relationship of France and the then existing Mali Federation, he noted, "The older or father nation—France, in this instance—places at the disposal of the sister nations seeking development, its knowledge, its productions, and organizational techniques. . . ." [13]

The leaders of the former British territories, sensitive to the condescending and often embarrassed nature of British rule, are more inclined to believe and to act on the belief that Britain is obligated by a sense of guilt to share her wealth with the new African states. Kwame Nkrumah expresses the attitude of many leaders of the former British territories. "The flowing tide of African nationalism sweeps everything before it and constitutes a challenge to the colonial powers to make just restitution for the years of injustice and crime committed against our continent." [14] In former British Africa, the African is more inclined to blame his economic and cultural backwardness on his former colonial

[13] Mamadou Dia, *African Nations and World Solidarity* (New York: Frederick A. Praeger, Inc., 1961), p. 95.
[14] United Nations General Assembly, Fifteenth Session (Sept. 23, 1960).

rulers, who are charged alike with prohibiting indigenous development and of failing to develop the country as their responsibility required.

A sense of racial hostility and inequality is also more apparent in former British than French territories, not only as a consequence of relatively greater European settlement, but as a product of the relative aloofness and segregation that characterized British colonial practice.

The leaders of former French Africa are inclined to view their interest and France's as mutual. Familiar with French institutions and culture as participants and contributors, they do not view the continued presence of expatriate administrators and association in the Common Market as a threat to their independence, or as a slight to their racial dignity. In the former British territories, however, independence has been followed by a tendency to sever the links that persisted after independence, and to replace the remaining British expatriates with a rapidity that has nearly everywhere threatened the stability of the new states. Among the former French territories, on the other hand, the continued presence of Frenchmen, French culture, and institutions is not regarded as a mortgage on independence.

In Tanganyika, Ghana, Uganda, and even Nigeria there seems to be a compulsion to eradicate all reminders of British culture and influence. Britain's motives are suspect and frequently challenged. Whereas the former French territories have supported French foreign policy even when it was inconsistent with African nationalism, Britain's former colonies have been quick to criticize British policy. Ghana condemned Great Britain's support of India in that Commonwealth member's border war with China. Uganda and Tanganyika censured Britain's role in the Katanga-Congo reunification crisis of late 1962. With tongue in cheek the Uganda spokesman raised the possibility of ousting Great Britain from the Commonwealth. Threats were made by Britain's former African dependencies to boycott British firms with interests in Katanga. The government-supported press in Ghana has accused Great Britain, along with the United States, of being responsible for the bomb attacks on President Nkrumah.

The reaction of former British Africa to associate membership in the European Common Market is particularly revealing. Whereas all fourteen members of the UAM are associate members in the Common Market, the former British territories have vehemently refused a similar arrangement.[15] Spokesmen from East Africa even questioned Britain's motives in attempting to bring her former African territories into the Common Market and suggested that they were only being used to further British interests. But the crucial argument is that there is a fear that involvement in the European Common Market might detract from their independence. Tom Mboya of Kenya expressed this view in an article written to explain

[15] Sierra Leone must be excepted.

why East African leaders were against European Common Market membership:

> This fact reveals the crude European colonial mentality of reaping advantages below the table, while claiming that they are serving our best interests. It also reveals the kind of encroachment on our political independence we are likely to experience again once we hand our economic institutions to European countries.[16]

In contrast to the French *Communauté*, which has had a chaotic past, the Commonwealth is firmly established, has a long and continuous history, and would seem to provide Britain and her former dependencies with an extraordinary opportunity to structure their relationships to mutual advantage. The Commonwealth, however, is undergoing considerable change, and in face of Britain's reappraisal of her obligations to the Commonwealth *vis-à-vis* entry into economic and political union with Europe, its very future is in doubt. The new African states have done little to strengthen the Commonwealth and have in fact on a number of occasions seriously weakened it in their efforts to further the African Revolution. The Commonwealth became multiracial in 1950 (to South Africa's open disgust), but it was Ghanaian and later Nigerian membership that signaled a marked change in this extraordinary international association.

Conscious of the dangers to the preservation of the Commonwealth from political dissension, Britain has traditionally sought to emphasize the economic implications of the Commonwealth bond and to avoid allowing it to become an arena for the expression of interstate conflict. The African members, however, are not so inclined, and since 1960 the Commonwealth has been battered and rent by political and racial discord. The presence of South Africa in the Commonwealth was particularly irksome to the new African members. The March 1961 Commonwealth meetings were viewed with considerable trepidation by Great Britain, for it was inevitable that an attempt would be made to expel South Africa. Great Britain sought acceptance of a compromise whereby apartheid would be roundly condemned but South Africa might be allowed to remain in the Commonwealth. For the new African states, however, the issue brooked no compromise, and Prime Minister Verwoerd led his country out of the Commonwealth before the Afro-Asian majority drummed it out.

Trade and historical links between South Africa, the United Kingdom, and other charter members of the club are considerable. Rather than sever these ties Britain retained the option of continuing informally to make available to South Africa the economic advantages of Commonwealth membership—as had been done earlier in the case of Ireland and

---

[16] *East African Standard* (Dec. 7, 1962).

Burma. The African members of the Commonwealth, and nationalist leaders in potential member states, however, were prepared to use every means at their disposal to force an irreconcilable breach between Britain and South Africa. In April 1961, a month after the disruptive meeting that witnessed the withdrawal of South Africa, Kenya's Tom Mboya warned publicly that any attempt by Britain to keep South Africa surreptitiously in the family might lead African and Asian states to reconsider the relative value of the Commonwealth tie.

The extraordinary number of African students studying in France and the United Kingdom is a guarantee that the relations between the metropole and the former dependencies will continue long into the future. But it is not simply the presence of thousands of young Africans in the United Kingdom and France that is significant. These expatriate African students are highly organized, and despite the thousands of miles that separate them from Lagos, Freetown, or Conakry, they are intimately involved in the political life of their respective nations and in the politics of African liberation.

The students are a political force in their own right, as every African politician realizes, and one of the most important constituencies in determining the success of a party or leader is to be found not in Africa but in London or Paris. African politicians exiled in London or Paris, awaiting either the advent of self-government or a coup d'état, build their reputations and followings among the African colony. In the universities and *bistros* tomorrow's philosophies and speeches are formed and sharpened, and in the process a new generation of party leaders emerges. Tribal, party, and regional factions, perfectly mirroring those at home, contest with one another for leadership and influence.

Some return home in triumph to important jobs and positions of influence. Others, either because they have failed to acquire the requisite educational credentials or because they are identified with the wrong faction or party, linger on as "professional students" or return home embittered and angry. The heavy flow of students to the metropole is not always well channeled and it is not always those that are capable of higher education that make the journey. It has been estimated that the number of African students who find their way to London without a place in a university or school is more than 30 per cent of the total.[17]

Until very recently, education abroad—almost anywhere—was a ticket to wealth and influence. But by 1963, only a few independence struggles remain to be fought. Available jobs in newly independent countries are being rapidly filled and more and more African students are anxiously contemplating their future. While they are in pursuit of knowledge and technology they see their relatively uneducated contemporaries filling the rapidly diminishing number of important jobs. As postwar revolutions in the Middle East and Southeast Asia have so vividly demon-

[17] *The New York Times* (April 3, 1962).

strated, unused intellectual capacity is a most powerful generator of
human destruction. Although it may seem somewhat premature to concern ourselves about an unemployed intelligentsia in Africa, the problem
may be nearer than we think, particularly in some West African countries. Within the next decade we may witness a second-generation revolution involving the toppling of the professional revolutionaries by the
returning intelligentsia since it is certain that a struggle for positions of
influence and decision between these two groups will take place. Too
young to have participated in the first revolution, these frustrated young
men with their London and Paris degrees, unless productively occupied,
may plan and execute the next one.

As we have pointed out, understanding and cooperation between
former French colonies and the metropole are considerably greater than
is the case with Great Britain and her former dependencies. Nevertheless the relationships in both instances are based upon a recognition—
either willingly or reluctantly accepted—of continuing mutual dependency. The relationship of independent African states to their former
rulers is a new and yet to be fully determined aspect of the international
relations of the latter half of the twentieth century. A successful reorder-
ing of these relations is crucial—not only to order and security in Africa
but in Europe as well.

PAN-AFRICANISM—OPPRESSED RACISM OR NEW UNITY?

New African states, through no fault of their own, are caught up in a
political dilemma inherent in the particular epoch in which they achieved
their independence. They aspire toward the most contemporary forms of
political organization—state socialism, mass democracy, and transnational
union—yet are reluctant to forego the strengths and follies which characterized the era of rampant European nationalism—jingoism, mer-
cantilism, and expansionism. At a time when Europe stolidly faces the
prospect of continental federation, African leaders are trying to create
a sense of national unity among traditionally Balkanized peoples. Yet
for more than a decade these same leaders have had an intense and
unique vision of a powerful and prosperous unified Africa.

Pan-Africanism, a convenient catchword for a sense of common destiny
shared by many African nationalists, has changed so much in emphasis
and meaning since the phrase was coined and conjures up so many
different and sometimes conflicting visions that it is difficult to analyze.
Our purpose here is to discuss some of the meanings that have become
attached to the term and evaluate the idea as a motivation for political
association in Africa.

In his outstanding work on Pan-Africanism, Colin Legum suggests a
possible parallel with Zionism, and it is true that both originated in the
"diaspora" and expressed the passionate longing of group suffering dis-

crimination for dignity and for a homeland.[18] Marcus Garvey, the Jamaican "Negro Moses," and spokesman for Negro unity and racism in New York during the early decades of the twentieth century, put forth a plan for establishing a Negro nation in Africa which has been described as "Black Zionism." [19] A Pan-African movement led by the late W. E. B. DuBois gained a large following at about the same time. DuBois significantly realized that race, as an organizing force among international Africans, was less important than the discrimination that color had brought to the black man. Although he played down race in favor of an emphasis on equality and civil rights in America and Africa, he effectively laid the basis for the larger international unity of colored people that has been frequently emphasized at Bandung and elsewhere since 1955.

The Fifth Pan-African Congress held at Manchester in 1945 marked the transition of leadership away from an emphasis on the solidarity of the colored peoples of the world toward African nationalism and unity. But though its functions and emphasis have changed somewhat, Pan-Africanism has remained a peculiar blend of Garvey's racialism and DuBois' social consciousness. In one sense, of course, these two themes are but opposite sides of the same coin. For confronted with the continued existence of colonialism and the emergence of neo-colonialism, and still smarting from the memory of his own period of serfdom, the Pan-African movement is inclined to deny "whites" a future on the newly discovered continent. Yet, in a more positive sense, Pan-Africanism represents a search for a new basis for personal and group pride. Making his color a virtue by necessity, the contemporary African emphasizes economic and political unity as a means of achieving continental self-control and international significance.

Of the independent African states, Ghana is by far the most conspicuously enthusiastic about a strong political and economic "United States of Africa." Nkrumah bases his philosophy on the fragmented nature of the independence struggles in the dependent and newly independent states of Africa. They are much more vulnerable, he argues, to neo-colonialism and imperialism through economic control by Western states, but if Africa were united, neo-colonialism would no longer be a threat.

Although there are serious cracks in the façade of Pan-Africanism, most African heads of state would agree with Legum's outline of a general "program" of Pan-African priorities—though they would differ on matters of means and timing. Shortened and paraphrased, these priorities

[18] Colin Legum, *Pan-Africanism: A Short Political Guide* (New York: Frederick A. Praeger, Inc., 1962).
[19] "Pan-Africanism: New Aspirations of an Old Movement," *Roundtable*, 49 (Sept., 1959) pp. 345-350.

make a good statement of what Pan-Africanism implies: (1) independence and no white domination in Africa, (2) African unity, (3) national over tribal loyalties, (4) "African" socialism, (5) electoral democracy (one man, one vote), (6) positive intervention (material and moral) in aiding independence movements, (7) anti-colonialism and solidarity of colored peoples, (8) international political noninvolvement except in Africa, (9) African cultural rediscovery and adaptation of Western progress to African personality.[20]

African unity attained new heights at Addis Ababa in 1963. On May 25, hereafter to be known as African Solidarity Day, thirty heads of state signed an all-African charter which provides for an Organization of African Unity composed of an Assembly of Heads of State, a Council of Ministers, a Secretariat, and a Commission of Mediation, Conciliation, and Arbitration. It is still not certain whether the new Pan-African organization will effectively eclipse existing groupings. But it is evident that the Casablanca and Monrovia divisions will no longer exist, at least in their present forms. On his return from the Conference, Tanganyika's President Nyerere is reported to have said that the new organization rendered all other charters, including PAFMECSA, unnecessary.[21] In August Guinea's Sékou Touré sounded the death knell when he officially renounced the Ghana-Guinea-Mali Union and the Casablanca Charter.

The Addis Summit Conference also brought agreement on strategy to be employed to rid the continent of the remnants of European domination. The heads of state called on all African countries to sever diplomatic and consular relations with South Africa and Portugal. A resolution was passed calling for the closing of all ports and airports to South African and Portuguese ships and aircraft. To translate words into action the conference established a nine-nation committee with its headquarters in Dar es Salaam to coordinate assistance from African states to national liberation movements.[22] Guinea's Sékou Touré urged that every independent African state subscribe 1 per cent of its budget for this crusade. The heads of state further resolved to establish and equip a volunteer corps in their respective countries to assist the liberation of the remaining dependent territories.[23]

It is certain that a number of fundamental secret agreements and plans were made on the strategy to be employed to end white domination in the South of Africa. There is reason to believe, for example, that the heads of state set a date by which all foreign rule must be ended if combined military action was to be avoided. Uganda's Prime Minister Milton

[20] Colin Legum, *op. cit.*
[21] *Tanganyika Standard* (May 27, 1963).
[22] The nine nations are Tanganyika, Ethiopia, Algeria, The United Arab Republic, Uganda, Guinea, Congo, Senegal, and Nigeria.
[23] The coincidence of the Addis Ababa Conference and the racial demonstrations in Birmingham, Alabama, led to a resolution expressing deep concern at racial discrimination, particularly in the United States.

Obote offered his country as a training base for the military forces, and it would appear that this offer was accepted.[24] In the economic field, the Addis Conference decided that a preparatory commission be established to investigate the possibility of an all-African free trade area, a common external tariff, a raw materials stabilization fund, coordination of transport, establishment of road, air, and maritime companies, an African payment and clearance union, and a Pan-African monetary zone.

Although Pan-Africanism is now a recognized slogan everywhere in Africa, it had its early strength in British West Africa. The French West African political leaders, however, are responsible for developing the parallel philosophy of *Négritude*—a term coined by the West Indian poet Aimé Cesaire. While the British West African idea of Pan-Africanism had its psychological appeal to an oppressed race, it was essentially pragmatic and its "program" was political in nature. Négritude, however, is a more esthetic and philosophical concept, best expressed through literature and scholarship. In the words of Léopold Senghor, its foremost spokesman, "Négritude is the whole complex of civilized values—cultural, economic, social, and political—which characterize the black peoples, or, more precisely the Negro-African world. . . . The sense of communion, the gift of myth-making, the gift of rhythm, such are the essential elements of Négritude which you will find indelibly stamped on all the works and activities of the black man." [25]

Some have styled Négritude as neo-traditionalism.[26] But it is too sophisticated and syncretistic to be left at that. Beier seemed puzzled that the French African should have taken up the idea of Négritude more enthusiastically than the British African, who was much less "won over" to British culture and whose native traditions had been given more chance to survive. Perhaps not a small part of the impetus toward Négritude was the influence of the existentialist emphasis of self-identity and purpose brought to West Africa by students returning from Paris universities. Certainly Négritude is an intellectual movement and has little mass appeal. Its basic limits were defined by Beier, "It became a battle cry, a slogan. It served to draw together all those who were striving to rediscover their African identity." Obviously, most Africans even in the French colonies had never had an opportunity to lose their "African identity"! These were the people Cesaire was cheering when he wrote:

Hooray for those who never invented anything. Hooray for those who never conquered anything, but who, in awe, give themselves up to the essence of things. . . .[27]

[24] Algeria offered 10,000 revolutionary veterans.
[25] Léopold Senghor, *West Africa* (Nov. 4, 1961), p. 1211.
[26] Ulli Beier, "In Search of an African Personality," *Twentieth Century*, 165 (April, 1959), pp. 343-49.
[27] *Ibid.*

Although the audience for existential poetry is understandably small, the movement has not been without its utility. In its championing of the underdog, it has provided the same kind of identity as DuBois' Pan-Africanism with the underdeveloped former colonial nations of Asia. Léopold Senghor has identified the bond among the *tiers monde* as "alienation" from the Western world, which not only exploited the colored peoples of Africa and Asia but continues to reject them.[28]

Although Africans from non-French territories have never evinced great enthusiasm for the esthetics or philosophy of Négritude, Nkrumah has popularized the related term "African Personality." The frequent reference to African Personality is not an attempt to define a national character common to the entire continent; it is rather more of a defense of syncretism and a refusal to be "ashamed" of indigenous culture and behavior. When the politician invokes the slogan of African Personality, he is affirming his confidence in the basic forces of creativity in his nation and among the colored races of the continent. It is an attempt to dramatize the fact that modern life in Africa is distinctive and not just a shabby copy of the Western world.

In short, the invocation of African Personality and Négritude is both a defense and an appeal: a defense before the West of apparent aberrations in familiar institutions, and an appeal to Africans to feel pride in their progress and not consider it merely "second-hand" and made in Europe.

Pan-Africanism is mainly the credo of those Africans who have been involved in a white society and to their discomfiture have found themselves categorized by color and continent rather than as individuals. Thus Négritude and Pan-Africanism are attempts to cope with an imposed and not a spontaneous situation. This distinction, though subtle, is important for it helps to explain the peculiarly detached concept of "black brotherhood."

Brotherhood through color-consciousness was not endemic to African society but was learned from the European, who presupposed communality based on color, since that seemed to be the most conspicuously "African" characteristic. Thus, racial consciousness as a basis for political, social, and economic unity is not inherent, and therefore is susceptible to human manipulation, as African leaders have been quick to see.

But Pan-Africanism is more than a slogan to be employed on the political hustings. There are in Africa and among Africans some basic similarities which give substance to the slogan and provide a sense of common identity. It is possible to identify five general areas of similarity which together provide focus and unity to Pan-Africanism viewed both as a philosophy and as a plan of action.

[28] Léopold S. Senghor, *African Socialism,* American Society of African Culture, New York (1959).

1. *A Common Colonial Experience.* Perhaps the most intensely perceived commonality is the realization that all of Africa was colonized. Thus independence in every case has meant the throwing off of an alien yoke. The unity Africans feel under the aegis of a colonial past is fired by a determination to join together to rid the continent of every vestige of European domination.

2. *The Timing of Independence.* If the new African states are unified by a shared history of colonial subjugation, they also have experienced cohesion by virtue of their having achieved independence within a very few years of each other; they have jointly made their mass debut into the international realm. Sharing a sense of inexperience, a need for a compensating bravo, and having been thrust suddenly into the vortex of historic international alignments and feuds, they have naturally moved closer together in recognition of a common need and mutual understanding of one another's problems. The simultaneous emergence of the new African states on the world scene has demonstrated to them the strength that their unity can wield. The changing character of the United Nations, from an arena for the exercise of Euro-American power politics to an organization dedicated to aiding the transition of dependent and underdeveloped nations, bears ample testimony to the potential of this newly emergent unity. Indeed the exciting discovery that together the African states can effectively apply moral and political pressure to force the mighty and privileged states to cater to African needs and interests has demonstrated the importance of unity to African states as disparate as Ethiopia and Ghana.

3. *Economic and Social Underdevelopment.* Although his was a documentary on the absence of unity, Habib Bourguiba of Tunisia nonetheless touched on an important factor of cohesion when he said that the Arab States "are united only in poverty." [29] Because they have been able to blame continental poverty on imperialist exploitation and colonialism, the African nations can regard their underdevelopment as a common challenge and not as an embarrassing disgrace. Thus the challenge and excitement of development also provide a degree of unity and common purpose. A realization that they are all in the same boat has given impetus to the formation of Africa-wide development institutions. To this end efforts are being made to establish an African Development Bank and an African Common Market. The United Nations Economic Commission for Africa (ECA), with its permanent headquarters in Addis Ababa, has rapidly assumed the lead in the attempt to coordinate African development. A UNESCO study and subsequent conference on higher education has provided a twenty-year plan to raise the number of students in higher education from the present 30,000 to 247,000.

The activities of the Commission for Technical Cooperation in Africa

[29] William S. Ellis, "Nasser's Other Voice," *Harper's Magazine*, June 1961, p. 58.

South of the Sahara provide further evidence of the unified nature of development. Formed in 1950 the CTCA is an organization comprising twenty-two member states, with the object of promoting technical co-operation within the countries of tropical Africa. Its activities have been manifold and varied. In 1962 it sponsored a symposium on the problems of unemployed youth. Representatives from most African states as well as delegates from the United Nations, ILO, and UNESCO met to exchange information and experience on a problem of increasing importance.

A more subtle but equally important aspect of the "politics of poverty" is the wide range of tolerance that even competing African leaders extend to one another. Because they share an acute knowledge of the problem of capital formation and budgetary brinkmanship, national leaders of every stripe condone the game of playing off the East against the West. There has evolved a kind of comradeship and tolerance built around the gamesmanship of procuring external assistance. In the life and death struggle for external aid, understandably very little significance is attached to the source of the assistance, and it is not treated as an indication of political alignment. On this score Africa's leaders have shown greater sophistication than observers from the East and the West. Whereas official American spokesmen were quick to write off Guinea as a Soviet satellite, the leaders of the neighboring African states rightfully, as subsequent events have shown, did not equate the acceptance of Russian aid with evidence of membership in the Soviet bloc.

4. *Racial Self-consciousness.* We have devoted an entire chapter to this important subject. Here we need only note its particular relevance to Pan-African unity. Racial consciousness permeates all the factors that tend toward a sense of Pan-Africanism. Colonialism and alien domination are important, but more important still is the fact that the oppressors in every case were white and the oppressed black. Pan-Africanism is above all else an expression of outraged pride that has grown up in response to the European assumption of inherent racial inequality.

5. *Communalism as an Indigenous Way of Life.* The spokesmen of Pan-Africanism are quick to claim that a predilection for continental unity flows naturally from an indigenous habit of communal life. "African socialism" in the last analysis is built upon this heritage of cooperation, and "socialist unity" is possible because of the universality of this phenomenon. To the extent to which this traditional communalism leads the new states to similar socialist societies it is conductive to closer union, for as Nyerere has written,

> Modern African Socialism can draw from its traditional heritage the recognition of society as an extension of the basic family unit. But it can no longer confine the idea of the socialist family within the limits of the tribe, nor indeed, of the nation. For no true African socialist can look at a line drawn on a map and say "the people on this side of the line are my

brothers, but those who happen to live on the other side of it can have no claim on me. Every individual on this continent is his brother." [30]

African socialism is quite unlike the scientific socialism of Marx, the totalitarian socialism of the Chinese People's Republic, or the philosophical utopianism of the Fabians. Above all it is pragmatic; its expression is dictated by the exigencies of the day-by-day African scene. In common with other aspects of the developing African political philosophy it is syncretistic—confusing to the intellectual purist but basically a sagacious approach that permits Africa's new leaders to tailor their politics to native cloth. Thus, even though African "socialism" is expounded in different languages and terms, as a general theory it rests less on economic doctrine then on the demand for social justice. It is a unifying foundation to African politics and an important concept in the universal discourse of Pan-Africanism.

SOME REFLECTIONS

In this chapter we have attempted to identify and describe the major forces promoting and obstructing unity and Pan-Africanism. We have found generally that the more radical mobilization regimes have laid claim to the spirit of Pan-Africanism and have deployed themselves to extend the influence of their highly centralized, relatively totalitarian systems.

The discrediting of colonially inspired transnational unions and institutions has led the African states to a quest for a new basis for cooperation and union. The frustrations inherent in the quest for unity are implicit in the remarks of a Congolese delegate at an all-African labor convention held in Dakar—"How easy it seemed to achieve African unity in the old days when the colonial regimes ruled almost the whole continent." [31] African unity was essentially a negative reaction to white racialism. For the vocal nationalists, Pan-Africanism is a political and psychological rebellion against a foreign culture perceived as the divisive influence that long precluded national unity.

Gone is the unifying glue of colonial oppression, while the glory of working for one another's liberation has turned into accusations of interference in the internal affairs of independent states. It is difficult to come to any other conclusion but that there is little in the past or current history of Africa to suggest that Pan-African unity is either natural or that it will be easily achieved.

The only basis of effective operational unity seems to be that based upon similar political ideologies and governmental systems. As the new nations tend toward greater rather than less divergence on this score, the

[30] Julius K. Nyerere, *UJAMAA, The Basis of African Socialism, Tanganyika Standard,* Dar es Salaam (1961).
[31] *The New York Times* (Jan. 14, 1962).

likelihood of Pan-African unity grows correspondingly dim. Aware that Pan-African unity requires compatible if not identical political systems and ideologies, Pan-Africanist leaders, as exemplified by President Nkrumah, have not hesitated to attempt to engineer the emergence of new African states accordingly. Within those independent states characterized by less militant political systems, the supporters of the Ghanaian model are busily at work encouraging alterations in the existing systems.

The late George Padmore had a vision of a United States of Africa that, despite the numerous maneuvers for personal and circumscribed national influence, still inspires a host of young Pan-Africanists who are determined, and who one day may succeed in turning this dream into reality.

In our struggle for national freedom, human dignity and social redemption, Pan-Africanism offers an ideological alternative to Communism on the one side and Tribalism on the other. It rejects both white racialism and black chauvinism. It stands for racial co-existence on the basis of absolute equality and respect for human personality. Pan-Africanism looks above the narrow confines of class, race, tribe and religion. In other words, it wants equal opportunity for all. Talent to be rewarded on the basis of merit. Its vision stretches beyond the limited frontiers of the nation-state. Its perspective embraces the federation of regional self-governing countries and their ultimate amalgamation into a United States of Africa. In such a Commonwealth, all men, regardless of tribe, race, colour or creed, shall be equal and free. And all the national units comprising the regional federations shall be autonomous in all matters of common interest to the African Union. This is our vision of the Africa of Tomorrow—the goal of Pan-Africanism.[32]

And whether Africa is to play a major role in world affairs and is to contribute to, rather than threaten, world peace depends in great part on the realization of that goal.

[32] George Padmore, *Pan-Africanism or Communism?* (London: Dobson Books Limited, 1956), p. 379.

VIII
Africa in World Politics

One need not be a prophet to predict that in the coming years the arrival at the United Nations of a wave of young nations, most of them African, will continue to shake the world's equilibrium.—Mamadou Dia.

We have sought up to this point to show, with the assistance of the general concepts outlined in the first chapter, how Africa's quest for order involves the cumulative impact of problems and challenges. This quest in turn is related to the myriad entanglements of the cold war, and to the interrelationships of that most extensive of all international organizations—the United Nations. The universal human quest for peace on earth is itself in no small part dependent upon the delicacy and sophistication with which the new African states, in Dia's words, "shake the world's equilibrium."

Because the success of this quest for racial dignity and for an improved standard of living (without which human dignity cannot be obtained) depends upon the participation of the entire world community, African development must be examined within the context of international organization and politics.

AFRICA IN THE COLD WAR

As the probability of thermo-nuclear warfare, as a once-and-for-all solution to the East-West struggle, becomes less and less likely, there is a discernable a shift to a contest for the support of the new nations of Africa and Asia. Both the USSR and the United States enter this phase of the cold war with firmly fixed assets and liabilities. The Soviet Union, for example, has effectively dramatized the capacity of a totalitarian government to transform a backward territory rapidly into a modern and powerful state. And to many African leaders it stands as proof that a poor and humiliated people, in the face of imperialist opposition, can turn itself in the space of a single generation into a highly developed and respected nation. An additional asset is Russia's good fortune in having been occupied elsewhere during the nineteenth-century scramble for Africa, with the result that it has not been tainted with the odium of colonialism.

On the other hand, Africa's inheritance of Western languages, political philosophies, and institutions must be chalked up on the debit side of the Russian ledger. This was vividly demonstrated at the 1963 Afro-Asian Peoples' Solidarity Conference hosted by Tanganyika. Although the Soviet and Chinese delegations were the largest and tended to dominate the Conference, English, French, and Arabic were the official languages. Official solidarity was effectively manipulated by the Communists, but after-hours solidarity—probably the most important—took place between French-speaking Guineans, Congolese, and Vietnamese, and between English-speaking Ghanaians, Nigerians, and Indians.

Even more detrimental to the Soviet Union's relations with the African states, is her colossal ignorance of the continent and its peoples. Even Pieter Lessing, who is greatly concerned about the Communist intrusion into Africa, writes that until 1958 the Soviet Union "not only had no organizations working anywhere in Africa south of the Sahara, except the small South African Communist Party, but the Soviet policy makers were so ignorant about Africa that they were incapable of shaping a coherent policy." [1] The continued popularity of the Soviet political and economic model, despite a remarkably inept African policy, indicates the genuine attraction of Communism to nation-building in Africa. The ugly Russian, in so far as Africa is concerned, is a more accurate stereotype than the ugly American and despite many built-in advantages, it is likely that the Soviet Union has been less successful in promoting its brand of economics and politics in Africa than anywhere else in the underdeveloped world.

The migration of thousands of African youth to American, French, British, Russian, and other universities is perceived by the host nations as a unique opportunity to expose the future leaders of the continent to their respective cultures and polities, and hopefully thereby predispose them, upon their return, to favor, support, or even emulate one system rather than the other. The exact number of African students abroad is unknown, but the total probably exceeds fifty thousand. The long-run significance of this extraordinary migration is still to be determined. Russia was relatively slow to grasp the potential political advantages inherent in the provision of higher education to a large number of African youths. In the late 1950's, however, the Soviet Union decided to enter the African field in a big way. Premier Khrushchev himself opened Moscow's Friendship University in October 1960. Lumumba University, as it was subsequently renamed, caters largely to African scholars and has facilities for approximately four thousand students. It is estimated that there are in the Soviet Union, as of 1963, at least eight thousand young African men and women. The Soviet Union's East European allies have also played a major role in the provision of educational facilities for African students. Radio Prague boasts that there are more than three thousand Africans studying in Czechoslovakia. In addition, there are as many as one thousand students in East Germany, and Bulgaria and Poland each have more than five hundred.

Despite the magnitude of this educational operation it has not, from the Communist's point of view, proven entirely successful. The Eastern bloc leaders are only now learning that indiscriminate recruitment of young Africans, with little reference to their intellectual motivation or educational background, is likely to return to Africa a number of disappointed and frustrated young men little inclined to think or speak well of the Communist ideology. In this field too, the Soviet Union's lack of experience in contrast to a long history of accommodating foreign students in Great Braitain, France, and the United States, has contributed to its ineptness and to numerous and costly mistakes. The tendency to cluster African students together in special institutions and dormitories has been interpreted by African students as racial discrimination. Whereas a black face is common in Chicago, Manchester, or Brussels, the appearance of Africans in Prague, Sofia, and Leningrad came as a shock, and from the Communist point of view far too many Africans discovered that racial discrimination was more pronounced on the East then on the West side of the Iron Curtain.

A most dramatic example of the failure of the Eastern bloc's policy of African education occurred in Bulgaria. In February 1963, nearly two hundred African students demonstrated in Sofia against a government ban on their newly formed All African Students Union. Unaccustomed to student demonstrations, the Bulgarian police employed considerable force and a number of African students were injured. The Ghanaian President and Ethiopian Vice-President of the proscribed association were arrested and instructed to leave the country.[2] The incident precipitated a mass exodus of African students from Bulgaria and as of March 1963, about two hundred of the estimated four to five hundred African young men and women had left this Eastern bloc country in anger and disgust. Many complained of racial discrimination which seemed to be condoned by the Communist authorities. Political indoctrination of two hours or more a week added to heavy doses of Communist Party history were aspects of their education which the African students had not anticipated and which they strongly resented. "We soon realized that to study in a Communist country is a bloody waste of

[2] *East African Standard* (Feb. 14, 1963).

time." [3] The Western states were quick to take advantage of this situation. The United States and Great Britain announced a willingness to find places in their universities for qualified students.

This and similar incidents suggest the impact of a Western oriented primary and secondary education on the personalities and values of young Africans. Thus the Communist bloc's policy of favorably influencing Africa through the provision of higher education is seriously hampered by inherited Western values which accompany the African students behind the Iron Curtain. African students already familiar with the ideas of Montesquieu and John Stuart Mill take for granted the right of free speech and assembly, and upon their arrival in the Communist world are struck by contrast. There is little that courses in Marxism and Leninism can do to alter this fact.

It is true that Soviet influence within the Casablanca bloc nations has been relatively considerable. But despite a predilection in Ghana, Mali, and Guinea for economic socialism, single-party totalitarianism, and vehement anti-imperialism, the Soviet Union has been unable to establish firm beach heads for the Communist cause. What seemed to many, including the Russians, to be a Soviet victory in Guinea subsequently turned into a humiliating rout when in 1961 President Touré, angered by discovery of the Russian Embassy's covert support of an emerging political opposition, ordered the expulsion of the Soviet ambassador. Since that date American and French technicians and assistance have been gradually supplanting Soviet aid and influence.

Since its founding late in 1957, the Afro-Asian Peoples' Solidarity Organization has served as a major instrument of Communist penetration into Africa. The permanent secretariat is headquartered in Cairo and the seven-man executive committee is composed of representatives from China, Guinea, Indonesia, Cameroon, Morocco, the United Arab Republic, and the Soviet Union.

In 1961 the related Afro-Asian Solidarity Fund was established and Ismael Touré, Minister of Works and brother of Guinea's President, was elected chairman. To this day Conakry is the financial headquarters of the organization and the source of untold covert contributions to revolutionary movements in African countries. Two bank accounts are maintained in the Bank of Guinea, one in foreign currency and the other in Guinean francs. Total assets are not public knowledge but it is known that at the inception of the Fund the Soviet Union contributed twenty thousand dollars. There are indications that the Fund and the Organization have been liberally employed to further the cause of parties and individuals relatively sympathetic to the East and critical of the West. During the Congo crisis, for example, the Soviet Union took the lead in the formation of a subsidiary International Committee of Aid to Algeria

[3] Statement by an African student upon arrival in West Germany from Bulgaria, *Kenya Sunday Nation* (Feb. 17, 1963).

and the Congo, and urged member organizations to send volunteers to the Congo to assist the Antoine Gizenga faction.[4]

Egypt's gradual disenchantment with Russia in conjunction with the Sino-Soviet rift, has damaged the effectiveness of the AAPSO. This was vividly apparent in Moshi, Tanganyika, during the Afro-Asian Peoples' Solidarity Conference of February 1963. The large Chinese delegation hardly veiled its attempt to take over the movement and even went so far as to seek the expulsion of the Russians on the basis that they were neither African nor Asian. Failing this the Chinese were successful in blocking the Soviet Union's attempt to invite East European observers. African delegates were button-holed in the hotel lobbies and reminded that the Russians were white and would when necessary, identify with the other white colonialists, whereas the Chinese were colored and shared with their African brothers a legacy of European colonial imperialism and exploitation.

Another factor limiting the effectiveness of the AAPSO is the increasing sophistication and pragmatism of Africa's leaders—an important augury of the future. Sophistication was much in evidence at the Moshi Conference. President Nyerere's opening speech, for example, was deliberately cast to warn his guests, particularly the Chinese and Russians, not to use the Organization as a platform for anti-imperialist propaganda or an arena for Sino-Soviet competition. Referring to the cold war and what he terms the "Second Scramble for Africa," Nyerere said,

> Imperialists, old and new, will exploit differences within African nations. . . . Neither should we allow ourselves to think of this new imperialism solely in terms of the old colonial powers. Imperialism is a by-product of wealth and power. We have to be on guard against incursions by anyone. . . . The socialist countries . . . are now committing the same crime as was committed by the capitalists before. On an international level they are now beginning to use wealth for the acquisition of power and prestige.[5]

Most African delegates were aware that the Conference was being used to further competing Communist ends and that the really important issue—liberation of the still dependent peoples of Angola, Mozambique, Southern Rhodesia, and South Africa—was receiving only slight attention.[6] The comments of Tanganyika's Minister for Home Affairs, Oscar

[4] *Afro-Asian Peoples' Solidarity Movement*, Publicity-Research Secretariat (Cairo: Del El-Hana Printing House, 1962), p. 130.

[5] Afro-Asian Peoples' Solidarity Conference, Opening Session, Moshi, Tanganyika (Feb. 4, 1963).

[6] Competition between the Russians and the Chinese sank to such a low level of intrigue that each reportedly sought (with some success) to interfere with the simultaneous translations and distribution of the other's prepared remarks. The Chinese are making a supreme effort to wrest control of the AAPSO from the Soviet Union, and there is evidence to suggest that they have successfully taken over the important Solidarity Fund.

Kambona, at a press conference at the conclusion of the Conference are most revealing. They clearly demonstrate the refusal of African leaders to be regarded as inferior or as a ploy in a game not of their making:

> I think it is high time now those overseas should take recognition that the Africans have also a brain. . . . We in Tanganyika agreed to play host to the Conference because we have confidence in ourselves. . . . We believe in our brain, we do not think that any other race has a more superior brain than ourselves. . . . I do not accept the argument put by our friends overseas that the Africans are the people to be won either by West or by the East. They cannot be played as if they are little boys to be won by whoever is clever.[7]

Although Soviet activity in Africa often appears ill-advised and badly managed it would be inaccurate to conclude that it is completely without effect. One must not lose sight of the fact that whereas the West has had a century or more of experience, serious Soviet involvement in Africa began only recently.[8] It was soon evident that orthodox Marxist-Leninist theory was inappropriate to Africa and that if the Soviet Union were to persist in its view that the African Revolution, had to include a class struggle and a subsequent victory for the proletariat, its policy would be without any effect whatsoever. This realization no doubt contributed to the extraordinary reinterpretation of political philosophy which has occurred in the Soviet Union over the past decade. Thus in one important sense the emergence of Africa has had an impact on the operation and evolution of world Communism. Having decided to join what President Nyerere has termed the second scramble for Africa, the Soviet Union was quick to establish the necessary institutions and programs to compete successfully. A multitude of Soviet-Africa Friendship Associations have been established, beginning with those arranged with the relatively sympathetic Casablanca states. Commissions for cultural cooperation and for communications and information were rapidly set up, and in 1961 Soviet trade delegations in increasing numbers began making the rounds of Africa's capital cities. The Russians have had their greatest success in attempting to manipulate the trade union movement in Africa.

African labor unions have played an important role in the independence struggles of new states. The struggle between the Communist-dominated World Federation of Trade Unions (WFTU) and the Western-dominated International Confederation of Free Trade Unions (ICFTU) has dominated the international labor scene for some years. In 1959 the Soviet Union's efforts to entice African trade unions away from the

---

[7] Press conference, Moshi, Tanganyika (Feb. 12, 1963).

[8] The growth of Russian academic interest in Africa commenced in earnest in 1959 and the establishment of the African Research Institute headed by Professor Potetkin, the doyen of African studies.

ICFTU into the WFTU orbit met with some success when Ghana Trade Union Congress disaffiliated from the ICFTU and, with the assistance and encouragement of the WFTU, took the initiative in establishing a Pan-African labor organization separate from the ICFTU. The argument used to considerable effect in support of an All African Trade Union Federation was that affiliation with the ICFTU was inconsistent with full independence and with a declared policy of cold-war nonalignment.

The influence of the Communist dominated ICFTU in the new All African Trade Union Federation (AATUF) was evident to all who cared to look; for example, four of the six secretaries were associated with WFTU unions. At the Federation's initial Casablanca meeting in May 1961, the arguments of those union leaders who supported continued association with the ICFTU but were nonetheless willing to join the AATUF as well were ignored. An AATUF charter, requiring member unions to disaffiliate from all international labor organizations within ten months was steam-rollered through the meeting after the Tunisian, Nigerian, and several other East and Central African delegates walked out in protest.

Ghana's volatile trade union leader, John Tettegah, declared "total war" on those unions that refused to disaffiliate from the ICFTU and explicitly warned that the new All African Organization would attempt to destroy unions affiliated with ICFTU from within their respective countries; this in fact has occurred.[9] In response to this threat those national unions that had refused to join the AATUF at the price of disaffiliation from the ICFTU met in January 1962 at Dakar where they established their own African Trade Union Confederation (ATUC), supported by labor organizations in the Congo, the former French West and Equatorial states (except Mali and Guinea) and East, Central, and South Africa. Whenever possible, the AATUF, under Ghanaian leadership and doubtless financed by the Afro-Asian Solidarity Fund, has sought to establish rival organizations in those states where the trade union movement is dominated by ICFTU-affiliated unions. While the Kenya Trade Union Federation, which has as its goal the destruction of "the foreigner aided Kenya Federation of Labor," is said to be financially supported by the funds from the WFTU, the Kenya Federation of Labor (KFL), which has been closely identified with the political career of Tom Mboya, is said to receive some four thousand dollars a month from the Western-dominated ICFTU.[10]

Africa's labor unions, in common with numerous other modern membership units, unfortunately are buffeted first one way and then the other by the conflicting currents of the cold war. The fact that most have

[9] Trade unions in Ghana, Mali, Guinea, Morocco, and the United Arab Republic all belong to the AATUF, as well as some small rival unions in countries where the major labor organizations are affiliated with the ICFTU.

[10] Reported by Hilary Ng'weno, *Kenya Daily Nation* (Nov. 9, 1962).

been able to maintain a relatively even keel is another testimony to the rapidly developing sophistication of Africa's young leaders.

In 1962 and 1963 the Chinese People's Republic considerably stepped up its activities in Africa. There is substantial evidence that the new African states will soon not only be required to pick their way through the hazards of the cold war but will be faced with the necessity of juggling the Sino-Soviet conflict as well. In many respects China is in a better position than the Soviet Union to win the support of the new African states. To many of the growing number of African visitors to China that country provides a more appropriate model of economic development and political organization than does the Soviet Union. Chinese trade delegations are today a common sight in even the more remote up-country African towns. Chinese broadcasts beamed to Africa, unheard of five years ago, today total more than seventy hours a week. Unencumbered by international regulations as to frequency modulation and transmission power, Radio China comes in loud and clear from the Cape to Cairo and from Mombasa to Monrovia. Chinese programs beamed in English to East Africa, for example, can be picked up more easily than the BBC or the Voice of America. The programming is excellent, informal, and breezy where The African Service of Radio Moscow, in contrast, is often pedantic and doctrinaire.

Apparently focusing its activities on East Africa, China has been quick to interject its influence into the economic life of Zanzibar, Tanganyika, and Uganda. The price received for cotton at the port of export in Tanganyika in 1963 has been significantly affected by the obviously politically inspired purchases by an agent of the Chinese Government. The price of cotton to the grower, though stabilized by marketing boards, depends in the last analysis on the world market. If China, for example, were to stockpile and then flood the market with cheap cotton, the resulting economic dislocation in Tanganyika and Uganda would surely have political implications. Chinese interest in Africa is definitely on the increase; it is likely that in the next few years Chinese attempts to influence the African Revolution, particularly in East and Central Africa and in Malagasy, will be greatly accelerated.

To some observers a willingness in the Communist world to supply arms and military technical assistance to opposition elements seeking to overthrow newly independent governments or to revolutionary forces attempting to liberate their countries from alien rule is a much more serious matter than subversion within the trade union movement. For obvious reasons it is difficult to document the extent to which such activities are carried on and it is likely that overt evidence of military assistance is but a fraction of the total. The Guinean Army, for one, has received considerable material assistance from the East and under the direction of a sizeable Czechoslovakian military mission has been re-organized along Soviet lines. A military academy established by this

Czechoslovakian military mission, in addition to training future Guinean Army officers, is thought also to be a major institution for instructing students from Angola, Mozambique, and South Africa in guerilla warfare and revolutionary tactics. One aspect of President Nkrumah's leftward shift subsequent to Ghanaian independence has been the substitution of considerable Russian military assistance and advice for British. Hundreds of Ghana's military cadets, for example, are sent to the Soviet Union for military training.

The United States, though honored for its own successful revolution against European imperialism and respected for its high level of material development, is often lumped together with its English- and French-speaking imperialist allies. There is no doubt that America's obligations to its NATO allies has been a constant irritant to Afro-American relations. The problem of balancing support for the important African issue of self-determination for Angola and Mozambique over against the maintenance of friendly relationships with Portugal, particularly in view of the significance to hemispheric defense of the Azores missile tracking base, has been particularly vexing and a frequent embarrassment to American foreign policy. The United States also has been accused, with some justice, of having provided its Portuguese and French NATO allies with arms and ammunition which were subsequently employed against Africans in Algeria and Angola.

Africans identify with the underdog and often take a position against the large and powerful states. This attitude permeates African relations with the West generally and toward the United States in particular; it is believed that Africa's ascendancy and the achievement of international and racial dignity are somehow predicated on a corresponding decline in the fortunes of the mighty. It is difficult to explain in any other way the extraordinary support that Cuba's position has received from many African states, despite the fact that its conflict with the United States is far removed from the African scene. The presence of a Cuban delegate is also indicative. Even more so was the thunderous ovation that greeted his abusive attack upon the United States: "The Cuban people . . . do not want war, and, because of that fight resolutely against Yankee imperialism, the most monstrous murderer of peoples, exploiter of peoples, practicing racial discrimination, lynching our Negro brothers on their territory, corrupting human dignity and blackmailing with atomic war." [11]

Additional aspects of the impact of the cold war on Africa's quest for order, as well as the significance of other international rivalries such as

---

[11] Third Afro-Asian Peoples' Solidarity Conference, Moshi, Tanganyika (Feb. 6, 1963). The author was fortunate to have been living in Moshi, Tanganyika, during the 1963 Conference and recalls vividly how emotionally moved a number of African delegates were by the tone and words of the Cuban speaker's attack upon the United States.

the Israeli-Arab conflict, are treated below in the section dealing with development. Before proceeding to the subject of African development in an international context, it is necessary to view the role of the newly independent African states in the United Nations.

AFRICA IN INTERNATIONAL ORGANIZATIONS

Few among that illustrious group of men that met at San Francisco in 1945 to write a charter for what they hoped would be a United Nations could have had the foresight to know that within seventeen years approximately one in every three of its member states would be African. The United Nations is often justifiably credited with having miraculously survived a number of difficult international crises; but certainly not the least of its accomplishments is the flexibility it has demonstrated in its absorption, since 1955, of thirty new African member states. When it is recalled that many critical General Assembly motions require two-thirds majority, the importance of the fact that as of 1963, 34 of the United Nations 102 member states are African, is more fully appreciated. Whereas in 1955 the African territories were a subject for discussion in the General Assembly, today they possess on many important matters a virtual veto in that august body. By 1965 there is a strong likelihood that Kenya, Northern Rhodesia, Nyasaland, Zanzibar, and Swaziland will swell this total to nearly forty. This number, when added to the twenty Asian member states, is more than enough to provide the Afro-Asian bloc with a simple majority in what a few short years ago was in effect a white man's club.

The year 1961, which saw the queuing up for United Nations membership of seventeen African states, marked the effective beginning of the African bloc as a power to be reckoned with in the United Nations. It is also from this point that we can usefully date the end of one era in the United Nations history and the commencement of another. The dominant Afro-Asian bloc intends to give the organization quite a different role from that of its traditional function as an arena for the cold war conflict. The Africans, supported by the Asian states, above all else are determined to employ the United Nations as an effective instrument to secure the liberation of the remaining European-dominated territories and to promote their own rapid economic development. As we noted earlier, the African Revolution is inconclusive as long as there is a vestige of white domination on the continent. Without this, national independence, racial dignity, and equality are incomplete. Thus, issues within the United Nations involving questions of colonialism and racial discrimination unite the African delegates to a man.

The 1962 meeting of the United Nations Food and Agriculture Organization (FAO) in Tunis illustrates the particular intensity with which the Africans view the liberation of the remaining European-dominated territories. It is this single-purpose obsession that has sometimes led new African states to employ the United Nations and its related agencies ruthlessly. At the Tunis meeting Ghana's Minister of Agriculture, Krobo Edusei, demanded that the South African delegation withdraw from the meeting. When the South African representative rose to defend the propriety of his presence in a purely technical nonpolitical conference, the African delegates walked out of the meeting. Upon their return they voted to expel the South African delegation. The racial issue, of course, had little to do with the technical subject under discussion, but it obviously was of considerably more importance to the African representatives than the technical purposes of the Conference. South Africa refused to withdraw, and as the African delegates would not meet in the presence of South Africa, the Conference was abruptly ended. The Tunisian chairman, in concluding the meetings, addressed his remarks to the South African delegates. "You have experienced the will of Africa to free itself." [12] In a similar fashion, the Economic Commission for Africa (ECA), meeting in February 1963 in Léopoldville, voted to expel the Republic of South Africa and Portugal and also to relegate France, Great Britain, and Spain to associate membership.[13]

The questions of South Africa, Southern Rhodesia, and Portugal's African territories have come to monopolize the energy of the African bloc in its struggle against the remnants of colonialism. In November 1962 the African bloc was successful in obtaining a sixty to sixteen (twenty-one abstentions) vote in the special political committee of the United Nations General Assembly, recommending that diplomatic and economic sanctions be leveled against South Africa to force it to abandon its policy of racial discrimination. In the ensuing debate in the United Nations Trusteeship Committee the tactics of the Africans brought protests from a Mexican delegate that they were treating the United Nations with contempt; he added that his "country, though sympathetic with the broad aims of the African and Asian nations, would be compelled to reconsider its attitude and abstain on the voting of their major proposals if delegates with different views were denied the right to speak. . . ."[14] Despite numerous private and public requests to temper their demands, if for no other reason than to give them more real effect, the African bloc's resolution urging that United Nation members break off diplomatic relations with South Africa, boycott its goods, and close all ports and airports to South African ships and aircraft was passed in the General Assembly with sixty-seven states voting in favor of the resolution, sixteen against, and twenty-three abstaining. At the same time that most African states were supporting the admission of the Chinese People's Republic they were also demanding the expulsion of the Republic of South Africa.

As even some African spokesmen have come to realize, there is a real danger that the African states, in their passionate insistence on utilizing

---

[12] *East African Standard* (Nov. 7, 1962).
[13] South Africa withdrew from the ECA in July, 1963.
[14] *Tanganyika Standard* (Nov. 3, 1962).

every weapon in the United Nations' arsenal to rid the continent of the remnants of white rule, will destroy the effectiveness of the United Nations in the process. For example, though few would condone Afrikaner apartheid policy in the mandate territory of Southwest Africa, it can hardly be considered a threat to world peace. Yet in November 1962 the African bloc successfully pushed through the General Assembly Trusteeship Committee a resolution calling for the establishment of United Nations observers in South-West Africa on the basis that the situation there was a threat to world peace. The U. S. delegation supported a move to amend the resolution to read that such a situation could lead to a threat to international peace but this was defeated, despite the fact that a paper submitted by a special committee charged with investigating the situation in South-West Africa had reported that the issue was not a threat to international peace.[15] The African states, by successfully engineering the passage of strongly worded resolutions condemning South Africa and calling for severe sanctions, are able to demonstrate their newly acquired power to themselves and to the outside world. The effectiveness of extreme resolutions to achieve these ends in questionable, however, the resolutions calling for sanctions against South Africa leave it up to each member state to take action as it seems fit. When a member of the Labor Party in the British House of Commons asked the Deputy Foreign Secretary whether the government would forbid the sale of arms to South Africa in view of this United Nations resolution, he answered "No." The British delegate to the General Assembly Trusteeship Committee reflected the views of many delegates: "Unsubstantiated accusations of genocide, of threats to the peace of the world and fables about industrial plots designed to keep the indigenous peoples in a position of subjection merely clogged the issues by their extravagance and undermined the clear case against the South African government." [16]

Possibly the Congo situation reveals even better the nature of the United Nations involvement in Africa and the manner in which the African states have sought to employ the United Nations to pursue their own ends. It provides one of the clearest illustrations of major power rivalry in the African arena and one of the machinations of neo-colonialism. The Congo has held center stage in the international arena since 1960. Its bizarre and violent history since its precipitous independence on June 30, 1960, is a Pandora's box of international intrigue, intertribal warfare, schemes of interlocking world-wide industrial cartels, and of competition for power between rival African states and blocs. For the United Nations it has been both challenge and catastrophe and, to the tune of ten million dollars a month, has threatened its very solvency.

[15] It should be added, however, that considerable controversy surrounds this investigation and report. Victorio Carpio of the Philippines, Chairman of the special South-West African Committee, subsequently denied that he had written or approved this controversial report.

[16] *The Sunday Telegraph* (Nov. 25, 1962).

Riots and scattered disorder in 1959 and an awareness that Britain and France were rapidly liberating their dependent African territories led Belgium, early in 1960, to examine the possibility of granting independence to the Congo. Once this issue had been raised there was no turning back, despite the fact that Belgium had done very little to prepare the way for a successful assumption of self-government by the indigenous peoples. At the very outset it was evident that a critical lack of unity, which neighboring independent states had been able to forge during their independence struggles, was to pose a serious threat to the stability of the new state. Rivalry between Lumumba and Kasavubu led to a compromise whereby the former became Prime Minister and the latter President.

There is considerable evidence that both the Soviet Union, through the agency of the Belgian Communist Party, and international capitalist interests were busy at work in the Congo during the five months preceding independence, seeking to enhance or to preserve their respective vested interests.

Less than a week after independence the only potential stabilizing factor in the Congo, the large and well-trained quasi-military Force Publique, revolted against its officers. In July, Belgian troops were parachuted into Léopoldville to protect the large European population eliciting the accusation that she was in effect reoccupying the country. A series of desperate and contradictory cables was flashed from the embattled Congo capital, still gaily decorated with Independence-Day bunting, to the United Nations and to various capital cities including Moscow, Peiping, and Washington. To complicate events further Moise Tshombe took advantage of the confusion to declare mineral-rich Katanga an independent state and himself its president. Stories of mass murder, rape, arson, and of imminent Russian intervention circulated among the nervous capitals of the world and in the corridors of the United Nations. The African delegates, fearful of Western and Communist intervention, were instrumental in bringing about an emergency session of the Security Council which on July 14 authorized the Secretary-General to take the steps necessary, in cooperation with the Central Congo government, to protect lives and property and to oversee the withdrawal of Belgian troops. It is important to note, however, that Dag Hammarskjöld deliberately sought to preclude the involvement of the United Nations in the internal affairs of the Congo.

United Nations troops began to arrive on July 15. For reasons that are still partially shrouded in mystery Lumumba expressed a dissatisfaction with the United Nations' efforts, did a *volte-face,* and cabled Premier Khrushchev to intervene and assist him in driving the Belgians out of the Congo. Despite a United Nations resolution strongly supported by the African bloc—which feared that the Congo debacle would open the door to a new wave of imperial conquest—that all assistance to the Congo should flow through the United Nations, the Soviet Union delivered one hundred three-ton trucks, fifteen troop transports and crews, automatic rifles, and two hundred technicians to Lumumba, at the same time denying their use to the United Nations command.

On September 5 President Kasavubu reacted by dismissing Premier Lumumba, who in turn dismissed the president, while the ensuing confusion permitted Colonel Mobutu to seize power. One of his first acts was to expel the Soviet and East European representatives. This was followed by the arrest and house imprisonment of former Premier Lumumba and then by the expulsion of the Ghanaian and Guinean ambassadors on the charge that they were assisting Lumumba.

In November rivalry between the Casablanca and Monrovia bloc took the form of determining whether to seat a Lumumba or a rival Kasavubu-Mobutu delegation. The African states split along predictable lines and a joint Casablanca and Asian bloc motion to seat the Lumumba delegation was defeated. A motion providing for the recognition of the Kasavubu delegation was accepted, with the stipulation that a special United Nations Committee composed of African states attempt to reconcile the differences between the two Congolese factions and assist in the establishment of a single unified government. It is impossible to tell whether or not the African states might have succeeded in this attempt to reconcile the warring factions; before they had an opportunity to leave for the Congo Lumumba disrupted the plan by escaping from his heavily guarded Léopoldville home. Although he was recaptured, his Vice-Premier, Antoine Gizenga, declared Stanleyville the proper Congo capital and himself Acting Premier in the absence of Lumumba. Gizenga held effective sway over the Eastern Province and at times over parts of Kivu and Katanga as well. The Eastern bloc nations recognized the Gizenga government and the Russian and Czech embassies, which had been thrown out of Léopoldville earlier, and were re-established in Stanleyville.

Stanleyville, Léopoldville, and Elisabethville became African outposts in the cold war. While French and Belgian advisers were actively assisting Kasavubu, Russian and Czech advisers and materials were focusing on Stanleyville. Anxious not to involve itself in the internal problems of the Congo, the United Nations reluctantly prepared to do so in order to avert a civil war which gave every indication of breeding an international holocaust. Things had reached such a state by January 1961 that it was evident the United Nations would either have to play a more powerful role in the Congo or withdraw completely. The Central government forces, those of the Casablanca and Communist-supported Stanleyville regime, as well as Tshombe's secessionist Katangan Army, were all in the field and eager for combat.

In February Lumumba was murdered. In March Katanga's Tshombe, President Kasavubu, and others met in the Malagasy Republic to agree upon and establish a federal arrangement for the Congo. At a subsequent meeting in Léopoldville during April, Tshombe was arrested by the Central government, the Tananarive Agreement was scrapped, and while Tshombe languished in jail a federal constitution was adopted and Cyrille Adoula was made president. In August, Gizenga had a change of heart and agreed to join the new federal government as one of the three vice-presidents, with the result that the Soviet bloc's Congo adventure came to a grinding and ignoble end.

After declaring his most recent intention of cooperating with the Léopoldville government, Tshombe was released and his promise evaded as soon as he made his return to his capital at Elisabethville. Meanwhile, in April, a General Assembly resolution in effect extended the United Nations role to include the task of reorganizing and equipping the Central government's army and authorized the use of force, if necessary, to prevent a civil war. By the summer of 1961 the Congo problem was rapidly shaping into a contest between the Central government, supported by the United Nations and the African bloc, against the copper-rich state of Katanga, which drew its strength from the far flung international interests of the Union Minière and less overtly from the Belgian and British Governments.

A serious outbreak of fighting occurred in August 1961 in the vicinity of Elisabethville between United Nations forces and the Katanga Army, led and augmented by hired European mercenaries. It was this crisis which brought Secretary-General Hammarskjöld to the Congo and, thus, to his tragic and untimely death in the mysterious crash of his personal plane. The Soviet Union's heavyhanded attempt to sabotage the United Nations executive by its insistence upon *Troika* and its effort to block the election of Secretary-General U Thant contributed to a further African disillusionment with Russia's African policy.

In November, with strong support from the African bloc, the General Assembly authorized United Nations forces to assist the Central government in its unification of the Congo and to put an end to Katanga's secession. But as the year ended United Nations and Katanga troops were once again engaged in combat. Throughout 1962 the situation remained confused with sporadic outbursts of violence and rioting in first one and then another part of the country as the specter of anarchy loomed ever closer. It was evident by the summer of 1962 that a solution to the Congo impasse was imperative and was dependent upon agreement between the major powers involved—the United States, Great Britain, Belgium, the two African blocs, and possibly the most powerful of all, the Union Minière. An agreement was gradually hammered out which provided for the integration of the Congo on the basis of a new federal constitution, the absorption of the Katanga gendarmerie into the Congolese Army, the channeling of a considerable part of Katanga revenue derived from the Union Minière into the coffers of the Central government, and a general amnesty for Tshombe and his fellow secessionists. Nevertheless it was evident that severe economic sanctions would have to be applied if Katanga was to be brought into line. Having made this threat the United Nations set a deadline for the acceptance of U Thant's unification plan, which Tshombe, in characteristic style, neither accepted nor rejected. The failure of economic sanctions and of Great Britain and Belgium to support the United States in backing the United Nations plan led to a decision to employ force to end Katanga's secession once and for all. It was evident that if the United Nations did not act quickly the Adoula government, under pressure from the Casablanca states, would fall. Early in December, U Thant summoned his twenty-man Congo Advisory Committee. A decision was subsequently reached that the United Nations was prepared to use considerable force to integrate the Congo and to implement U Thant's plan. It was evident in December that a large-scale final effort strongly supported by the United States would be made to bring the stalemate to a successful conclusion. With the support of the United Nations Secretariat, the United States sent a military mission to the Congo to determine the amount of support that would be required. On December 19, the United Nations General Assembly overwhelmingly supported the World Court judgment that all member states should share the costs of the peace-keeping force, and by so doing dealt another blow to the African policy of the Soviet Government, which along with France had refused to contribute to the costs of the Congo exercise.

The extraordinary emergence of an African personality in the United Nations has strengthened the neutralist bloc. Relatively unconcerned with what are often perceived as the useless bickerings of the East and the West, the African delegates have strongly urged that important issues of the African liberation and economic development be given priority over issues of the cold war. To many observers and delegates the African behavior in the United Nations frequently appears to be inconsistent and based on a double standard. While the newly independent states of Africa practice the right of acting in their own and their collective self-interests, they frequently demand that other states orient their policies to serve the ends of racial equality, anti-colonialism, and African development. While Africa's leaders argue the right of self-determination for South-West Africa and Angola, they are quick to deny its application to Rwanda, Burundi, or Katanga. From the African point of view, however, there is no inconsistency here; the related issues of racial equality, the furtherance of African strength through unity, and the liberation of the remaining white-dominated territories are of such magnitude that they are perceived in a unique category. Thus reasonable men might differ about the rival claims of Israel and the United Arab Republic or about the merits of the Cuban situation, but from the African point of view there can be no difference with respect to the question of race, anti-colonialism, and African development.

THE INTERNATIONAL POLITICS OF AFRICAN DEVELOPMENT

The highly developed nations of the East and the West, in their preoccupation with competing cold war tactics and ideologies, are often dangerously unaware of the more fundamental implications of the revolution of rising expectations that today liberates the energies of millions of long dormant peoples.

Spokesmen for the world's two billion ill-fed, ill-housed, and ill-clothed have come to power on the wave of a powerful message of human equality and dignity that requires—better still, demands—that the extraordinary discrepancy between the style of life of the few and the many be narrowed. The United States has about 6 per cent of the world's population but consumes 40 per cent of its income. The underdeveloped countries of Africa, Asia, and Latin America, on the other hand, the home of two of every three human beings, account for less than one-fifth of the world's income. The great mass of have-nots has suddenly become knowledgeably articulate and insistent that there be a redistribution of the world's resources; more important still is the postwar emergence of organizational, ideological, and material power to force such a redistribution. Thus, the African Revolution, as a territorial aspect of the larger revolution of rising expectations, will either be assisted by those already in possession of the fruits of such a revolution, or in the last analysis that revolution will be directed against them.

The attitude of the United States and other Western powers reflects a realization that a failure to assist the great majority of humanity to realize its expectations of enhanced dignity, comfort, and equality will contribute to frustration and bitterness and consequently to the destruction of the political and economic systems inherited from the West. The USSR and its other Eastern bloc nations are also seeking to channel the revolution of rising expectations to their relative advantage, with the goal of promoting the Communist style of development for the new African states. Russian and East European developmental aid is designed to eliminate the inherited dependency of the African states on the franc, sterling, and dollar blocs. Only after complete economic independence has been achieved and neo-colonialism eradicated can the new states, it is argued, take their rightful place in the growing universe of socialist peoples' republics. While the Western governments urge their free enterprise institutions to invest in the new African states, Soviet spokesmen encourage the new states to confiscate and nationalize foreign capital investments.

The enormous task of narrowing the gap between the rising expectations of Africa's millions and the realities of poverty, ignorance, and disease is staggering. However great the magnitude of international resources, they may well be insufficient to the task.

Africa's economic development has not kept pace with its political

revolution. This discrepancy, coming as it does in a period of rapidly
rising expectations, poses a dangerous threat to political stability.
Problems and Levels of Development. The economies of the newly
independent African states are peculiarly dependent upon the export of
a few primary products purchased almost exclusively by the highly developed industralized countries of Europe and North America. Thus, the
underdeveloped African states are at the economic mercy of these industrial giants, who, in effect, can control the prices that African exports will
bring. The successful effort over the past decade to increase African
export production, in an attempt to meet rising expectations by lifting
the standard of living, has been largely negated by a corresponding fall in
African commodity prices on the world market. The value of major
African products, for example, fell 6 per cent between 1958 and 1960, and
another 3 per cent between 1960 and 1961. Thus, while exports increased
by 6.5 per cent between 1960 and 1961, the effective gain was minimal for
total export earnings only increased from 6,380 million dollars in 1960 to
6,530 million dollars in 1961.[17]

Although development plans for most African states call for an agricultural revolution that will rapidly expand exports, the control of the
commodity market by the industrial buyers, a gradual fall in commodity
market prices, and a relatively inflexible demand for African exports
suggest that economic plenty and security for most African states will
depend more upon a capacity to attract external assistance and investment
than upon an increase in the production of primary products.

Space does not permit a detailed account of the extraordinary human
and technical investment that will be required if Africa is to achieve
sufficient momentum for economic take-off. Education requirements may
be the most critical. As of 1960 fewer than 40 per cent of eligible children
were enrolled in primary schools, only 3 per cent in secondary schools and
an infinitesimal .2 per cent in institutions of higher learning.[18]

A twenty-year 1960-1980 educational plan for the entire continent blue-
prints to an increased attendance (in percentages) as follows:

	1961-62	*1965-66*	*1970-71*	*1980-81*
Primary school	40	51	71	100
Secondary school	3	9	15	23
Higher education	.2	.2	.4	2.0

By 1965 this plan will require the expenditure of about one billion
dollars and more than two and one-half billion dollars by 1980, a sum

[17] Of this increase the greater part was accounted for by the Republic of South
Africa. United Nations E/CN.14/202, p. 11.
[18] Economic Commission for Africa, Fifth Session, Léopoldville (February-March,
1963). E/CN.14/210 (January, 1963).

about half the value of total exports from Africa south of the Sahara, excluding the Republic of South Africa in 1961.

The amount of external assistance that will be required to make this increase in educational output possible by 1970 is estimated to be nearly one billion dollars, while public assistance of every sort to all African countries in 1960 was about 1.4 billion dollars.

With the exception of aid from metropolitan France and Great Britain to their former dependencies, the great bulk of external assistance to Africa comes from the United Nations and its related agencies, the United States, the Soviet Union and its East European allies, and, of increasing significance, Israel, West Germany, and Japan.

United Nations. The African states have a powerful voice in the United Nations and are able to influence decisions on the nature, direction, and purpose of developmental assistance. Thus it is not surprising that the African bloc unanimously supports an increase in multilateral aid through the United Nations in preference to bilateral assistance with real or fancied strings attached. In fact, the African bloc at the United Nations constantly exerts its influence to alter those aspects of the organization and procedure of the United Nations which act to restrict the weight that their numerical strength might otherwise carry. For example, African delegations have been in the forefront of the movement to amend the United Nations Charter to secure permanent African representation on the Security Council.

Of the five major regions of the world receiving United Nations technical assistance, Africa ranks first. Also indicative of the emphasis that the United Nations places on African development is the extraordinary number of specialized agencies with regional offices on the continent.

During the two-year period 1961-62 the United Nations Expanded Program of Technical Assistance, at a cost of more than twenty million dollars, sent 1,632 experts to Africa and awarded 1,618 fellowships; the United Nations Special Fund during this same period allocated forty-two and one-half million dollars for fifty-three projects in Africa, and from 1961 to 1962 the International Bank for Reconstruction and Development lent nearly nine hundred million dollars to Africa.[19]

The United Nations Economic Commission for Africa (ECA) established in 1958 and described in some detail earlier in the preceding chapter, is rapidly assuming a major role in determining Africa's developmental needs and has been instrumental in establishing the machinery for inter-African economic cooperation. The small scale of many African national markets and the absence of a correlation between political boundaries and national economic regions places a premium on coordina-

---

[19] United Nations Organization, Office of Public Information, External Relations Division, *The United Nations and Africa,* New York (1962), p. 13.

tion of national planning, particularly with respect to education and communication.

Cognizant of the extraordinary organizational requirements that African development will require, the ECA has concentrated considerable energy and research on training Africans in the field of development planning and administration. As a United Nations regional commission the ECA serves as the agency for a variety of United Nations programs of technical and material assistance. The Economic Commission for Africa has also taken the initiative in promoting increased inter-African trade and has sought to promote the development of complementary industries and products.

The many African economies, developed largely in relationship to their respective European metropoles, are not at all complementary. With the exception of the East African and the West African Customs Unions and trade patterns between the Central African Federation and South Africa, there is hardly any inter-African trade at all. Total inter-regional trade in 1960 was only valued at 540 million dollars—less than 8 per cent of total trade.

Total private and public capital investment in Africa is currently running at about two billion dollars per year, of which three-quarters is derived from public and only one-quarter from private investment. More important still, of the approximately 1,400 million dollars of public assistance to Africa only 146 million, or roughly 10 per cent is channeled through the United Nations and its related agencies.[20] It is evident, therefore that international assistance, critical to Africa's development, depends more heavily upon bilateral arrangements than it does on the efforts of the United Nations and its related agencies.

East Side—West Side. France, the United States, and the United Kingdom—the largest contributors of economic assistance to Africa—together in 1960 accounted for more than 80 per cent of all aid granted.[21]

Total assistance to Africa contributed by the Soviet bloc in 1960 was 285 million dollars, down slightly from 1959. The greater part of this amount was contributed by the Soviet Union.

The bilateral aid of the major donor countries tends to flow in predictable patterns. Soviet bloc aid, for example, over the past five years has gone largely to the United Arab Republic, Ethiopia, Ghana, and Guinea. Predictably, France has concentrated its assistance on its former dependencies. In 1960 a total of nearly 685 million dollars in French grants and loans was distributed as follows: 48 per cent to Algeria, 46 per cent to the former tropical African dependencies, and the remaining 6

---

[20] *Ibid.,* p. 142.
[21] *Ibid.,* p. 144. France—732 million dollars; the United States—231 million dollars; the United Kingdom—144 million dollars. The amounts do not include unidentified contributions from the Soviet bloc, nor do they include technical assistance from the United States.

per cent to Tunisia. About two-thirds of Italy's 1960 assistance of 25 million dollars went to the United Arab Republic and the remaining one-third to Somalia. Nearly one half of 144 million dollars made available for African developmental assistance in 1960 by the United Kingdom went to the East African dependencies (50 million) and to Nigeria (27 million); the remainder was almost equally divided among Sudan, Somalia, Sierra Leone, the Central African Federation, and Libya.

It is not possible here to analyze the amounts, purposes, and organization of American developmental assistance to Africa in detail. From the end of World War II through 1963, United States grants and loans have totaled approximately two billion dollars. Of this total about 40 per cent has been in the form of long-term loans and the remainder as grants.

Though not without significance, economic aid to Africa over this fifteen-year period has accounted for only 2.4 per cent of total United States economic assistance. The portion of external aid directed toward Africa has increased rapidly since 1960, and by 1963 nearly 14 per cent of foreign economic aid from the United States was finding its way to Africa.[22]

The major benefactors of the 1.7 billion dollars of American economic aid to Africa from 1946 to 1963 were: Morocco (21 per cent), Tunisia (17 per cent), Libya (11 per cent), Ghana (9 per cent), Liberia (8 per cent), Ethiopia (7 per cent), Congo (6 per cent), Sudan (4 per cent), and Nigeria (3 per cent). It is worth noting that nearly half of this assistance went to the three North African countries of Tunisia, Morocco, and Libya, leaving approximately 50 per cent for all of tropical Africa.

The form and direction of American developmental assistance is determined by a variety of factors. In 1961 and 1962, for example, famine conditions developed in a number of African countries in the wake of a rapidly increasing population, economic and political instability, and a spate of unseasonal weather. American assistance in the form of famine relief and other emergency aid during this two-year period averted serious starvation in Tanganyika and Kenya. The magnitude of this assistance is illustrated by the fact that in 1961 famine relief of one form or another accounted for more than one-third of the total American economic assistance to Africa. From April 1961 to January 1963 the United States shipped more than 90,000 tons—about twenty pounds per person—of maize to Tanganyika alone.

The investment of private American capital in Africa, long relatively insignificant, is currently reaching major proportions. Generally, such investment gravitates to the extractive industries, where a substantial and quick return can be anticipated. American interests in iron ore in Liberia, in copper and chrome in Central Africa, and in gold and lead in South Africa are substantial. In 1961 private American investment in Africa for the first time reached the billion dollar mark (1,070 million

[22] Based on the proposed program for the fiscal year 1963.

dollars). More significant, however, is the rate of increase, up to 16 per cent over 1960, and the trend toward a relative increase in investment in East and West Africa in contrast to traditional interests in South and Central Africa.

Islam and Zion. The Muslim world has had a long association with Africa and in many regions of the continent the impact of Islam has been far greater and possibly more permanent than that of the Christian West. It is important to keep in mind that the word of the prophet swept south and west into the interior of Africa and provided the base for a number of large and powerful African kingdoms in the sixteenth and seventeenth centuries. In addition to the countries of the North African littoral a majority Muslim population can be found in the Sudan, Tchad, Niger, Mali, Guinea, Senegal, Zanzibar, Mauritania, and Somalia; a large minority in Nigeria, Cameroon, Ethiopia, and Tanganyika.

Egypt has long demonstrated a particular interest in its neighbors to the south. Heir to a long tradition of involvement in the affairs of the Upper Nile, Gamul Nasser is acutely aware of the history of Mohammed Ali's extension of Egyptian hegemony and influence up the Nile almost as far as the present frontiers of Uganda. And like Mohammed Ali, Colonel Nasser seeks for Egypt a critical role in the affairs of Africa and the Middle East alike. Modern Egypt's attempts to influence, if not to direct, the African Revolution are centered in the "African Association," with its headquarters in Cairo.[23] Cairo has long served as a "home away from home" for exiled African nationalists; more than one of the continent's present-day rulers can nostalgically recall his "days of waiting" in Cairo.

To the faithful, Cairo's Al Azher University is the center of Islamic learning and has attracted Muslim scholars from the interior of Africa for many centuries. But not only the Muslims journey to the Nile Delta in search of an education; at present more than four thousand African students study in Egyptian schools and universities—nearly as many as in the United States. Despite its centuries of experience, Egypt too has recently learned that dynamic African youth cannot be taken for granted. A number of East African students sent to the United Arab Republic on scholarships in 1962 and 1963 complained that they had not received university placements as they had been promised and that the Egyptian government was discriminatory in providing them with only eleven dollars a month maintenance allowance, whereas students from other countries received more than one hundred dollars.[24]

The Voice of Free Africa, beamed from Cairo's powerful transmitters in twenty-two languages for ninety-one broadcasting hours per day effectively saturates the entire continent. The new African states are

[23] For a timely and concise treatment of this subject see Jacques Baulin, *The Arab Role in Africa* (Baltimore, Md.: Penguin African Library, 1962).

[24] *East African Standard* (Sept. 21, 1962).

buffeted by the tides of the cold war and find themselves caught up in the conflict between the Arab states and Israel. Radio Cairo transmits a never ending anti-Israel diatribe to its African receivers while the Cairo-based Afro-Asian Peoples' Solidarity Organization is employed by Egypt to enlist the support of the African states in its anti-Israel crusade. Treaties of friendship are sought with the states of tropical Africa, and in the predominantly Muslim countries Egypt has had some success in obtaining at least verbal support for its policies. The signing of a treaty of friendship in 1961, for example, between the United Arab Republic and Mali, replete with a million-dollar loan, was followed by a Mali pronouncement that it too believed Israel to be an imperialist bridgehead in Africa.[25]

Surrounded by a hostile world, Israel has been quick to establish friendly relations and trade agreements with the newly independent African states, and her assistance to African development, given the limits of her own resources, is most extraordinary. Ghana's pride—the Black Star Line—for example, was made possible by Israeli technical and material assistance. Other Israeli ventures in the politics of African development include pilot training facilities in Ghana and the Cameroon, a medical mission in the Congo, and teachers for Sierra Leone.[26] The Israeli Government has carefully concentrated its energies on relatively inexpensive projects which take advantage of its specialized skills and which affect a maximum number of people, e.g., a school for women in Kenya to train social workers, technical assistance to the cooperative movement and to agricultural settlement schemes in Tanganyika and Kenya, advice and assistance to the labor organization in Kenya, and agricultural help for the Congo.

Israel has found most African states receptive to offers of developmental assistance and mutual trade agreements. Unlike aid from the East or the West, Israeli assistance can be accepted without the suspicion that ideological strings are attached. Furthermore, the scale and nature of Israel's extraordinary economic development are peculiarly pertinent to Africa's problems. Israel's experience in the field of agricultural development, cooperation, and national and regional planning are particularly appropriate to the African environment.

The Arab states have noted with increasing anxiety Israel's remarkably successful African policy and have launched a propaganda program to convince Africa of the evils and dangers of Zionism. African states with a Muslim majority are appealed to in the name of Islam to boycott Israeli goods and to refuse offers of assistance and friendship. But most African states are no more inclined to involve themselves in the Arab-Israeli conflict than they are to align themselves in the cold war. While Afro-Asian Peoples' Solidarity Conference was gathering in the small

[25] Baulin, op. cit., p. 78.
[26] Ibid.

town of Moshi, Tanganyika, to resolve, among other matters, that "All Afro-Asian Peoples and nationalist parties exert pressure on their governments for the abrogation of bilateral treaties . . . and the prevention of new ones . . . with Israel, the dangerous tool of neo-colonialism," [27] Mrs. Golda Meir, Israeli Foreign Minister, had just departed from Moshi on her way to Dar es Salaam, where she concluded an agreement of friendship and technical cooperation between her country and Tanganyika.

In an attempt to counter the growing Israeli influence in Africa, the United Arab Republic in 1961 established the Arab Company for Foreign Trade with offices in a number of African capital cities. There is also some evidence that in its campaign against Israel the United Arab Republic has made use of the World Muslim Congress. In September 1962 Sheikh Yahya Hussein, East African representative of the World Muslim Congress, launched a campaign to stop the "infiltration into East Africa of Jewism." [28] As he claimed that his campaign was officially and financially supported by the United Arab Republic, Sheikh Hussein in effect raised the issue of Egyptian interference in the internal affairs of Kenya and Tanganyika. Accusations of interference brought a reply from the United Arab Republic's Chargé d'Affaires in Tanganyika that Sheikh Hussein's campaign was not officially supported by the United Arab Republic.[29]

The major powers, acutely aware of the suspicion that surrounds their activities in Africa, are inclined to encourage aid by their satellites or by smaller states that share either political ideology or common policy goals. The Soviet Union in this manner encourages and assists the East European Peoples' Republics to provide technical and material assistance to African states. As long as Russian and Egyptian policy in Africa coincided, the Soviet Union in part pursued its goals in Africa through the agency of the UAR. On the other hand, the United States is constantly urging its NATO allies and Japan to contribute more to African development. Some Western observers feel that Israeli influence in Africa should be encouraged and even assisted as long as it continues to promote ends and values consistent with those of the West. G. Mennen Williams, Assistant Secretary of State for African Affairs, in a major address in January 1963, praised Israel's policy of assistance, stating "Of particular importance, Israel's work is not tied to the efforts of any of the larger powers who sometimes are charged with neo-colonialism by the ardently independent Africans." [30]

[27] Third Afro-Asian Peoples' Solidarity Conference, Moshi, Tanganyika, February 4-11, 1963—Resolution on Palestine.

[28] Quoted in the *Kenya Daily Nation* (Sept. 20, 1962).

[29] *Kenya Daily Nation* (Sept. 20, 1962).

[30] In a speech before the national conference of the Organization for Rehabilitation Through Training, quoted in *Tanganyika Standard* (Jan. 21, 1963).

West Germany, Japan, et al. In recent years West Germany has demonstrated that there still exists in that country a strong interest in Africa and African affairs. West German assistance to Africa is increasing rapidly and in some areas is assuming major proportions. During 1962 West German economic assistance to Africa totaled about two hundred million dollars. An interesting aspect of this revival of German involvement is the re-establishment of strong ties to her former colonies. The Federal German Government, for example, is playing a major role in the external financing of Tanganyika's current developmental plan. In September 1962, an agreement between the two governments provided for a grant of more than four million dollars and for the provision of technical assistance in general planning and other fields. Furthermore, it is probable that as much as one-third of the approximately eight hundred million dollars of assistance slated by ECM for its African associate members will be contributed by West Germany. West Germany's decision to participate in major programs of developmental assistance in the new nations, and particularly in Africa, necessitated the establishment of the Federal Republic's new Ministry of Economic Cooperation.

The Japanese, too, are turning their attention toward Africa and have had considerable success in introducing their textiles into the growing African market.[31] Early in 1963 the Japanese Trade Fair ship made a number of extended calls along the East African coast; an agreement between Nigeria and Japan, concluded in November 1962, provides for the provision of technical assistance and for mutual trade. Under a similar agreement concluded with Ghana, Japan has provided technicians and materials for a substantial center of technology. The rapid growth of Japan's involvement in the African market is indicated by the remarkable increase in trade with Northern Rhodesia from 3.4 million dollars in 1958 to 22.4 million dollars in 1961.

A number of other states have joined in the unprecedented international endeavor. Italy, like Germany, is particularly interested in re-establishing close ties with its former dependencies and has extended considerable development assistance to Somalia. Early in 1963 closer relations with Ethiopia were resumed, and an agreement providing for fourteen million dollars of aid and considerable technical assistance was signed.

Tito's Yugoslavia has long sought to play a commanding role in the bloc of nonaligned nations and, given its limited capacity, has taken an active interest in developing close ties with the new African states. A substantial number of African students are studying at Yugoslavian universities, and many relatively small assistance projects have been undertaken, such as the negotiation of a long-term loan for Tanganyika to cover the purchase of three hundred tractors.

[31] Film slides in East African movie houses skillfully and colorfully advertise Japanese made *kangas* (a traditional East African dress) in Swahili.

Sweden, Finland, Denmark, and Norway have combined their assistance to Africa in the "Nordic Council," and in December 1962, concluded an agreement with Tanganyika providing for the establishment of an agricultural institute, health center, and secondary school. The entire project, costing nearly two million dollars, was financed by the four Scandinavian countries. Interestingly enough the occasion of the signing of this agreement was the first time that a minister for one Nordic country was empowered to sign an agreement on the behalf of all.

THE NEVER-ENDING QUEST

Man's quest for certainty, security, and harmony knows neither beginning nor end. And men everywhere establish and maintain political systems to regulate and regularize their interrelationships so that they may walk without fear, rest assured in their possessions, and take pride in their unity.

But one era's order may be another's disorder and chaos, and we speak of the "African Revolution" because of the swiftness with which events and ideas propel the quest for new memberships and institutions. This process of institutional formation and dissolution lies at the heart of the quest. Although this age-old process involves all human organizations and institutions in modern Africa, it particularly involves the ordering and functioning of the nation state and its constituent elements.

The new order, seeking to emerge, draws its sustenance from a legacy of European conquest and from an imposed and alien order as well as from Mother Africa. The rapid disintegration and subsequent integration that characterize the quest severely try human endurance and capacity, shattering status and interest, demanding a revolution in leadership; governments' fortunes and egos are made overnight. Violence, just under the surface, erupts here and there as the limits of human endurance and capacity to reorder are exceeded or are knocked askew by the intervening pressures of an external world, which itself is characterized by a powerful quest for some sort of order. Devoid of generations of sanctity, the new institutions and leaders, as they seek the proper path, are extremely vulnerable. In 1962 hardly an African premier or president could report that his assassination had not been attempted.

One powerful theme, that of race, dominates the entire African Revolution. It is apparent in the form and function of the countless new African associations and in the non-African ones which form in opposition. More than any other single element, race threatens the emergent new order, for its emotional irrationality puts a premium on violence, insecurity, and disorder and, unlike other ideologies, it seems to cut to the very marrow of interhuman relations. The impact of race ranges from domestic interpersonal relations to those between groups and blocs of states; it permeates the streets of Salisbury and the corridors of the United Nations alike. Until black, brown, and white men are successful in their quest to order their interrelationships on a foundation of mutual trust and equality, and in the absence of either guilt or insecurity, the world will know no peace. The African Revolution is reaching its most critical stage. The remaining bastions of white domination, which must be destroyed if the real fruits of the revolution are to be won, are few. But the most powerful bastions are always the last to fall, and it is becoming more and more evident that they will be taken only by storm. The effect of a climax of large-scale violence upon the continent's new and fragile institutions and values, and upon the future relationship of men of different colors everywhere in the world is incalculable.

Even when finally won, the revolution must still be consolidated. We can anticipate a long period of confusion as African states, regions, institutions, and associations sort themselves out, combine and disintegrate, and recombine in Africa's quest for order.

COUNTRIES	Area (in thousands of square miles)	Population (in millions)	Density (per square mile)	Per Capita Income (in U.S. dollars)	Literacy (percent)	Principal exports	Political status	Present/former Metropole	Date of Independence	Capital	Principal political parties	Major leaders (1963)	Membership in principal international associations
Angola	481	4.6	9	100.		coffee diamonds	D	Port.		Luanda	UPA MPLA	Holden Roberto Dr. Antonio Neto	
Basutoland	12	.7	58	100.		wool	D	G.B.		Maseru	NP BCP	Paramount Chief Moshoeshoe, II Ntsu Mokhehle Chief Leabua Jonathon	
Bechuanaland	225	.3	2	100.		cattle	D	G.B.		Lobatsi	BPP BPFP	Seretse Khama Kgaleman T. Motsete	
Federation of Cameroon	183	4.3	24	86.	15	coffee cocoa	I	FR.	1960	Yaoundé	UPC DC	Pres. Ahmadou Ahidjo V.P. John Ngu Foncha F.Min. Charles Okala	Brazzaville Grp. ATUC Monrovia Grp. EACU UAM EEC
Central African Republic	238	1.2	5	40.	8	coffee cotton	I	FR.	1960	Bangui	MESAN	M. David Dacko	Brazzaville Grp. UAM Monrovia Grp. ATUC FC EEC EACU
Congo (Brazzaville)	132.	.8	6	40.	10	timber palm oil nuts	I	FR.	1960	Brazza-ville	UDDIA PPC	Mr. Matsika Mr. Alphonse Massamba-Debat	Brazzaville Grp. UAM Monrovia Grp. EEC FC EACU ATUC
Congo (Léopoldville)	905	13.7	15	90.	40	uranium diamonds copper	I	Belg.	1960	Léopold-ville	ABAKO	Pres. Joseph Kasavubu Cyrille Adoula	EEC

*The Addis Ababa Conference of May 1963 resulted in the establishment of the Organization of African Unity (OAU) to which the independent African states have subscribed with the result that the Brazzaville, Monrovia, and PAFMECSA groups are formally dissolved.

Country													Leaders	Affiliations
Dahomey	45	1.7	38	40.	20	palm oil nuts	I	FR.	1960	Porto Novo	PDU		Pres. Hubert Maga Sourou Migan Apithy Colonel Sog lo	Brazzaville Grp. WACU / Monrovia Grp. EEC / UAM ATUC
Ethiopia	400	21.8	54	44.		coffee tobacco	I	Italy 1936-1941	11th C., B.C.	Addis Ababa	None		Emperor Haile Selassie, I / Crown Prince Alfa-Wossen Haile Selassie	Monrovia Grp. / PAFMECSA
Gabon	102	.4	4	200.	6	manganese oil iron	I	FR.	1960	Libreville	BDG USG		Pres. Leon Mba / F.Min. Jean-Hilaire Aubame	Brazzaville Grp. UAM / Monrovia Grp. EEC / ATUC EACU / FC
Gambia	4	.3	70	65.	20	nuts	D	G.B.		Bathurst	UP PPP		P. S. N'Jie / David K. Jawana	ATUC
Ghana	92	6.7	73	194.	25	cocoa gold	I	G.B.	1957	Accra	CCP		Pres. Kwame Nkrumah	Casablanca Grp. / BC AATUF / UAS
Guinea	95	2.7	29	58.	10	bauxite iron gold	I	FR.	1958	Conakry	PDG		Pres. Sékou Touré / Min. P.W.: Saifoulaye Diallo	Casablanca Grp. / UAS / AATUF
Ivory Coast	125	3.1	25	180.	16	coffee cocoa	I	FR.	1960	Abidjan	PDCI		Pres. Felix Houphouet-Boigny	Brazzaville Grp. UAM / Monrovia Grp. EEC / ATUC WACU
Kenya	225	6.6	29	96.	50	coffee pyrethrum	I	G.B.	1963	Nairobi	KANU KADU		Jomo Kenyatta / Tom Mboya / Ronald Ngala	PAFMECSA / ATUC
Liberia	43	2.5	58	159.		iron rubber	I		1847	Monrovia	TWP		Pres. William U.S. Tubman	Monrovia Grp. / ATUC
Malagasy	228	5.2	23	75.	20	coffee vanilla	I	FR.	1960	Tananarive	PSD AKFM		Pres. Philibert Tsiranana	Brazzaville Grp. FC / Monrovia Grp. EEC / UAM ATUC

COUNTRIES	Area (in thousands of square miles)	Population (in millions)	Density (per square mile)	Per Capita Income (in U.S. dollars)	Literacy (percent)	Principal exports	Political status	Present/former Metropole	Date of Independence	Capital	Principal political parties	Major leaders (1963)	Membership in principal international associations
Mali	464	4.1	9	53.	10	ground nuts cotton	I	FR.	1960	Bamako	US	Pres. Modibo Keita Maria Kone	Casablanca Grp. UAS AATUF WACU
Mauritania	419	.7	2	46.		iron copper	I	FR.	1960	Nouakchott	UNM	Pres. Mokhtar Oulo Daddah	Brazzaville Grp. Monrovia Grp. ATUC UAM EEC WACU
Mozambique	298	6.3	21	100.		sugar copra cotton	D	Port.		Lourenço Marques	FRELIMO	Eduardo Mondlane	ATUC
Niger	490	.9	2	40.	2	ground nuts millet	I	FR.	1960	Niamey	PPN	Pres. Hamani Diori	Brazzaville Grp. Monrovia Grp. ATUC UAM EEC WACU
Nigeria	357	35	98	88.	25	iron tin coal	I	G.B.	1960	Lagos	NPC AG NCNC	Alhasi Sir A.T. Balewa Nnamdi Azikiwe Obafemi Awolowo	Monrovia Grp. ATUC BC
Northern Rhodesia	288	2.3	8	163.*		copper zinc lead	SG	G.B.		Lusaka	UNIP ANC	Kenneth Kaunda Harry Nkumbula	PAFMECSA ATUC
Nyasaland	45	2.8	62	163.*		tobacco tea	SG	G.B.	1964	Zomba	MCP	Dr. Hastings Banda	PAFMECSA ATUC
Rwanda	11	3.0	272	40.	25	coffee tin	I	Belg.	1962	Kigali	PARME-HUTU	Grégoire Kayibanda	PAFMECSA ATUC UAM

*Over-all computation for Central African Federation.

Country													
Burundi	10	2.5	250	60.	25	tobacco pyrethrum	I	Belg.	1962	Usumbura	UPRONA PDC	Andre Muhirwa Pierre Ngendandumwe	PAFMECSA ATUC
Senegal	76	3.1	41	177.	25	ground nuts fish	I	FR.	1960	Dakar	UPS	Pres. Leopold Senghor	Brazzaville Grp. FC Monrovia Grp. EEC ATUC UAM WACU
Sierra Leone	28	2.5	90	70.	12	diamonds iron coffee	I	G.B.	1961	Freetown	SLPP	Sir Milton Margai John Karefa Smart	Monrovia Grp. EEC BC ATUC
Somalia	246	2.0	8	42.	10	bananas livestock	I	Italy	1960	Mogadiscio	SYL	Aden Abdullah Osman Abdi Rashid Shermarke	Monrovia Grp. EEC PAFMECSA ATUC
South Africa	473	14.7	31		35	gold diamonds	I	G.B.	1910	Pretoria	NP UP	Hendrik Verwoerd Albert Luthuli Robert M. Sobukwe	
Southern Rhodesia	150	3.1	20	163.		tobacco chrome	SG	G.B.		Salisbury	ZAPU RF	Joshua Nkomo Rev. N. Sithole Winston Field	ATUC
South-West Africa	318	.6	2	427.		diamonds	D	S.A.		Windhoek	NP SWANU SWAPO	Chief Hosea Kutako Sam Nusoma Siriretundu Kozonguizi	
Sudan	968	11.7	12	95.	5	cotton	I	G.B. Egypt	1956	Khartoum	None	Ibrahim Abboud	Arab League
Swaziland	7	.3	38			cattle	D	G.B.		Mbabane	SPP	Sobhuza, II J. J. Nquku	
Tanganyika	363	9.2	26	59.	15	sisal cotton coffee	I	G.B.	1961	Dar es Salaam	TANU	Julius Nyerere Rashidi Kawawa Oscar Kambona	PAFMECSA ATUC BC
Tchad	514	2.7	5	40.	3	cotton rice	I	FR.	1960	Fort Lamy	PPT	Pres. François Tombalbaye	Brazzaville Grp. UAM Monrovia Grp. EEC FC ATUC

COUNTRIES	Area (in thousands of square miles)	Population (in millions)	Density (per square mile)	Per Capita Income (in U.S. dollars)	Literacy (percent)	Principal exports	Political status	Present/former Metropole	Date of Independence	Capital	Principal political parties	Major leaders (1963)	Membership in principal international associations
Togo	22	1.5	68	73.	15	phosphate	I	FR.	1960	Lomé	CUT JUVENTO	Nicolas Grunitzky Antoine Meatchi	Monrovia Grp. ATUC WACU EEC
Uganda	94	7.0	75	68.	40	coffee cotton	I	G.B.	1962	Entebbe (Admin.) Kampala (Comm.)	UPC KY DP	Milton Obote Kabaka, Mutesa II Joseph Kiwanuka	PAFMECSA ATUC BC
Upper Volta	106	4.0	38	40.	3		I	FR.	1960	Ouagadougou	UDV	Pres. Maurice Yameogo	Brazzaville Grp. Monrovia Grp. ATUC UAM EEC WACU
Zanzibar (incl. Pemba)	1	.3	300	110.		cloves nuts	I	G.B.	1963	Zanzibar	ZNP ASP	Mohamed Shanti Shiekh Othman Shariff	PAFMECSA

ABBREVIATIONS EMPLOYED

I. Political Status
    I = Independent
    D = Dependent
    SG = Self-Governing

II. Present/Former Metropole
    G.B. = Great Britain
    FR. = France
    Belg. = Belgium
    Port. = Portugal
    S.A. = South Africa

III. Principal International Associations
    UAM = Union Afro-Malagasy
    ATUC = African Trade Union Confederation
    AATUF = All African Trade Union Federation
    EACU = Equatorial African Customs Union
    WACU = West African Customs Union
    FC = French Community
    EEC = European Economic Community
    BC = British Commonwealth
    UAS = Union of African States
    PAFMECSA = Pan-African Freedom Movement of East, Central, and South Africa

IV. Principal Political Parties

ABAKO = Alliance des Bakongo
AG = Action Group
AKFM = Ankoto Kongresyny Fahalevatanana Malagasy
ANC = African National Congress
ASP = Afro-Shirazi Party
BCP = Basutoland Congress Party
BDG = Bloc Démocratique Gabonais
BPFP = Bechuanaland Protectorate Federal Party
BPP = Bechuanaland Peoples' Party
CCP = Convention Peoples' Party
CUT = Commité de l'Unité Togolaise
DC = Democrates Camerounais
DP = Democratic Party
FRELIMO = Mozambique Liberation Front
JUVENTO = Mouvement de la Jeunesse Togolaise
KADU = Kenya African Democratic Union
KANU = Kenya African National Union
MCP = Malawi Congress Party
MESAN = Mouvement pour l'Evolution Sociale de l'Afrique Noire
MPLA = Movimento Popular de Libertaçao de Angola
NCNC = National Council Nigeria and Cameroons
NP = Nationalist Party
NP = National Party (Basutoland)
NPC = Northern Peoples' Congress
PARMEHUTU = Parti d'émancipation des Hutus
PDC = Christian Democratic Party
PDCI = Parti Démocratique de la Côte d'Ivoire
PDG = Parti Démocratique de Guinea

PDU = Parti Dahoméen de l'Unité
PPC = Parti Progressiste Congolais
PPN = Parti Progressiste Nigérien
PPP = Peoples' Progressive Party
PPT = Parti Progressiste Tchadien
PSD = Parti Sociale Democrate
RF = Rhodesian Front
SLPP = Sierra Leone Peoples' Party
SPP = Swaziland Progressive Party
SWANU = South-west Africa National Union
SWAPO = South-west Africa Peoples' Organization
SYL = Somali Youth League
TANU = Tanganyika African National Union
TWP = True Whig Party
UDDIA = Union Démocratique de Défense des Intérets Africains
UDV = Union Démocratique Voltaique
UNIP = United National Independent Party
UNM = Union National Mauritanienne
UP = United Party
UPA = Uniao das Populacoes de Angola
UPC = Union des Populations du Cameroun
UPC = Uganda Peoples' Congress
UPRONA = Parti de l'Unité et du Progrès National du Burundi
UPS = Union Progressiste Senegalaise
USG = Union Sociale Gabonaise
US = Union Soudanaise
ZAPU = Zimbabwe African Peoples' Union
ZNP = Zanzibar Nationalist Party

SPECTRUM  BOOKS

S-1   THE CAUSES OF THE CIVIL WAR, edited by Kenneth M. Stampp
S-2   IMMIGRATION AS A FACTOR IN AMERICAN HISTORY, edited by Oscar
      Handlin
S-3   PSYCHOANALYSIS AND PSYCHOTHERAPY: 36 SYSTEMS, Robert A.
      Harper
S-4   FALLACY: THE COUNTERFEIT OF ARGUMENT, W. Ward Fearnside
      and William B. Holther
S-5   THE GREAT DEBATE: OUR SCHOOLS IN CRISIS, edited by C. Winfield
      Scott, Clyde M. Hill, and Hobert W. Burns
S-6   FREEDOM AND CULTURE, Dorothy Lee
S-7   UNDERSTANDING TODAY'S THEATRE, Edward A. Wright
S-8   GOLDEN AGES OF THE THEATER, Kenneth Macgowan and William
      Melnitz
S-9   THE SEARCH FOR AMERICA,* edited by Huston Smith
S-10 THE GREAT DEPRESSION, edited by David A. Shannon
S-11 WHAT PRICE ECONOMIC GROWTH?* edited by Klaus Knorr and
      William J. Baumol
S-12 SCARCITY AND EVIL,* Vivian Charles Walsh
S-13 JUSTICE AND SOCIAL POLICY, Frederick Olafson
S-14 CONSTRUCTIVE ETHICS, T. V. Smith and William Debbins
S-15 LONELINESS,* Clark E. Moustakas
S-16 KNOWLEDGE: ITS VALUES AND LIMITS,* Gustave Weigel, S. J., and
      Arthur G. Madden
S-17 THE EDUCATION OF TEACHERS,* G. K. Hodenfield and T. M. Stin-
      nett
S-18 LITERATURE, POPULAR CULTURE, AND SOCIETY, Leo Lowenthal
S-19 PARADOX AND PROMISE: ESSAYS ON AMERICAN LIFE AND EDUCATION,*
      Harry S. Broudy
S-20 RELIGION IN AMERICA: PAST AND PRESENT, Clifton E. Olmstead
S-21 RELIGION AND THE KNOWLEDGE OF GOD,* Gustave Weigel, S.J., and
      Arthur G. Madden
S-22 INTUITION AND SCIENCE, Mario Bunge
S-23 REVOLUTION, EVOLUTION, AND THE ECONOMIC ORDER,* Allen M.
      Sievers
S-24 AN ANATOMY FOR CONFORMITY,* Edward L. Walker and Roger
      Heyns
S-25 SCIENCE AND THE NATION,* J. Stefan Dupré and Sanford A. Lakoff
S-26 POLITICS IN AFRICA: PROSPECTS SOUTH OF THE SAHARA,* Herbert J.
      Spiro
S-27 THE FIRST RUSSIAN REVOLUTION: ITS IMPACT ON ASIA,* Ivar
      Spector
S-28 MASTERY OF THE METROPOLIS,* Webb S. Fiser

* Also available in limited clothbound edition.

S-29   JOHANN SEBASTIAN BACH: AN INTRODUCTION TO HIS LIFE AND WORK,* Russell H. Miles

S-30   IN DEFENSE OF YOUTH,* Earl C. Kelley

S-31   HEROES, VILLAINS, AND FOOLS: THE CHANGING AMERICAN CHARACTER,* Orrin E. Klapp

S-32   COMMUNIST CHINA'S STRATEGY IN THE NUCLEAR ERA,* Alice Langley Hsieh

S-33   SOCIOLOGISM AND EXISTENTIALISM,* Edward T. Tiryakian

S-34   PHILOSOPHY OF SCIENCE: THE LINK BETWEEN SCIENCE AND PHILOSOPHY, Philipp Frank

S-35   FREE WILL: A BOOK OF READINGS, edited by Sidney Morgenbesser and James J. Walsh

S-36   NINE MODERN MORALISTS,* Paul Ramsey

S-37   THE IMPORTANCE OF LANGUAGE, edited by Max Black

S-38   SOCIAL JUSTICE,* edited by Richard B. Brandt

S-39   EXISTENTIALISM AS PHILOSOPHY, Fernando Molina

S-40   TRUTH, MYTH, AND SYMBOL, edited by Thomas J. J. Altizer, William A. Beardslee, and J. Harvey Young

S-41   GOVERNMENT AND POLITICS OF THE MIDDLE EAST,* Maurice Harari

S-42   ART AND EXISTENTIALISM,* Arturo B. Fallico

S-43   THE PHILOSOPHY OF MIND, edited by V. C. Chappell

S-44   THE AMERICAN LABOR MOVEMENT, edited by Leon Litwack

S-45   DISCRIMINATION,* Wallace Mendelson

S-46   MAN'S DISCOVERY OF HIS PAST,* edited by Robert F. Heizer

S-47   LOUIS SULLIVAN: AN ARCHITECT IN AMERICAN THOUGHT,* Sherman Paul

S-48   THE FAITH TO DOUBT,* M. Holmes Hartshorne

S-49   UNDERSTANDING OTHER CULTURES,* Ina Corinne Brown

S-50   CLASS IN SUBURBIA,* William M. Dobriner

S-51   A GUIDE TO THE WORLD'S RELIGIONS,* David G. Bradley

S-52   PSYCHOTHERAPY IN OUR SOCIETY,* Theron Alexander

S-53   POSITIVE PROTESTANTISM: A RETURN TO FIRST PRINCIPLES, Hugh T. Kerr

S-54   CONTINUING CRISIS IN AMERICAN POLITICS,* edited by Marian D. Irish

S-55   THE NEGRO LEADERSHIP CLASS,* Daniel C. Thompson

S-56   THE NATURE OF SCIENTIFIC THOUGHT,* Marshall Walker

S-57   PSYCHOANALYSIS AND HISTORY,* edited by Bruce Mazlish

S-58   THE PROBLEM OF RELIGIOUS KNOWLEDGE,* William T. Blackstone

S-59   SLAVERY DEFENDED: THE VIEWS OF THE OLD SOUTH,* edited by Eric L. McKitrick

S-60   THE REALITIES OF WORLD COMMUNISM, edited by William Petersen

S-61   THE BOLSHEVIK TRADITION: LENIN, STALIN, KHRUSHCHEV,* Robert H. McNeal

S-62   LENIN, STALIN, KHRUSHCHEV: VOICES OF BOLSHEVISM,* edited by Robert H. McNeal

* Also available in limited clothbound edition.

S-63   THE SHAPING OF MODERN THOUGHT, Crane Brinton
S-64   HISTORY AND FUTURE OF RELIGIOUS THOUGHT: CHRISTIANITY,
        HINDUISM, BUDDHISM, ISLAM,* Philip H. Ashby
S-65   ALFRED NORTH WHITEHEAD: ESSAYS ON HIS PHILOSOPHY,* edited
        by George L. Kline
S-66   TRIUMPH IN THE PACIFIC: THE NAVY'S STRUGGLE AGAINST JAPAN,
        edited by E. B. Potter and Chester W. Nimitz
S-67   THE CHALLENGE OF LEISURE, Charles K. Brightbill
S-68   PLATO: TOTALITARIAN OR DEMOCRAT?,* edited by Thomas Landon
        Thorson
S-69   THE TWENTIES: FORDS, FLAPPERS, AND FANATICS, edited by George
        E. Mowry
S-70   THE POTEMKIN MUTINY, Richard Hough
S-71   AN INTRODUCTION TO THE LAW,* C. Gordon Post
S-72   THE PROGRESSIVE MOVEMENT 1900-1915, edited by Richard Hof-
        stadter
S-73   STIGMA: NOTES ON THE MANAGEMENT OF SPOILED IDENTITY,* Erving
        Goffman
S-74   SOCIOLOGY ON TRIAL, edited by Maurice Stein and Arthur Vidich
S-75   NOTES FOR A YOUNG PAINTER,* Hiram Williams
S-76   ART, ARTISTS, AND SOCIETY: ORIGINS OF A MODERN DILEMMA,*
        Geraldine Pelles
S-77   MICHELANGELO: A SELF-PORTRAIT,* edited by Robert J. Clements
S-78   RACIAL CRISIS IN AMERICA: LEADERSHIP IN CONFLICT,* Lewis Kil-
        lian and Charles Grigg
S-79   AFRICA'S QUEST FOR ORDER,* Fred G. Burke
S-80   WORLD PRESSURES ON AMERICAN FOREIGN POLICY,* edited by
        Marian D. Irish
S-81   PSYCHOTHERAPY: THE PURCHASE OF FRIENDSHIP,* William Schofield

                    The American Assembly Series

S-AA-1 THE FEDERAL GOVERNMENT AND HIGHER EDUCATION,* edited by
        Douglas M. Knight
S-AA-2 THE SECRETARY OF STATE,* edited by Don K. Price
S-AA-3 GOALS FOR AMERICANS: THE REPORT OF THE PRESIDENT'S COMMIS-
        SION ON NATIONAL GOALS
S-AA-4 ARMS CONTROL: ISSUES FOR THE PUBLIC,* edited by Louis Henkin
S-AA-5 OUTER SPACE,* edited by Lincoln P. Bloomfield
S-AA-6 THE UNITED STATES AND THE FAR EAST (Second Edition), edited
        by Willard L. Thorp
S-AA-7 AUTOMATION AND TECHNOLOGICAL CHANGE,* edited by John T.
        Dunlop
S-AA-8 CULTURAL AFFAIRS AND FOREIGN RELATIONS,* edited by Robert
        Blum

* Also available in limited clothbound edition.

S-AA-9 THE UNITED STATES AND LATIN AMERICA (Second Edition),* edited by Herbert L. Matthews

S-AA-10 THE POPULATION DILEMMA,* edited by Philip M. Hauser

S-AA-11 THE UNITED STATES AND THE MIDDLE EAST,* edited by Georgiana G. Stevens

Classics in History Series

S-CH-1 FRONTIER AND SECTION: SELECTED ESSAYS OF FREDERICK JACKSON TURNER,* *Introduction and Notes by Ray Allen Billington*

S-CH-2 DRIFT AND MASTERY: AN ATTEMPT TO DIAGNOSE THE CURRENT UNREST, Walter Lippmann, *Introduction and Notes by William E. Leuchtenburg*

S-CH-3 THE NEW NATIONALISM, Theodore Roosevelt, *Introduction and Notes by William E. Leuchtenburg*

S-CH-4 THE NEW FREEDOM: A CALL FOR THE EMANCIPATION OF THE GENEROUS ENERGIES OF A PEOPLE, Woodrow Wilson, *Introduction and Notes by William E. Leuchtenburg*

S-CH-5 EMPIRE AND NATION: JOHN DICKINSON'S "LETTERS FROM A FARMER IN PENNSYLVANIA" AND RICHARD HENRY LEE'S "LETTERS FROM THE FEDERAL FARMER," * *Introduction by Forrest McDonald*

S-CH-6 THE SUPREME COURT AND THE CONSTITUTION,* Charles A. Beard, *Introduction by Alan F. Westin*

S-CH-7 SOCIAL DARWINISM: SELECTED ESSAYS OF WILLIAM GRAHAM SUMNER,* *Introduction by Stow Persons*

S-CH-8 WEALTH AGAINST COMMONWEALTH, Henry D. Lloyd,* *Introduction by Thomas C. Cochran*

S-CH-9-10 HISTORY OF THE UNITED STATES DURING THE ADMINISTRATIONS OF JEFFERSON AND MADISON,* Henry Adams, *Abridged with an Introduction by George Dangerfield and Otey M. Scruggs*

Science and Technology Series

S-ST-1 THE ATOM AND ITS NUCLEUS, George Gamow

S-ST-2 ROCKET DEVELOPMENT,* Robert H. Goddard

S-ST-3 STARS AND GALAXIES: BIRTH, AGEING, AND DEATH IN THE UNIVERSE,* edited by Thornton Page

* Also available in limited clothbound edition.

27

DATE DUE

Twentieth Century Views*

S-TC-1   CAMUS, edited by Germaine Brée
S-TC-2   T. S. ELIOT, edited by Hugh Kenner
S-TC-3   ROBERT FROST, edited by James M. Cox
S-TC-4   PROUST, edited by René Girard
S-TC-5   WHITMAN, edited by Roy Harvey Pearce
S-TC-6   SINCLAIR LEWIS, edited by Mark Schorer
S-TC-7   STENDHAL, edited by Victor Brombert
S-TC-8   HEMINGWAY, edited by Robert P. Weeks
S-TC-9   FIELDING, edited by Ronald Paulson
S-TC-10 THOREAU, edited by Sherman Paul
S-TC-11 BRECHT, edited by Peter Demetz
S-TC-12 EMERSON, edited by Milton R. Konvitz and Stephen E. Whicher
S-TC-13 MELVILLE, edited by Richard Chase
S-TC-14 LORCA, edited by Manuel Duran
S-TC-15 HOMER, edited by George Steiner and Robert Fagles
S-TC-16 DOSTOEVSKY, edited by René Wellek
S-TC-17 KAFKA, edited by Ronald Gray
S-TC-18 BAUDELAIRE, edited by Henri Peyre
S-TC-19 JOHN DONNE, edited by Helen Gardner
S-TC-20 EDITH WHARTON, edited by Irving Howe
S-TC-21 SARTRE, edited by Edith Kern
S-TC-22 BEN JONSON, edited by Jonas A. Barish
S-TC-23 YEATS, edited by John Unterecker
S-TC-24 D. H. LAWRENCE, edited by Mark Spilka
S-TC-25 HARDY, edited by Albert J. Guerard
S-TC-26 JANE AUSTEN, edited by Ian Watt
S-TC-27 F. SCOTT FITZGERALD, edited by Arthur Mizener
S-TC-28 EMILY DICKINSON, edited by Richard B. Sewall
S-TC-29 EZRA POUND, edited by Walter Sutton
S-TC-30 MARK TWAIN, edited by Henry Nash Smith
S-TC-31 BYRON, edited by Paul West
S-TC-32 DRYDEN, edited by Bernard N. Schilling
S-TC-33 WALLACE STEVENS, edited by Marie Borroff
S-TC-34 HENRY JAMES, edited by Leon Edel
S-TC-35 SWIFT, edited by Ernest Tuveson
S-TC-36 THOMAS MANN, edited by Henry Hatfield

* Also available in limited clothbound edition.